S0-BJN-467

Harmon KILLEBREW

Ultimate Slugger

Steve Aschburner

Library of Congress Cataloging-in-Publication Data

Aschburner, Steve.
Harmon Killebrew : ultimate slugger / Steve Aschburner.
p. cm.
Includes bibliographical references.
ISBN 978-1-60078-702-7 (hardback)
1. Killebrew, Harmon, 1936–2011. 2. Baseball players—United States—Biography. I. Title.
GV865.K49A64 2012
796.357092—dc23
[B]

2012010208

This book is available in quantity at special discounts for your group or organization. For further information, contact:

Triumph Books LLC
814 North Franklin Street
Chicago, Illinois 60610
Phone: (312) 337-0747
www.triumphbooks.com

Printed in U.S.A.
ISBN: 978-1-60078-702-7
Design by Patricia Frey

For an era when sluggers bulked up on milkshakes,
and for the timelessness of being a gentleman

Contents

Foreword

The first time I ever heard of Harmon was through Charlie Manuel. Manuel was our hitting instructor in Cleveland, then he was the manager. I used to hear Charlie talk about this guy Harmon Killebrew. And I remember hitting a home run in Cleveland and Charlie said, "Man, that reminded me of a Harmon Killebrew home run." And I said, "What do you mean?"

He goes, "Well, it was a high home run. It looked like it would never come down. It just kept going..." I had always heard Harmon's name through Charlie, and then when I signed in Minnesota and was able to go to spring training with the Twins, there was Harmon.

I'm glad that someone is writing a book about Harmon because he's a legend. It was a thrill to meet him—he's a huge baseball icon. But then, when I had the opportunity to talk to him, I saw a man. *This guy is like my dad or my grandfather,* I thought. You could sit down and he would talk to you about anything. What really stood out was that Harmon had time for everybody—it wasn't something that was an act. He truly, genuinely liked being around people. That was his personality.

I watched how he'd handle our young guys on up to the veteran guys. I know that when he was going through the struggle with his illness, even then he always thought of other people first, which is a testament to his character.

Unfortunately, he and I really never got to talk about hitting. There was maybe one time when he stood around the cage and he said something like, "This is what I used to try to do in BP..." His theory was, he tried to hit home runs in BP because he was a home run hitter. Charlie Manuel used to tell me, too, you have to *practice* hitting home runs. But Harmon wasn't one of those guys who just came in and started talking about what he knew. If the subject of hitting came up, he would do it. But he wanted to get to know the person and build from that, maybe build a relationship and then get into the hitting or the player end of it. That was unique.

As much of a gentleman as Harmon was, he was very, very firm about the steroid era. I agree with him. That was a part of the era I played in. Guys did it, let's face it. But as I've always said, not *every* guy did it and you shouldn't punish everybody. Unfortunately, I think there's a little bit of a sour taste for some older players; they're a little bit bitter. And Harmon was one of them. You've got to respect the way a guy feels about it—it's not right, it wasn't right—and Harmon definitely stood for what he believed in. No question.

I've been told that Harmon took awhile to get his 500th home run, and I can understand what he might have been going through. The journey for me [to 600], I've had back issues, I've had some injuries where I went on the DL a couple of times. I take nothing for granted at this stage. When you get older and you've had some injuries, it makes you appreciate so much more the things you accomplish. I never sat there, two away, going, "Oh, it's going to happen." You approach every game as if it could be your last.

Someone said it took Harmon 23 games to go from 498 to 499 and 14 more to go from 499 to 500. Those big numbers have been kind of tough for me, too, looking back. Going from 495 to 498—you know, when you're there but you're still not there—I needed eight days to get to 496 but I got 496, 497, and 498 pretty quick. Three days, I think. Then it took me another three or four days to reach 499. And I'll never forget getting to 500 because my wife was pregnant with our son and we had three games in Chicago against the Angels and then we were going on the road. I'll never forget that Sunday, the last day of the homestand, she said to me as I left the house, "Hey, could you do it?" Joking, right? "It sure would be nice if I didn't have to go to Kansas City."

Well, I ended up doing it on my last at-bat on a walk-off, and it was very special.

The night Harmon hit 500 he also hit 501, and I totally understand that. It's a huge burden off your back when you accomplish it. A couple of nights after I hit 500, I hit two more in Kansas City. I remember, after you hit a big milestone—500 or even 400—how much more relaxed you feel afterward.

Harmon talked about never getting to 50 home runs—though he had one in Boston in 1969, when he hit 49, that hit the top of the wall and was ruled a double. I can remember hitting a ball in Cleveland that hit an iron railing in left-center field and the umpires missed it. You always look back and go, "Oh, if I'd just gotten that one," or, "That was the one the wind knocked down." You're always looking back on those handful of homers you didn't get. That's what makes hitting home runs so special—it's not something you can try to do. You've just got to let your swing do it. Harmon might have disagreed. It's a fine line.

It's flattering when people say I remind them of Harmon. It has to do with being a "slugger," and it has to do with our defense. Let's face it, I wouldn't be sitting here talking to you if it hadn't been for the

DH. The DH has given several guys in the latter stages of their careers an opportunity to reach milestones that normally might not have happened. It has given guys like, say, Eddie Murray, myself, Harmon, Tony Oliva, and Paul Molitor the opportunity to hang on and not put as much stress on our bodies compared to going out and grinding every day on the field. Harmon only had three years with the DH, and the Twins had Tony then, too. But I'm all for the DH, because I've reaped the rewards from it, no question.

Harmon was fortunate to play all but one season with one franchise. I've moved around more. But it's been a great journey, and it's been a great ride. I feel very fortunate. I mean, think of the people I've met in the game. There have been rivals. Legends, too. There's been Mike Schmidt with Philly. There's been Bob Feller with Cleveland. In Minnesota, it was Harmon and Tony. All those guys, they came back and gave their time to the game. It's important that guys today appreciate that. You're talking about the living legends.

Harmon is still a living legend to me.

—Jim Thome
August 8, 2011

Acknowledgments

Clyde Doepner, the first-ever curator for the Minnesota Twins, is a man who has forgotten more about Harmon Killebrew than this book ever could hope to include. His foresight in salvaging artifacts that otherwise would have been lost, tossed, or sold off, and maintaining them through three ballparks in the Twin Cities across four or five decades was vital to this or any other retelling of Twins history. So was his generosity in sharing access to the team's files and in tapping his own reservoir of Killebrew knowledge. "Clyde the Collector" kick-started this project on a 2011 summer weekend in Minneapolis.

Thanks also to Molly Gallatin, Dustin Morse, and Mike Sherman of the team's media relations department and others in the organization whose efforts and support were so helpful. Especially to Dave St. Peter, the Twins' president, for his enthusiasm for the book, his advocacy in presenting the project to Nita Killebrew and, way back when, his remembrance of Killebrew as an alumnus, legend, and icon.

Special thanks to Jeff Idelson, president of the National Baseball Hall of Fame and Museum, and his Cooperstown crew. Jeff reached out to Hall of Famers with interview requests not once but twice, and he helped with info about the Hall and Harmon's days as one of its most spirited members. The staff in the library, meanwhile, provided me with a steady supply of white gloves when I dropped by the Hall library to tap their Killebrew archives.

Thanks to Henry Aaron, George Brett, Jim Kaat, Charlie Manuel, Phil Roof, Jim Thome, and the many others I spoke to or corresponded with for the book. They also were generous with their time and their anecdotes, putting flesh, blood, and feelings to the raw numbers by which most folks otherwise would know Killebrew.

But thanks for those numbers, as well, specifically as accessed through Baseball-Reference.com. The depth of statistical data maintained there is unmatched in scope and ease of use. Frankly, the Sports Reference websites across all the major U.S. sports are so helpful overall, it's a mystery how any of us authors or sportswriters managed to function before they were created.

Thanks to Charley Walters of the *St. Paul Pioneer Press,* a sportswriter who knew Killebrew from the inside out—they were teammates during Walters' brief stay with the 1969 Twins as a hard-throwing fellow nicknamed "Shooter"—and a good friend. Thanks to all the baseball writers at newspapers in the Twin Cities, Washington, Idaho, and Arizona for the legwork and deadline wrestling they put into penning the first drafts of Killebrew's biography. Special thanks to Dr. Wayne Anderson, whose extensive biography of the Twins slugger on the heels of Killebrew's MVP season focused as much on his family and religious lives, providing a portrait of the man in full.

Thanks to Bob Killebrew, Harmon's loving brother who revealed himself within minutes to be the family's comedian, as well. Also to Ron Manser and others from Payette, Idaho, and Ontario, Oregon, who "knew Killebrew when," several of whom are convinced that if he hadn't chosen baseball over football, he simply would be enshrined in Canton rather than Cooperstown.

Thanks also to Adam Motin, managing editor at Triumph Books, for his guidance, patience, and flexibility in bringing this project home, and to associate editor Karen O'Brien for the same, along with her craftsmanship in shepherding the manuscript. Thanks to the Triumph staff overall, who made my first experience with the *Good, Bad, & Ugly* Twins book so satisfying.

Thanks to Mark Heleker, the principal of Payette High and committed Killebrew fan, for his information and hospitality in introducing me to my subject's hometown, the sort of place where we all wish we had grown up, particularly as it was in Harmon's time. For that, thanks also to Ann Curtis, administrator of the Payette County Historical Society. It's too bad every Twins fan can't leaf through the Payette High yearbooks and know the surprise of finding photos of young Harmon—with a full head of wavy brown hair.

Finally, thanks to my wife, Wendy, the baseball fan I married.

Introduction

From the start, there was some debate over the title of this book. One early version was *Killer: The Harmon Killebrew Story,* which would have required constant explaining—not to mention air quotes and italics—to make sure people didn't get the wrong impression about the man. Yes, some people referred to Killebrew by that inconvenient nickname. It was a by-product of his family name, it was easy and, for those who actually knew him, it packed its own wink: *Harmon? A killer? Bwahahahahahaha! Not in this or any other lifetime! See, that's the joke.*

Problem was, not everyone knew Killebrew—certainly not every potential book buyer, many of whom weren't even born when the Hall of Famer played his final games in 1975. They might indeed judge the book by its cover and dive in with the wrong idea about the friendly fellow's personality. They might get turned off by the presumed harshness and pass on the book entirely, an even bigger problem for the folks back at Triumph Books headquarters.

My own thought was to go with something more nostalgic and big-picture, titling the book, *Harmon Killebrew: The Last Slugger.* A case could be made, frankly, that Killebrew did represent the end of an era in Major League Baseball. He was a flannel-wearing, fence-busting, milkshake-drinking big leaguer who talked softly but carried a big stick. He got his strength naturally, the old-fashioned way, wrangling 10-gallon milk cans off the back of a truck in Small Town, U.S.A. He went year to year with his contracts, bound by the reserve clause, driven by the very real threat of a pay cut if he somehow failed to live up to the lofty expectations he had set in previous seasons.

Killebrew played in a different time, before interleague play, before *SportsCenter*, before cable and satellite TV penetrated many American homes. That left him somewhat mythic, a Paul Bunyan from flyover country in the Upper Midwest, a Casey-at-the-Bat-type who actually did deliver for the Mudville Nine. And yet, he wasn't precisely the "Last Slugger," not when a look-alike, swing-alike guy like Jim Thome can come along, become Killebrew's friend, surpass his home run count as a member of the Twins, and even write the foreword to his biography.

Finally, the suggestion came. "How about, *Harmon Killebrew: Ultimate Slugger*?" Hmm. That seemed to cover it all. Ultimate, as in final. Ultimate, as in utmost. Consummate, absolute, supreme. Sure, that would work. It might have made the Hall of Famer blush a bit, but it was pretty darn accurate. Not just as a slugger, either.

In writing this book, I learned that Harmon Killebrew was considered the ultimate lot-of-things by those who knew him best, from ultimate teammate and role model to ultimate friend and partner. He had his flaws, he had his failures like any person, and given the chance to do a few things over, he might have lobbied to set right twice that many. But what Minnesota manager Ron Gardenhire said—after getting to know Killebrew, the Twins legend, in the last decade of his life—was repeated in one form or another by so many. "There aren't too many people who met Harmon," Gardenhire said, "and walked away disappointed."

Hopefully, some of that will rub off on this book, as it helps folks know Killebrew who might otherwise have missed the chance. This project didn't begin until late summer 2011, a few months after Killebrew's death from esophageal cancer that May. As a result, it couldn't be an autobiography or an "as told to" book, a transcribed version of the former ballplayer's recorded memories and reminiscences. There was, however, a trove of source material available, and numerous friends and teammates eager to talk about him.

Killebrew's baseball career spanned an impressive arc in MLB history. He broke in with the old Washington Senators when Ted Williams, Yogi Berra, and Early Wynn were American League stars and stuck around long enough to compete with Robin Yount, Goose Gossage, and Dennis Eckersley. When Killebrew arrived, Babe Ruth held both the career and single-season home run records; when Killebrew exited, the Babe held neither. In 1954, only one AL team (Chicago White Sox) was located as far west as the Central time zone. By 1975, Killebrew's final season, seven of the AL's 12 teams resided somewhere besides the East.

Individually, Killebrew changed cities twice, clubbed 40 home runs or more eight times, was an 11-time All-Star, earned the 1969 MVP award, and played in one World Series and two more playoff series. When he did retire, he reigned as the AL's all-time home run leader among right-handed batters—a title he held for 37 years (from passing Jimmie Foxx in 1972 to being passed by Alex Rodriguez in 2009).

Yet the arc of Killebrew's life was impressive, too, as a son himself, as a husband to Elaine and then Nita, as the father of five children, and eventually a grandfather. As a friend, Harmon could turn every conversation about him around to something about you, how you were doing, right to the end. His humility as he fought his rough, frightening final battle with cancer was humbling to those who knew him then.

I first met Harmon in 1987, while covering the World Series–bound Twins as part of the *Minneapolis Star Tribune*'s baseball crew. He was broadcasting for them then, enjoying the championship he never quite reached as a player. Before that, as a kid growing up in Chicago, I only knew him as the most intimidating bat in that ridiculously powerful lineup from Minnesota that tormented the White Sox across state lines in the Midwest.

Later, though, my favorite memory of Killebrew came at a baggage carousel at Phoenix's Sky Harbor International Airport. He had flown from the Twin Cities home to Scottsdale, I was traveling on an NBA assignment, and we'd managed to say hi and chat briefly. Then the belt began to grind and bags started to drop, grabbing our attention.

As one suitcase slid down right where Killebrew was standing and began its trek around the carousel, an elderly lady called out, "Please grab that! That's my bag!" Dutifully, Harmon reached over and plucked it from the belt in time. The old gal thanked him, without recognizing just who her strong helper was. Immediately, other ladies in her traveling party began instructing Killebrew which bags where theirs, asking him to grab those as well so they wouldn't have to chase or wait for them to come all the way around.

Harmon obliged, smiling and making small talk with them the whole time. I half-expected one of them to offer him a tip, not that he'd take it. I think his bag already had dropped, but he finished the job.

That's the person I hope this book captures, even though *Harmon Killebrew: Ultimate Skycap* wouldn't have cut it at the bookstores.

Chapter 1

Payette, Home Again

Driving into Payette, Idaho, the signs of Harmon Killebrew are easy to spot. They hang high, front and center at the town's entry points, clear sources of pride for the locals and maybe a little surprising for out-of-staters who happen to be passing through on the interstate highways and major roads that veer through the town on the state's western border.

In most locations, draping from lampposts, there's a vertical banner on the left that reads, "Welcome to Payette / Home of the Pirates," complete with a cartoonish figure and all the accessories you'd expect—skull and crossbones on his hat, eye patch on his face, stiletto clenched in his teeth. It's a Pittsburgh Pirates–Tampa Bay Buccaneers–Oakland Raiders type of vibe, and it's tied into the local high school's sports nickname.

Right next to it, though, the one on the right features the photo of a smiling, affable big leaguer in a relaxed 1960s pose. This one gets the job done for a favorite son: "Welcome to Payette / Hometown of Harmon Killebrew."

Immediately, an image forms—a happy mix of black-and-white newsreel footage and Kodachrome snapshots—of a fellow who reached the major leagues under Eisenhower and exited under Ford. From Joe McCarthy to Patty Hearst, from *I Love Lucy* to *Saturday Night Live*:

Harmon Killebrew—legendary slugger for the Minnesota Twins (with brief stays at the start and end with the Washington Senators and the Kansas City Royals)—573 "all-natural" home runs, ranking fifth in big league history when he retired and still ranking 11th as the 2012 baseball season began—high, majestic "moon shot" blasts that, modest as he was, even Killebrew would stand and admire for a couple seconds before trotting around the bases—forearms, biceps, and wrists that would have Popeye reaching for more spinach.

Eight seasons hitting 40 homers or more—six American League home run titles—ranked third all-time in home run frequency upon his retirement (one every 14.2 at-bats, behind Babe Ruth's 11.76 rate and Ralph Kiner's 14.11)—nine seasons with 100 or more RBIs, 1,584 RBIs in his career—the AL's Most Valuable Player in 1969—trips to three postseasons with the Twins (1965, '69, '70)—enshrinement into the National Baseball Hall of Fame in Cooperstown, New York, in 1984—a soft-spoken gentleman whose ill-fitting nicknames, "Killer" and "Harm," instantly and forever felt ironic—friend and neighbor whose battle at age 74 with esophageal cancer began late in 2010 and ended on May 17, 2011.

If you're coming in from Boise, about 60 miles southeast from Payette, you can branch off to the right at the "Welcome to…" banner and head north along US–95. Soon enough, you will see a second tribute on your left. "Harmon Killebrew Field," the two-piece sign reads. "Idaho's Athlete of the Century." And just to make sure there's no confusion—Huh? Which century?—the bottom of the sign features a sketch of Killebrew in multiple images and poses, taking a powerful cut at the plate in his Minnesota Twins prime and smiling out in portrait mode as a youthful, pleasant—and unmistakably 1950s—high school player.

Beyond the ballfield, you'll see the high school, long and flat and too modern to have been the place where Killebrew sat in classes and walked the halls. The old school—closer to the center of town—succumbed to wear, tear, and eventually a fire that took with it some trophies from Harmon's teams at Payette High School. Beyond the school, or more accurately rising up next to it, is the white geodesic dome of the gymnasium. It's modern and vintage all at once, poking up like a huge golf ball half-buried in a bunker or a tin of Jiffy Pop popcorn, ready to eat. In Cold War times, it might have been a radar center, scanning the sky for Soviet missiles. These days, however, it is simply the roof atop the gym and an opportunity missed.

Once upon a time—back in 1985—a brainstorm to honor one of Payette's most famous natives was hatched by local businesswoman and historian Dee Klenck and her husband, George. They called it the Killebrew Art Project, and their plan was simple. Paint large red "stitches" on the white gym dome to make it resemble a baseball and then position Harmon's famous, elegant autograph—writ large—between the seams. Killebrew was hot at the time, having recently been elected to Baseball's Hall of Fame, and the Klencks felt that creating the world's largest tribute to a sports celebrity would be just the ticket to draw some national attention to Payette and perhaps lure tourists, as well.

What the Klencks hadn't counted on, however, was a high school full of kids who barely remembered Killebrew as an active major leaguer, never mind the all-time slugger who had made their parents' generation so proud. The kids gave a collective shrug, though some took it further, picketing the Maudie Owens Café one day in April 1985 while George Klenck was inside pitching his project yet again to the town's Chamber of Commerce.

The objections, on top of a lukewarm initial response, embarrassed Killebrew, who initially had given his permission to the couple to pursue their idea. So he withdrew his participation. A few days later, the Klencks pulled the project's plug "due to the majority opposition of the high school kids and the general lack of support from the community." Dee and George apologized to Harmon and gave him a copy of a petition with names of neighbors who supported the idea. But they refused to back off on the notion as anything but one swell tribute. "By using Harmon's success in baseball as the example, we were wanting to show that in America we can excel in any endeavor we choose," George Klenck said. "However, if this project is ever to realize completion, I'm afraid it will have to be done by those who are in a position to do so."

The setback wasn't a total loss. Within three years, Dee Klenck came up with an idea for an Idaho Hall of Fame. Some of those who objected to the Killebrew tribute claimed that Payette had other natives deserving of recognition, which planted the seed for the proud Idaho booster. "I was determined that there was nobody as great as Harmon Killebrew," Klenck said in 2000. But as she heard or was reminded of folks from Payette or nearby communities such as Joe Albertson, Sen. James McClure, Chief Joseph, and Lana Turner, Dee Klenck's vision grew.

"We said, 'Alright, let's bring the attention of the world to those we are loaning to them," she said. Harmon was among those inducted on the inaugural ballot in 1995, though the Hall is largely honorary—without a permanent brick-and-mortar location, it exists primarily in cyberspace. Whenever she saw Killebrew after that, until her death in December 2009, she would tease him about withdrawing from the dome plan, saying, "Harmon, if it weren't for you—oh boy—see how things happen?"

Mark Heleker still has big dreams of a big baseball. The principal of Payette High and a member of the city council, Heleker thinks the logistics of getting Killebrew's distinctive signature on the dome is as big a challenge as finally, after all these years, getting the approval and momentum to achieve it.

"We're kind of reviving that," Heleker said on a January morning as he walked the halls of the high school. There are three trophy cases on site honoring Killebrew. One has hardware commemorating various tournament and game victories of his football, basketball, and baseball teams. Another houses his No. 12 baseball jersey. The third honors Killebrew alongside Payette High heavyweights James McClure, the former U.S. senator, and Warren McCain, who rose to be CEO of the Albertson's grocery store empire.

"We're talking about having two different cranes," Heleker continued, "and how nowadays with projectors, we could maybe project an outline of his actual signature onto the dome. A local radio station has been working with me a little bit, and I'm working through the city council. I would really like to see it up there."

The Minnesota Twins had a similar Killebrew autograph in white against the green backdrop of their outfield wall displayed as a tribute to the late slugger during the 2011 season.

Heleker has done much to revive the connection between Payette and its most famous sports personality. Harmon Killebrew Day was established on April 16, 2005. It was a brainstorm that swelled out of an innocent conversation Heleker had one day in 2004 with the school's baseball coach, Tracy Bratcher, about ways to raise awareness and boost local enthusiasm for the Pirates program. "He and I always felt that Payette was a baseball town, and we were talking about ideas to promote Payette baseball," Heleker said of the men's "Eureka!" moment, "and all of a sudden it was like, 'Harmon!'"

As Bratcher told the *Idaho Statesman* in May 2011, "My generation missed his playing days, but we grew up to the stories and reading the backs of baseball cards and reading old newspaper clippings that your grandma cut out. One thing I noticed when I became the coach is that the next generation was really kind of clueless about who Harmon Killebrew was."

More than just the passage of time had brought about some separation between the hero and his hometown. For most of Killebrew's career through the 1960s, the '70s, and beyond, he and his family had lived in a home in Ontario, Oregon, just across the Snake River at the Idaho border. About five miles southwest of Payette along Interstate 84, Ontario's slogan is, "Where Oregon begins."

It almost became the place where Payette ended, however. At least in an economic sense.

* * *

Primarily a farming community, supplying Heinz and other food companies with the same sort of russet potatoes, sugar beets, and onions that Idaho farmers provide, Ontario also began to grow its retail economy via the lack of a state sales tax. That lured shoppers from Payette, Fruitland, and New Plymouth first, then merchants second. When big-box stores such as Home Depot and Wal-Mart came into the "micropolitan" market, they set up—you guessed it—in Ontario. Even residents uprooted, following their finances to the more favorable side of the river/border.

"Oh yeah, Payette used to be so much bigger than Ontario," said Ron Manser, a classmate and teammate of Killebrew in high school and a lifelong resident of their hometown. "At one time, Payette had every car manufacturer, every dealership here. People of Ontario would come over to this side to shop. It was a big thriving metropolis, as far as any of the towns around, much bigger than Ontario. We had everything here—four grocery stores. We had specialty shops like meat markets, shoe stores, dry goods—three or four of them. Then our good legislature passed the sales tax law, and Ontario did not have a sales tax.

"The business just completely dropped. Everybody started closing down and leaving. There's one auto dealership left. We [owned] a Ford dealership and I sold out in '91, and they consolidated it with the one in Ontario. It all went across the river."

Manser was head of the Chamber of Commerce for a time and commissioned a study. It found that because property taxes in Oregon were higher at that time, merchants still charged more for goods and services, on average, than the Payette price even after the 3 percent sales tax. Didn't matter. "We advertised the daylights out of it," Manser said. "But *noooo!* They weren't paying any sales tax! They'd pay more for their goods before they'd pay that."

A rivalry between the two towns intensified, and the Killebrews took a hit for that. They had moved over to the Oregon side for a number of reasons, placing their five children in the Oregon school system and basing the auto dealership, Killebrew Motors, in Ontario. Some of those left behind—or at least those who felt that way—didn't take kindly to it and began to harbor a bit of a grudge.

"We kind of had a thing with Ontario because they kind of stole our glory," Heleker said, "and then Killebrew establishes a home there and raises his kids there. Some people felt, 'Harmon doesn't consider us his hometown anymore. He must not because, look, he's over there.' I was a little kid at that time, so to me none of that mattered. He's still Killebrew, he's my idol, he's the man, so anything he does or says ... nobody else's word means anything to me.

"But now that I'm older and one of the community leaders, I realize how wearing that was on our communities at the time. 'Our favorite son was in Ontario, too, and when he's back in the area, that's where he goes.' I really think there *was* a period of time where people around here, even though they still respected him and thought Harmon was the greatest thing that ever came out of Payette, there were some hard feelings. He came out of Payette, left Payette, and went to Ontario. And Harmon kind of felt that."

When Killebrew bought a home in Meridian (closer to Boise), he still felt concerned and wondered about the locals' grudge. It came up when Heleker contacted Killebrew with his brainstorm for Harmon Killebrew Day. Killebrew appreciated the lifeline thrown back to his true home. "He would say, 'I'm really happy that we're doing this because I want to be Payette. I just don't want to be from this area. I want to be Payette.' You could tell that was a very strong feeling he had."

By that time, the feeling was mutual. The grudge has lessened, and the wounds had scabbed over. By April 2005, the Killebrews were gone from Ontario. Their children were grown, and Harmon and Elaine divorced years earlier. Harmon spent most of his time in Scottsdale, Arizona, with his second wife, Nita.

Plus, kids like Heleker were the grown-ups now. That put the high school principal in a position to make things happen with a small-town advantage in getting things done—he had been both assistant principal and mayor for several years before flipping into the principal and city councilman role. Wearing multiple hats streamlined a lot of processes in taking the idea from plan to action. Heleker also had a connection to Killebrew that would make the whole vision possible.

Pat Heleker, Mark's father, worked for the U.S. Postal Service in town for 38 years. Off-duty, though, he played semi-pro baseball for the Payette Packers in the Idaho/Oregon Border League and later officiated baseball at all levels throughout the Treasure Valley. In fact, Pat Heleker was 12 years older than Killebrew and was seen as something of a mentor and role model when the younger man joined the Packers for games after his senior season at Payette in 1954. Killebrew's own father, Clay, had died during his junior year.

"Harmon played just a short time with them before the major leagues stole him away," Mark Heleker said. "But since my dad was a little ahead of him, my dad used to brag, 'For a while, I was Killebrew's hero.' He used to tag around with my dad and talk baseball."

The elder Heleker and young Killebrew kept in touch after Harmon left for the big leagues—Harmon even counseled his friend against pursuing a career as a professional umpire because of the strain the traveling and time commitment would put on Heleker's family back in Payette. That friendship gave Mark Heleker some currency with his friends as Killebrew's star climbed in the 1960s.

"I had a big brag. How many kids, when they pick up the mail at their house, see a letter from Harmon Killebrew?" the principal said, thinking back to the days when he would scour box scores in the morning paper to see how his favorite player had done. "So I'd always tell my friends, 'Yep, another letter from Harmon came today.'"

Pat Heleker was 80 years old by the time his son, Mark, pulled together the inaugural Harmon Killebrew Day in Payette on April 16, 2005. "The first couple of Killebrew days, my dad was still alive and he and Harmon kind of reunited, so that was fun," Mark Heleker said.

For the first celebration, the hometown pretty much blew it out for its old baseball hero. They arranged a banquet at the very un-Payette price of $50 per plate. The new middle school in town offered the biggest venue available, and they still had to cut off the number of tickets sold. They brought back favorite teammates and neighbors who had known Harmon back when, and they even held a parade. The next day, the Pirates had a home baseball game and made it special with a community barbecue beforehand. The first 200 people attending the barbecue received bobblehead dolls designed with Killebrew in his Payette uniform. "The only thing Harmon said to me about it was that he hoped the proceeds would go to support Payette baseball," Heleker said. "He didn't want to see anything. He just said, 'If we're making any money, let's put it to baseball.'"

Heleker ran the event, serving as the go-between for Harmon and Nita with the fans. At the barbecue, the plan had been for the Hall of Fame slugger to sign autographs for a fixed period of time. "We had all these rules and regulations, that, 'Mr. Killebrew will stop signing autographs at this time,' and, 'No one will bother Mr. Killebrew at the game,'" Heleker said. "Harmon wouldn't go for that at all. He started signing autographs at 4:00 in the afternoon and he signed them up until we're trying to get the game started. He was set up right behind the school, and I was going back and forth to the field, and when I told him we were getting close [to the first pitch], he said, 'Hey, they're just going to have to wait. I still have a few people in line here.' I said, 'All right, it's your day. Whatever you want to do.'

"Then during the game people are coming to talk with him. And he stayed after and signed more things. Nita has been at each of these Killebrew Days and she's had to kind of be his watchdog because I'm sure wherever they traveled, that's what her role was. She would come up to me and say, 'Okay Mark, I would like you to tell these people that at this time…' I said, 'That's what I tried to do, Nita, and he wouldn't go along with that.' Finally she said, 'I know. He won't let you. That's why you have to just make the announcements.'

"That's what we ended up doing because, you know, if Harmon were here for three days, he would spend every minute of it meeting and greeting people and signing [autographs]."

Harmon Killebrew Day has continued each year on the third Saturday in April. The program has changed a little—there's a golf tournament on Friday followed by a $25 prime rib dinner catered by the school's baseball players. Their parents cook, it's held in the middle-school commons, and Killebrew's old classmates continue to be invited and introduced at the game.

Bratcher and Heleker fondly recalled the second or third edition of the event when they pried Harmon away from the last of the autograph seekers and delivered him to the cafeteria for a question-and-answer session with the ballplayers. "These kids, their eyes are *this* big and their jaws all dropped," Heleker remembered. "Tracy, being a baseball coach, knew some great questions to ask. We'd pick out a pitcher, we'd ask Harmon, 'When you faced Don Drysdale ... ?' And the kids would go, 'You batted against Don Drysdale?' And he'd say, 'Yeah. I hit my home run in the World Series off Don Drysdale.' And these kids were going, 'Wow!'

"It was just so much fun. Any question the kids had, he got up and showed them his stance. And why he did things a certain way. And how he adjusted if the pitcher did this or that. They were in complete awe. Harmon would have done it clear through the game but we had to get him out of there so they could warm up. Tracy told them, 'Now go out and do what Harmon Killebrew taught you!' If I remember right, in the game we got down early, but the kids came back and hit home runs and scored 16 runs, and we won."

Killebrew committed to attend the event each year, but he needed excused absences a few times. In 2010, for instance, he was in Minnesota for the opening of Target Field, the Twins' new open-air ballpark in downtown Minneapolis. It was an exciting time—a return to the team's natural roots. Killebrew had worked as a broadcaster and he had paid a visit as a Twins alumnus to the Hubert H. Humphrey Metrodome, but that artificial, Teflon-covered, multi-purpose facility never held a whiff of nostalgia for him or any right-minded baseball fan. He had wrapped up his career in Minnesota, first as a Twin (1974) and one year later with the Royals at Metropolitan Stadium in suburban Bloomington. That was the site of The Killer's greatest feats, the place where he had played for the host team in a World Series, two AL playoff series, and an All-Star Game.

For longtime fans, Target Field, a state-of-the-art baseball park at its 2010 opening, intentionally evokes memories of the Twins' original home. And it showcases a number of Killebrew mementoes and reminders. His retired uniform No. 3 (the first Twin so honored) hangs high above the field. There are displays of many of his baseball artifacts in museum-like cases within the park and, most striking of all, his bronze likeness—in full, powerful swing—stands outside one of the gates.

Killebrew missed his "day" in 2011 while battling the esophageal cancer that would end his life a few weeks later. But the celebration went on, his new friends and old school chums understood, and at that time, they still rooted for his recovery. The plan is to continue the annual event as part of Payette's civic calendar—even if the guest of honor no longer can attend. There are Killebrew family members to invite and pals such as former Green Bay Packers great Jerry Kramer, an Idaho native who lives not far from Boise, as well.

Heleker grimaces a little when he thinks of all the years lost before the light bulb came on in 2005. But then, the better way to think about it is to focus on the Harmon Killebrew Days that they did have with the slugger on board, making life tough on the organizers with his endless autograph signings, boosting the profile and coffers for Payette baseball, and putting a little pride back into those who never strayed far from home.

"Everything he's meant to Payette, it's just...there should not be a disconnect," the high school principal said. "There never should have been. And I'd like to think that was completely done away with through this."

There still is work to be done, of course. There still is the unfinished business of a huge baseball just waiting to be painted and signed.

Chapter 2

Payette Back Then

The math seems off. If Harmon Clayton Killebrew Jr. was born in 1936 and Harmon Clayton Killebrew Sr. was 42 at the time, then this claim floating around about Culver Killebrew—Jr.'s *grandfather*—being renowned as the "strongest man in the Union Army" couldn't possibly be true.

Or could it?

It's a tale—seems like a broken time-machine boast—that appears again and again in background stories, magazine pieces, and biographies about Harmon Jr., the most famous of the Killebrew men for his power and accomplishments as a big league ballplayer and eventual inductee to the Baseball Hall of Fame in Cooperstown, New York. And yet chronologically, it seems out of whack. Union Army. That label, rather than simply U.S. Army or National Army, suggests a specific land force at a specific point in American history—the army of both professional soldiers and volunteers that waged battle with the Confederate States Army in the American Civil War from 1861 to 1865.

But if Culver Killebrew was the strongest man in blue for some period during those years, wouldn't he more likely have been Harmon's and his siblings' great-grandfather?

"Our father wasn't born until our grandfather was in his sixties," said Bob Killebrew, Harmon's older brother by three years. Bob was the second son of Harmon Sr. and Katherine Pearl Killebrew, and he still lives close to their hometown in Caldwell, Idaho, just west of Boise.

In his sixties? A visit to some genealogical databases disputes that number but confirms the overall truth. Culver Killebrew was a vibrant and virile fellow, both in his prime and later in his life. He was born on April 15, 1839, which would have put him at the peak of his physical prowess during the Civil War—he was also said to be the Union's heavyweight wrestling champion, which would explain the "strongest man" claims—and made him 54 at the time his eighth son and last of 10 children was born in October 1893.

"Culver was married three times," Bob Killebrew said, launching into a favorite story. "My grandmother was an old-maid school teacher. She was 30 or 35 years old when they got married. And they had two sons by that marriage. Culver's first wife died from eating poison mushrooms. Second wife died from eating poison mushrooms. The third wife, she died because she wouldn't eat the poison mushrooms."

At that, Bob laughed heartily, thrilled to have snared another unsuspecting listener. But there was some truth in what he said, in terms of the timeline, if not the autopsy reports on wife No. 1 Mary Elizabeth Harpole, wife No. 2 Mary Ann Miller, and wife No. 3 Frances Alice Weaver. Culver was a two-time widower by the time he married Frances Alice in December 1885. He and Mary Elizabeth had three children before she died in 1865. Culver and Mary Ann had five kids between 1867 and 1878 before she passed away in 1884.

Fourteen months later, the big man married for the third and final time. Son Thomas was born in April 1887, and six years after that—by which time Culver's first child Susan already was 32 years old—Harmon Clayton Sr. arrived. Culver lived until December 1917, when he passed away at the ripe old age of 78, well beyond the average U.S. life expectancy for a male at that time.

It is important to pin down the details of the Killebrew family tree in order to learn more about its most famous branch. Harmon's strength as a major league slugger came from somewhere and, contrary to many long-ball hitters that followed in his footsteps 20 or 30 years later (and eventually passed him in raw numbers), it most definitely did not come from the end of a syringe or a smear of "cream" or "clear." Some of his power was nurtured, the result of a childhood and adolescence spent outdoors in a rugged part of the country, playing each sport as the seasons changed, and working part-time jobs that required manual labor. But a large portion of his power was a result of nature.

Culver Killebrew was born and died in Calhoun, Illinois. In addition to his family life, he found time to become a successful farmer and livestock trader—successful enough that he was able to build a 22-room mansion just outside of Nebo, Illinois, according to Harmon's niece, Diane Killebrew Holt, in the April 2005 edition of *Idaho Magazine*. Culver Killebrew's extraordinary strength became the stuff of legend, and it was said that he could stand flat-footed and jump over a horse.

Apparently, Culver never met a man who could do anything better than him—but based on a story handed down through generations, there was one thing. As the story goes, some "little shrimp" in Culver's Union Army brigade demonstrated that he could run, leap, and do a handspring onto a horse's back. When the big man tried that one, he was lucky not to break his neck.

Fortunately, Harmon Jr.'s paternal grandfather survived to produce Harmon Sr. Preferring to be known by his middle name, "Clay," he was the prototype for the eventual Hall of Fame ballplayer. Clay stood 5'11", weighed about 190 pounds, and was built thick and strong, a gifted all-around athlete but especially accomplished in football and track. He lost sight in one eye before his freshman year in high school, though the cause is in some dispute. A 1959 story in the Jacksonville, Illinois, newspaper reported that Clay inadvertently pierced his right eye with a thorn while trimming a hedgerow. But Harmon's first wife, Elaine, said years later that she was told the accident stemmed from the use of a specific poison being used in the hog pens on his family's farm back in Nebo, Illinois. In 1971, she told Wayne Anderson, author of the book, *Harmon Killebrew, Baseball's Superstar,* that she often would sit near Clay to watch Harmon's games. Already shy, she added, "If I were sitting on the side where he had no vision, he wouldn't notice that I was there."

Clay reached All-State status at Jacksonville High, playing with the Crimson in 1913 and 1914. He went on to become a punishing fullback at West Virginia Wesleyan in 1915, crossing paths with coach Greasy Neale (who would go on to enshrinement in the Pro Football Hall of Fame). Clay also played at Millikin University in Decatur, Illinois. After earning an honorable-mention spot on Walter Camp's All-American team in 1916, Clay played professionally for a couple seasons with the Wheeling (West Virginia) Steelers. One of the teams the Steelers faced was the Canton Bulldogs with sports immortal Jim Thorpe.

"He said one time he tackled Jim, and well, my father's nickname was 'Killy,'" Bob Killebrew recalled early in 2012. "After he tackled him, Jim Thorpe got up and said, 'Killy, you're a good old boy. You let Jim run!' Dad said, 'Let him run, hell. It took me 40 yards to catch him.'"

* * *

It was fitting, considering the role sports had played and would play in the Killebrew family, that Clay and Katherine Pearl May were married on their way home from a football game in St. Louis in 1917. Not long after that, with son Gene on the scene and a family extended with in-laws and Katie's grandmothers, the whole bunch moved out West for greater opportunities. In 1920, they settled for a time in Portland, Oregon, where Clay got busy in the Amateur Multnomah Wrestlers League, competing in matches up and down the West Coast. In probably his biggest match, he took on Ted Thy for the Pacific Coast championship and lost their battle. There is a photo from around that time of Clay dressed in a suit and facing the camera while an equally well-attired friend stands perched on Clay's shoulders.

By 1924, the family had settled in Payette. Clay served as sheriff there but stayed active physically, as well. In the magazine article by Bob's daughter, Diane, she wrote that Clay would take on (and usually beat) circus boxers as they came through the area. He even got an offer to hire on as one. Later, Clay started a house-painting business, working for neighbors and others around Payette. He was said to be an avid reader of philosophy, exploring the works of Homer, Socrates, Plato, and Cicero.

"My parents would hire him when they needed some painting done," recalled Ron Manser, a childhood friend of Harmon who would exit Payette High one year sooner—class of 1953 to Harmon's '54. "I can remember their dad coming over—he always had candy in his pockets for the kids. And he made root beer. I guess in Minneapolis, they have a root beer now that Harmon's son is involved with." (Killebrew Root Beer is available back in the Twin Cities and is sold at Target Field.)

The Killebrews' old house on the town's northwest side still existed in early 2012. It was a cream-colored, story-and-a-half structure with a tiny porch, no garage, and was in need of some repair. "That house was built in 1913," Bob said. "I think the termites are the only thing holding it together."

Katie Killebrew lived there almost to the end. For many years, daughter Eula stayed there, as well, moving in after Eula's husband died suddenly while the couple was expecting their third child. The Killebrew men were considered to be the athletes in the family—Katie stood all of 4'10"—but the matriarch of the house was known as a good sport in her own right.

One of her most common expressions was, "The game was always at the Killebrews."

When it came to the large Sunday dinners that sometimes grew to include extended family and friends, she liked to say, "You don't need an invitation. Just be on time."

She was popular in Payette for her work with the American League Auxiliary, the Order of the Eastern Star, the Portia Club, the Payette County Historical Society, and the Republican Women's League. She joked that she never was old enough for the Senior Citizens Center, though she was 95 when she died in March 1990.

Much of Katie's time was spent as wife and mother. Eugene was the oldest, born nearly 20 years before Harmon. Next came Eula, 15 years Harmon's senior. Patricia was born in 1931 and died at three months old. Bob came along in 1933, followed by Harmon on June 29, 1936.

It did not take Bob long to notice the little stranger in their midst. "I was only about three years old before I figured out he was there and what he was doing," Harmon's closest sibling said. "He was crawling around on the floor getting into my blocks, messing up my fine edifices that I was building. One day I looked up at my mother and said, 'Are we going to keep him all winter?' That was one of my first lines! I don't know why we did, but we kept him around for a few more years."

All of the Killebrew kids took tap dancing and piano lessons. They fished, rode horses, and spent long days at a farm in the area that belonged to their Aunt Anne and Uncle Charlie. The boys built rafts for adventures on the Snake River. Many times on weekend nights, Clay would take Bob and Harmon to the movies, stop for an ice cream cone afterward, and then race them back home to the house on Seventh Street. He laced them up in boxing gloves and taught them lessons about temperament and sportsmanship that became part of Harmon's fabric as a major league star.

Bob said, "Harmon found out at a very early age, 'If you lose your temper, you lose the game.' That was from our father.... He was very good at instructing us. He'd tell us, 'You've got to figure out what you're trying to accomplish and not be distracted by this, that, or anything.' So no, Harm never threw a bat or took off and threw his helmet or cussed out an umpire. No. That was never part of his ego.... Several guys who played against him were his very good friends, and that's one of the reasons."

The love Clay and Katie had for the children and their development came shining through one day when a neighbor lady tsk-tsked about the wear and tear going on at the family's inviting yard. "We always had something going on out in the front yard," Bob recalled. "She said, 'Mr. Killebrew, those kids are tearing up the grass.' He said, 'That's all right, we're raising boys, we're not raising grass.'"

Some 40 years later, Harmon used that tale in his Hall of Fame induction speech at Cooperstown, though in the re-telling, it was Katie expressing her concerns for the lawn. After all, the sentiment and Clay's comeback were what really mattered.

Grass wasn't the only thing in jeopardy at the original "Killebrew field." Oldest son Gene, the former newspaper editor, once wrote about the family's bay window. "I was the first one to break Dad's window—when I was four years old in 1921. And from then on it really took a beating. All types of balls went through that window in the next 35 years, footballs, baseballs, snowballs, golf balls, and numerous rocks of assorted sizes. Each time the window was broken, Dad quietly went to town and got another pane and put it in. He never once told us kids that we couldn't play ball in the yard."

Katie wasn't as calm, it turned out, especially when the weather turned cold or when replacement glass had to be ordered for the big picture window, requiring a temporary canvas or wood cover. Bob recalled, "Our father finally figured it out, he put in [a French window with] small panes. So you'd only have to replace one pane instead of the whole window."

As the boys grew older, the sports grew more organized. And the bulk each packed as an athlete grew more apparent. One photo of Bob and Harmon in their Payette High football uniforms in the autumn of 1950 is especially telling and shows what Bob was talking about when he said, "Harmon was three years younger and 20 years bigger than me." Bob was a senior by then—the Snake River Valley All-Conference Halfback of the Year, in fact—and Harmon was just a freshman. But by appearances, they could be reversed; the younger brother stood about 6" taller and probably 20 pounds heavier than Bob.

"Harmon was the only person that I recall who graduated from Payette High with four letters in all four years," his friend, Manser, said. "He lettered in football, basketball, baseball, and track every year. Heck, that's all we had. That was in the days before tennis and tiddlywinks.... He was just an ordinary, hard-working kid. And from the time I'd known him as a little kid until he passed away, he hadn't changed any. He was just the same person all his life."

In those days, given the size of Payette's population, grammar schools on the town's east and west sides had classes through sixth grade. Then seventh and eighth grades were held in the same building as the senior high. "So you knew everybody," Manser said. "The school was on the east side, too, and a lot of us lived on the west. But you got an hour for lunch and you'd just walk home."

Harmon hummed along as an athlete, rapidly earning spots on the varsity of each sport he pursued, then starring on the American Legion baseball team in the summer. As a quarterback, he was said to be equally effective throwing and running with the ball, and when a possession did end poorly, Killebrew would bail out the Pirates as their punter. His greatest on-field challenges came from a pair of knee injuries, one as a sophomore and the other as a senior, that cut into Payette's seasons and were the early versions of ailments and physical setbacks that would plague him throughout his major league days.

Nothing in sports, however, compared to what Harmon and the rest of the family went through on February 25, 1953. Sometime after 1:00 AM, Harmon—at 16 years old he was the only child still living at home then—heard his mother scream. Clay was having an apparent heart attack and, try as they might to help him given the limited options of the day, Clay died in a matter of minutes.

In the newspaper obituary, Clay's focus on his children and their athletics received the acclaim it deserved. "'Clay' is survived by three sons who upheld the family name on the field of play. Gene and Robert actively participated in sports events. Youngest son, Harmon, has added the most recent honors to the collection with his tremendous work this year on the championship Payette Pirate football 11 and his fine play with the basketball squad."

Manser remembered that Mr. Killebrew's death hit hard a number of families and friends who circled the wagons to help them all get through it. "We were playing for the district championship, the tournament was in Boise, and his dad had just passed away just as the tournament started," Manser said. "And his mother and sister insisted that he go play in it. Our coach came to me—I had an automobile at the time—and said, 'I want you to drive your car to the tournament and I want you to take Harm with you. And as soon as the tournament's over, take him back home so he can be with his mother.'"

Harmon and classmate Elaine Roberts were constant companions at that point. They had known each other for years, and Harmon finally took extra interest in the pretty blonde cheerleader and majorette. When Clay Killebrew died, Harmon and Elaine were high school sweethearts. Soon, she would become his first wife and the mother of his children.

"For three or four days of the tournament, I drove him and Elaine back and forth," Manser said. "And we'd come back at night, come by Elaine's house—she lived across town from us—and stop to let her out, and Harm would get out and say, 'I'll walk home.' It was hard, losing his dad, because they were awfully close. Clay'd get out there and work with him, Bob, all the time. I remember they had a tire set up in the backyard, hanging up so Harm could throw [footballs] through that tire. They were tearing up the lawn pretty bad, and Harm's mother got on Clay about it..."

There's that story again.

* * *

Harmon's multi-sport career peaked in the 1953–54 school year at Payette High. He earned recognition as a member of All-American high school squads, was voted conference MVP in basketball, and batted .375 to lead the Pirates to the conference championship. His football coach, Jack Dailey, called him the "greatest athlete I ever coached" during an awards ceremony.

Larry Lynch, the son of former *Ontario Argus-Observer* columnist Don Lynch, wrote in May 2011, "My first memory of Harmon is the sight of his bulk carrying half our football team toward the goal line in the fall of 1953. He didn't have much blocking and never made a touchdown in that game, which we won 40–0. But he went on to be named Idaho's No. 1 high school running back. A victory over Ontario was about all he was to be denied that year."

Back on June 21, 1954, it was the elder Lynch sharing in print a tale from Harmon's brother, Gene, on Clay's influence on the youngest child-turned-budding-man, "Young Harmon had chores to do at home as a boy, and sometimes when he was playing sandlot baseball his mother would send the father to fetch the son home for family duty. If Harmon was playing ball, his father just couldn't bear to interrupt. He would come home quietly and do the chores himself so his prospective 'big leaguer' could get in a few minutes more of precious practice."

"My father helped me—not only with baseball but football, basketball and some track," Harmon said years later. "And he used to teach my brother and I how to punch a punching bag and skip rope and do lots of things."

Bob said, "Our older brother played football, basketball, baseball, too. But nobody wanted to become a professional other than Harmon. I think that was his ambition since he was little, and he worked at it. He worked at everything, be it throwing a basketball through the hoop or horseshoes or ping-pong, whatever. He worked at it 'til he could beat you. I don't mean he carried it to extremes—he knew how to lose a game, be a good sport. But he had a little different attitude about it all from the rest of us."

The physical side took care of itself, given the genetics, the desire, and Harmon's part-time job wrangling milk cans. They were more like milk drums, in fact.

"Back in those days, the milk trucks would run around with the milk in cans—10-gallon cans," Ron Manser said, recalling the neighbor who hired Harmon to do the heavy lifting. "You'd pick up those cans and throw 'em on the truck. You'd leave empty ones—they all had numbers of them, so you'd get 'can No. 171' from the farmer and take another '171' off and leave it. He got a lot of strength that way as a kid. And also, in the fall, we had classmates that had farms. We'd go buck onions and buck spuds in the sacks, and throw 'em up on the beds of trucks and someone would be up there stackin' 'em. But that was just life."

Killebrew did those sorts of things all through high school. "That will put muscles on you even if you're not trying," Killebrew told the *Washington Post* in 1984.

It's not as if they all were choir boys, by the way. They would go cruising in the 1930 Model A Ford that Manser got for $875 in his sophomore year. "I was making $30 a week working at the service station for my dad, and my car payment was $25 a week. That left me $5 to buy gas," Manser said. Then there was the Letterman's Club at Payette, which had a little bit of an initiation ritual.

"On the last day, they'd take you up into the hills, blindfold you on the way up, then turn you loose. You'd be left up in the hills there, trying to find your way out," Manser said. Once in a while, the phone would ring late and an angry parent or coach would be frantic, wondering where their boy was. "Never lost any for good, though," Manser said.

Manser, Killebrew, and the rest of their friends treasured their youth in Payette. But real life was quickly approaching. The kid with the Model A wound up going into the car business himself, getting married and starting a family soon after graduation. Bob Killebrew went to college for a year, then entered the service and spent 18 months in Korea. By the time he graduated from Payette, Harmon faced some grown-up decisions, too.

At that moment, he just knew he had outgrown the American Legion league in which he was accustomed to playing. "Whoever was the higher-up in Legion ball thought he hit the ball too hard for him to play Legion. He might kill some third baseman," said Cliff Massengill, who would become Killebrew's teammate at the semi-pro level.

Harmon often played sports with and against older boys, which was not only a nod to his abilities but helped to develop them. But he was 17, and as his days at Payette High neared their end, he needed to move his game up and take on some full-grown men.

"I don't know if I ever really reached that point where I felt like I had what it took," Killebrew once said. "But I always had the desire to be a professional baseball player. I wanted to play baseball for a career. I'm not sure that I knew even when I signed a major league contract that I had what it took to be a major leaguer."

It wasn't long before Killebrew would get the chance to find out. But it took a while before he could answer his own question.

Chapter 3

The Senator and the Senators

"When the legend becomes fact, print the legend."

That's a line from *The Man Who Shot Liberty Valance,* the 1962 John Ford movie that starred John Wayne, James Stewart, and Lee Marvin. Stewart had a prominent role as a United States senator, but his character, Ransom "Rance" Stoddard, was purely fictional.

Herman Welker, on the other hand, was a real-life, flesh-and-blood lawmaker and politician whose place in Killebrew's story, and thus in a small corner of baseball history, packs at least as much legend as fact.

Welker was a former prosecutor and private-practice lawyer from Cambridge, Idaho, who settled in Payette after serving in the U.S. Air Force. He spent two years as a member of the Idaho State Senate and was elected to the U.S. Senate in 1950. Once in Washington, Welker gained a reputation as one of America's most conservative—and anti-communist—legislators. The Republican became an ally of the notorious Joe McCarthy (R-Wisconsin), known best for fanning suspicions and paranoia at the height of the Cold War with his investigations into notable Americans and their political leanings.

Welker also dedicated a good chunk of his time to the national pastime, frequently attending Washington Senators games at Griffith Stadium. He regularly dropped in at the office of Clark Griffith, the Senators' owner. Nicknamed "The Old Fox," Griffith had been born in Clear Creek, Missouri, in November 1869 and made his pro pitching debut with the Milwaukee Brewers of the Western Association in 1888. He got to what was considered the big leagues in 1891 and stayed around for 20 seasons, compiling a 237–146 record. Griffith also managed the ballclubs on which he played his final 12 seasons, and he kept going as a skipper through the 1920 season. When he took over in Washington in 1912, he received a 10 percent ownership stake in the operation. Over time, Griffith became team president and the Senators' majority owner.

Griffith was 80 years old but still very much in charge by the time Welker got to Washington. The freshman senator cultivated a friendship with the senior baseball lifer. And as sportswriter Francis Stann noted in the July 1959 edition of *Baseball Digest,* four years after Griffith's passing, "[Welker] had been a frequent visitor to the office of the late Clark Griffith. It was quite by accident, a jest in fact, that led to Killebrew's acquisition, his historic signing as the [Senators'] first bonus baby, his recent deeds."

Welker often boasted to Griffth that he had discovered Vern Law, a pitcher from Meridian, Idaho, who had been pursued by nine major league teams. "I got Law his chance through Bing Crosby," Welker claimed, dropping the name of the famous crooner who happened to be a part-owner of the Pittsburgh Pirates. Law won a total of 13 games for the Pirates in 1950 and 1951, strengthening Welker's claims. Law would win the Cy Young Award in 1960 (20–9, 3.08 ERA) to help Pittsburgh beat the New York Yankees in the World Series before wrapping up his career with a 162–147 mark in 16 seasons.

"Well, why don't you find me a good player?" Griffith was reputed to have said. "Last one we had out of Idaho was Johnson."

That, of course, would be Hall of Fame pitcher Walter Johnson, arguably the greatest pitcher of all time with a 417–279 record, 2.17 lifetime ERA, and 3,509 strikeouts. Gifted with wicked velocity, Johnson was born in Kansas and moved with his family to California and he pitched in Tacoma, Washington, before winding up in Weiser, Idaho, playing semi-pro ball. In 1907, his second season there, he went 14–2, posted a 0.55 ERA, and struck out 214 batters in 146 innings. Johnson's stellar season attracted considerable attention, and the Senators were the quickest to pounce. Manager Joe Cantillon sent an injured catcher, Cliff Blankenship, to scout Johnson. Blankenship came through, persuading the quiet right-hander to sign by agreeing to purchase a round-trip train ticket for him—just in case things didn't work out with the Senators.

It isn't clear whether Griffith was humoring Welker, if he thought the Idaho politician was onto something, or if he considered him to be a pest. Because it surely sounded like a hometown boast when the Senator came especially hard at the team owner one day, claiming, "There is a boy who is the greatest slugger since Mickey Mantle. He runs as fast. He can throw better than Mantle."

Mantle was the exciting phenom of the Yankees and pretty much the whole American League, a two-time All-Star by the spring of 1954 who had amassed 57 home runs and 244 RBIs before his 22nd birthday. He had come from America's heartland, Commerce, Oklahoma, and he had raw, jaw-dropping power at the plate.

So whether Griffith's curiosity truly had been piqued by Welker or he simply wanted to call the boaster's bluff, he dispatched a former big league third baseman then in Washington's front office, Ossie Bluege, to Payette. Years later, Harmon recalled, "I think more than anything else just to keep Senator Welker quiet, Mr. Griffith sent Ossie Bluege out to see me.... And I really think that he just intended to invite me to come to Washington for a workout with the club, not thinking about signing me at that time."

Killebrew already had a plan by then, anyway. He was going to spend the summer after graduation working a maintenance job for the local school board and playing for the semi-pro Payette Packers. Then in the fall he would begin classes at the University of Oregon in Eugene, Oregon, going on a football scholarship but planning also to play baseball the following spring.

"The interesting thing is, Oregon wanted me to take over at quarterback for George Shaw, who played for the Vikings and Colts," Killebrew recalled. "I didn't go to Oregon, but four years later Oregon went to the Rose Bowl. I always wondered, 'If I had been there, would they have gotten to the Rose Bowl?'"

According to Killebrew's classmate Ron Manser, "He was probably a better football player than he was a baseball player in high school. He was one helluva quarterback. Had an arm that wouldn't stop. But one of the things was, he had bad knees. I thought he'd probably be another Namath. His knees just wouldn't do it. So to end up in baseball, that was a smart move."

Baseball *was* Killebrew's first love, and he still hoped for a career in the sport at some level. He began tearing up the semi-pro Border League almost immediately, and anywhere from nine to 12 of the 16 teams in the American and National leagues at that time were said to have scouted or at least heard of Killebrew. That was starting to provide something of a distraction from his college plans.

"I'd give him an 'A' in football, a 'C' in basketball, and an 'A+' in baseball," Tony Villanueva said shortly after Killebrew's death. Villanueva, a peer and rival from nearby Emmett, Idaho, competed against him from seventh grade right through high school and on into semi-pro ball. In the summer of 1954, Harmon was hitting better than .600 for the Payette Packers, while Villanueva topped the Emmett Loggers with a .517 average.

On one particular day, Villanueva recalled, Killebrew launched a ball from Emmett pitcher Stan Bollinger so high and far that Villanueva lost sight of it. "I think it was the first UFO in history," he said. When it was Villanueva's turn to pitch for Emmett, he had a strategy for facing Harmon. "I can always say I remember when he had trouble hittin' off of me," said the longtime Emmett educator and councilman. "But I had to throw it so far outside he couldn't reach it."

The Boston Red Sox seemed to be serious about Killebrew, sending scout Earl Johnson to see him and gifting him with a few Ted Williams–style bats. There was one potential snag: Lou Boudreau was the Boston manager at the time and apparently wasn't interested in having any "bonus babies" taking up roster spots. Baseball's rules mandated that any player receiving a bonus of $4,000 or more had to spend his first two pro seasons in the major leagues, rather than being farmed out to better learn the game.

In that sense, the Washington Senators might have had an unfair advantage in their pursuit of the Payette slugger. After all, their dugout already was full of players who might have been better off back in the minor leagues. The Senators weren't like other teams—they were much worse. From 1934 (the season after the club lost the World Series to the New York Giants) through 1960 (its last in the nation's capital before moving to Minnesota), Washington finished at or above .500 only five times and placed last or next-to-last 13 times.

A story in *Sports Illustrated* in October 1965—by which time the Senators had re-located and transformed themselves into the Twins—poked fun at three decades of misfortune. "The Senators' 30-year record of total ineptitude is unequaled in the annals of modern sport,"

Russell Baker wrote. "Any team, after all, can win a pennant. Even the St. Louis Browns did it in 1944. But to outwit the law of averages for 32 years, to finish with unparalleled consistency in the cellar, to lose 100 games year after year without letdown—that is a distinction."

How woeful were the Senators? Almost nothing went right for them. For instance, before one season, management decided that the team needed to boost its home run totals, so bleacher seats were added in left field to effectively move in the fence. Sure enough, home runs at Griffith Stadium soared. But of the 168 that were hit that season, only 63 were hit by Washington batters.

As Ossie Bluege made his arrangements to scout this kid named Killebrew, the Senators were headed to another dismal finish. The team went 11–17 in May 1954 and would lose more than it won in each subsequent month, settling at 66–88 for sixth place and 45 games behind the first-place Cleveland Indians. The Senators wound up seventh in home runs and batting average, third in runs and hits allowed, and they committed the fourth-most errors in the AL. Attendance was a mere 503,542, an average of 6,456 fans per game, and attendance had dropped nearly 200,000 in just two seasons. Clearly, Washington needed something to boost performance on the field and interest at the box office.

It rained in Payette the day Bluege flew into Boise and then rented a car to drive the final 60 miles or so. It rained the next day and the day after that, too. The games went from iffy to postponed, leaving the scout and the prospect to sit in the car and talk. That's when Killebrew told Bluege that he was headed to Oregon to play football and baseball.

They might have left it there except that having a big league scout travel to Payette to see a local kid wasn't an everyday thing for Killebrew's friends and neighbors. This wasn't just a big chance for him—it felt like a big chance for the whole town. Word got around that Bluege was in town to see Harmon play baseball and, by gosh, that's what he was going to see. In what sounds like a scene from a Hollywood movie—not a Western this time but something from Frank Capra—a number of Payette residents pitched in to give Bluege something to scout after all. They groomed the muddy field once the rain stopped and even burned gasoline on the infield to dry it faster.

When the Packers did play, Killebrew drilled one ball so hard that it hit the right fielder in the shin and caromed back toward the infield. But it was a home run that he hit to left, over what had seemed for all the years Killebrew played at that park to be an unreachable fence, that grabbed Bluege's attention. That incredible shot earned Harmon the payday that was about to come.

Baseball was a big deal in Payette, and it had a big ballpark to match. These days, the area has been turned into the high school's track with a football practice field in the middle. But back then, the location was all about baseball. A sizable L-shaped grandstand had a roof, which was unusual for that level of play. The outfield dimensions were vast with a beet field beyond the fence in left where Killebrew sent that particular baseball.

Curious to know how far the blast actually traveled, or at least to make a good guess, Bluege showed up at the park the next morning and walked off the distance. His verdict was 435'—by a 17-year-old boy.

At the end of the three games Bluege saw in Idaho, Killebrew was 11-for-13 with four home runs, two triples, and a double. The Senators' scout raced for a telephone, eagerly informing Griffith and getting the necessary authorization to bid serious money in hopes of landing Killebrew before any of Washington's rivals.

Convincing Harmon that his future was in professional baseball rather than on the college campus in Oregon wasn't too difficult once the young fellow began to run the numbers. On one side of the ledger were the years he would be devoting to the Ducks and other obligations. "If I go to college now, that's four years," Harmon thought.

"And in those days, guys were apt to go to the service for a couple of years. And then, if I did sign, I might be 28, 29 years old before I had the chance to get to the major leagues."

On the other side of the ledger were the fat round numbers tossed at him by the Senators, a bonanza now only a few pen strokes away—$30,000 in salary and bonuses over three years. It was an unusually big offer, the sort of money spent in Washington by politicians but not by ballclubs. Unlike other big-league owners, Griffith's sole source of income was his baseball team. He was known for his penurious tendencies.

Because Harmon was still a minor, Bluege sought out his mother to talk business. Katie referred him to Gene. The oldest Killebrew child liked what he heard and told their mother to sign the contract for Harmon. Gene and Don Dibble, coach of the Payette Packers, found Harmon at the high school where he was busy painting the gym. "In his T-shirt, with all those muscles squirting out, he looked like a Jimmie Foxx reborn," Bluege was quoted later, mentioning another Hall of Fame slugger and member of the 500 home run club that Killebrew one day would join.

Killebrew was wowed by the amount of Washington's offer—he realized quickly how much the money could ease things for his family and speed up his plans to marry Elaine. He eagerly told her the news and also phoned Johnson, the Boston scout who had shown interest in him. The former pitcher told Harmon the offer sounded good, better than what the Red Sox could do. And that's the deal Killebrew received—salaries of $6,000 for each of the 1954, 1955, and 1956 seasons, along with $4,000 in bonus money for each year of the deal. He became the first "bonus baby" in Senators history and thus would be headed directly to the parent club.

The final paperwork was dated June 18, 1954, and signed by Clark Griffith, AL president William Harridge, and Mrs. H.C. Killebrew.

Vernon Daniel, Welker's law partner back in Payette, sent a Western Union telegram to the Senators when the deal was officially complete and notified them to arrange transportation for Harmon to meet the team in Chicago, its latest stop on a 19-game trip. Washington's publicity department wrote up a news release, sharing the information that "the Washington Club has made a successful bid in landing the greatest potential infielder, Harmon Killebrew…"

There were skeptics, even from Harmon's side of the deal. Don Lynch, the newspaper writer from Ontario, Oregon, wasn't moved by Bluege's predictions that Killebrew could become one of the great hitters in baseball. "This is just a bunch of bulls---," Lynch thought, though he softened that slightly when he told Harmon's brother Gene, "This guy is trying to lead you on." For years after, Lynch felt that the Senators had stunted Killebrew's development by sending him right into the major leagues rather than letting him grow his game in the minors.

The move was a gamble for the Senators and a pricey one at that. But how does the old baseball saying go—desperate teams require desperate measures?

The scout's brother, Otto "Squeaky" Bluege (who briefly played in the big leagues with Cincinnati), met Killebrew at the airport in Chicago and whisked him downtown. The scenery, needless to say, was a little different from what the teenager was used to back in Treasure Valley. An Associated Press wire service photo from that day, June 22, shows Killebrew chatting with Senators manager Bucky Harris at the team's hotel in Chicago. The caption reads, "Killebrew, batting sensation of Idaho semi-pro ball, is reported to have cost $50,000." The dollar amount was wrong—a number of media outlets overstated his initial contract—but the clamor over the new kid was about right.

A group of writers peppered him with questions, and Killebrew admitted that he was a little scared at the prospect of being dropped into the deep end of baseball's swimming pool. He also told them that his favorite player at that time probably was Cleveland's Al Rosen because of the pop in Rosen's bat and his position (third base). But it wasn't as if the Killebrew home had regular access to watch or follow Rosen's career with the Indians. Rosen just happened to have been the AL's Most Valuable Player in 1953, so he was a lot of young guys' favorite player.

Another wire photo taken a few hours later shows Killebrew in the visitors' dugout at Comiskey Park, the home of the White Sox, holding a bat while standing next to Senators first baseman Mickey Vernon. He was introduced to veteran Johnny Pesky, the former Boston shortstop who was twice Killebrew's age and would be his new roommate. The kid from Payette was issued uniform No. 25. Several Washington players took him to the field for batting practice, where he mostly slapped the ball to right field against a young left-hander named Dean Stone. Then, during an infield drill, Killebrew handled some ground balls hit to him by coach Heinie Manush, who'd had a Hall of Fame career from 1923 to 1939 as an outfielder with six teams.

"I know how he feels," Harris told one of the sportswriters while Killebrew was in the batting cage. "He's shaking in his boots. This is the first major league park he has seen, and Stone is showing him better pitching than he has seen. He'll look better tomorrow when some of the nervousness wears off, and in a week or so he'll start catching up with the pitching."

It was a lot to absorb in a day—his first time on an airplane, his first glimpse of a big league ballpark or game. And that's all Harmon had to do that first night. He watched—part nervous, part excited—as the Senators lost 7–5.

The next day, however, Killebrew made his big league debut—as a pinch runner, of all things. The man who, during his 22 seasons, would never lay down a sacrifice bunt and would steal only 19 bases, was sent in to run for Clyde Vollmer in the second inning of a game in which Washington already trailed 5–2. He edged off first base, the Sox's Ferris Fain to his left, second baseman Nellie Fox to his right. Killebrew and the other two runners watched Eddie Yost pop up, and he moved up on a wild pitch by Chicago's Jack Harshman before Pesky flied out to end the inning. Reliever Gus Keriazakos came out of the bullpen to plug the ninth spot in the order, and Killebrew's first AL appearance was over.

It went like that for a while. The Senators traveled next to Detroit, Philadelphia, and New York with their wide-eyed spectator in tow. As the trip ended—7–12 overall, 3–9 with the kid aboard—Killebrew finally got a look at the ballpark that he would call home for all or parts of the next five seasons.

"I'll never forget when I got to Washington," Killebrew recalled in an extended interview for the Baseball Oral History Project, part of a 2008 book, *They Would Have Played for Nothing*, by former MLB commissioner Fay Vincent. "The next day, they wanted to throw me some batting practice and see if I could hit the ball at all. So there was a veteran left-hander on the mound.... In those days, the Griffith Stadium left-field fence was 405' down the left-field line—long, long, biggest park in baseball. This pitcher [journeyman Johnny Schmitz, 33, in the midst of an 11–8 season] threw me everything up there: curveballs, sliders, fastballs. I don't know if he threw any knuckleballs or not. But I hit quite a few up in the seats, and they seemed to be impressed with that. I really didn't think much about it, because I thought all the ballparks were like that in the big leagues."

It would be another month before the Senators played at Boston, giving Killebrew his first look at Fenway Park and the Green Monster wall so close in left that it tantalized many right-handed batters. His first thought, "Gee, maybe I signed with the wrong team." (Eventually Killebrew would punish the Red Sox by hitting 37 home runs at Fenway, the most he hit at any road park.)

More than three weeks passed between Harmon's debut and his next action. It, too, was as a pinch runner; in fact, all three of Killebrew's appearances in July came as a sub on the base paths. He scored once, but the Senators lost all three of those games. By this time, some of Welker's claims about the strong boy had proved false. For instance, while Killebrew ran better as a teenager than he did later in his career, he was no match for Mantle in speed. He had an awkward throwing motion—half football quarterback, half girl—that needed to be refined. And while the slugger broke in as a second baseman, his range and footwork made it obvious that the middle infield wasn't going to figure into his future. Frankly, Killebrew didn't look like a natural fit anywhere on the diamond with a glove in his hand. He was always better in the batter's box, especially when he could jog around the bases.

Killebrew stepped to the plate for the first time on August 18, pinch-hitting for pitcher Connie Marrero with two out and a man on first in the bottom of the 11th inning. He hit a groundball off lanky Red Sox right-hander Sid Hudson to Billy Goodman at second base, ending the Senators' 9–8 loss. The next day it was more of the same. He pinch hit for Camilo Pascual to lead off the bottom of the sixth with Boston already in front 9–1. He grounded out to short, then took a seat.

It wasn't until the next week, on August 23, that Killebrew started a ballgame for the first time in the majors. Harris kept the situation as non-threatening as possible, It was the second game of a Monday doubleheader with only 2,094 in the stands at Connie Mack Stadium and the Senators facing the even-worse Philadelphia Athletics that day. Killebrew started at second base, batted eighth, and went 3-for-4 with a double, two RBIs, and a walk. He also grounded into a double play, but after the Senators won 10–3, he remembered clearly thinking, "Gosh, this is going to be easy."

Not so much. The next two days, Killebrew faced White Sox pitching and went 1-for-7, driving in one run, walking once, and striking out three times. His first taste of the majors ended there—a .308 average (4-for-13)—when Harris permitted him to leave the ballclub early to begin the fall semester at the University of Idaho. By the time Killebrew would report to spring training, he and the Senators would have a new manager. Calvin Griffith—nephew and ward of Clark Griffith, with increasing involvement in the ballclub's daily operations—replaced Harris with Charlie Dressen. And the salty Dressen wasn't keen on living with Killebrew's flaws nor was he a fan of bonus babies in general.

Still, at a certain level, the young player's achievement already was a success. Clay Killebrew would have been proud that Harmon actually had made it to the major leagues with a contract to stick around longer. Herman Welker could boast to others that his baseball acumen had paid off for the Washington club. On June 30, just a week after Killebrew's arrival, the Senator sent a note to Clark Griffith:

My dear Mr. Griffith:

Your nice letter of June 29th came today and with it the season pass you sent. I cannot thank you enough for your thoughtfulness. I know that I will get a good deal of use out of the pass as I don't intend to miss a single game if I am within reasonable distance of it.

I also want to again express my appreciations for your including me in the luncheon for Harmon yesterday. It was a privilege to be there and to be able to appear on the television broadcast with the two of you.

With warmest personal regards, I am,

Sincerely,

Herman Welker

U.S. Senator, Idaho

Welker was gone from Washington before Killebrew and the Senators were. While he was around and going to the ballpark in 1955 and 1956—Harmon sat for all but 38 games in his second season and got into 44 in his third—the Senator would sometimes goad Dressen from his box at Griffith Stadium to "put Killebrew in!" Dressen posted a record of 116–212 before he was fired early in 1957.

Welker had also been "fired" by then, losing his 1956 bid for re-election to Democrat Frank Church. (Welker's pal McCarthy blasted President Dwight Eisenhower for not doing enough to support the Idaho Republican's campaign.) In January 1957, he returned to his home state intent on resuming his law practice in Boise. But Welker fell ill, and in October he was diagnosed with a brain tumor. The one-term senator died later that month at age 50. Griffith was gone, too, dying at age 85 in October 1955.

But the precocious slugger the senator and the team owner had helped deliver from the great state of Idaho was just getting started.

Chapter 4

Bonus Baby

For a period in baseball history, everybody—from real, honest-to-goodness players to clock-punching dreamers sitting in the grandstand—wanted to become a "bonus baby." From 1953 through 1957, however, a series of talented young prospects learned that it wasn't much fun to actually be one.

Becoming a bonus baby meant playing well enough as an amateur ballplayer to attract the attention of major league scouts, sifting through their competing offers, and then signing a lucrative contract that, by the rules in force at the time, assured the young man of spending at least his first two professional seasons in the American or National League.

Being a bonus baby, however, meant sitting instead of playing. It forced young players to learn the game in the glare of spotlights at baseball's highest levels with expectations and impatience crushing down on them. It pushed them into competition, on those rare occasions when they got a chance, against the game's most seasoned and savvy veterans.

Being a bonus baby also meant risking hard feelings from a fellow's own teammates and manager. You show up to the major league clubhouse guaranteed a roster spot—that means another player who has friends on that team has to go. Those left behind might also resent the new kid for the size of his contract or the threat he poses for playing opportunities. As for the manager, he's not thrilled to provide on-the-job training to some youngster prone to mistakes, not when mistakes can lose games and losses can get a skipper fired.

About the only thing worse than the bonus baby rule in practice was its conception, which was nothing more than an early attempt by baseball team owners to restrain their spending. If teams wanted to avoid all the unsavory effects cited above, they would limit their bids for top prospects to an amount below the threshold that triggered the rule. (This was all before the creation of the amateur draft.) And if a team hit or passed that threshold, then it was penalized via the loss of that roster spot and a limit on the player's development.

This, of course, could hurt both the player and the team.

"Looking back, I think I would have been a better ballplayer if I had spent those first two years in the minors," infielder Reno Bertoia told Brent P. Kelley in his 2006 book, *Baseball's Bonus Babies*. Bertoia signed with Detroit in 1953 for $23,000, got one at-bat that season as an 18-year-old stuck on the Tigers' roster, and was out of the big leagues at age 27. "I think, emotionally, sitting on the bench as a kid and not playing and wondering whether you belong there, then being put into situations where you're not comfortable—that was tough on a young kid.... I think it was the stupidest rule that was ever made, although you've got guys like Kaline and Koufax—they're one in a million."

Detroit outfielder Al Kaline was a bonus baby who made it all the way to the Hall of Fame. Dodgers pitcher Sandy Koufax got there, too, but only after some churning early in his career. Harmon Killebrew followed a path to the Hall more reminiscent of Koufax than Kaline.

Killebrew's hurry-up-and-wait beginning didn't necessarily damage his career in a significant way, unless you want to sweat some theoretical home runs he might have hit beyond No. 573 or the runs he might have driven in to push his career total past 1,600. But the approach did complicate his journey from Idaho strong boy to reliable major league slugger and eventually to AL All-Star and MVP. It threw a few curves at him and his family as he tried to establish himself with the Washington Senators. And it added stress that might not have been there had he taken a more traditional route, starting in the minor leagues and climbing out in the right order.

"To me, I don't really think it did that much damage," Killebrew said, looking back. "It was a rule that didn't help the player or the club, but as far as hurting me, I don't know. I was so young and I still was able to go to the minor leagues and get the experience that I needed and that's the only way you can get it, by playing every day. I could have just as well got it with the Washington club because they weren't going anywhere. But because Eddie [Yost] was there, I think that was the main reason I went to the minor leagues.

"I learned things playing every day that you can't learn by just sitting on the bench watching. You've got to be in there and learning those things playing every day. They can talk to you and in practice you can do all kinds of things, but unless you're in a competition and getting that experience, you aren't really learning."

Killebrew's 1954 season had been something of a lark, mostly because it started late. He signed with the Senators in June, met the team on the road, stuck around for a couple of months, and was allowed to leave early to enroll in fall semester college classes.

But in 1955, Harmon was on board from start to finish, from his first taste of spring training through the dead days of September for a team that lost 101 games, finished last, and was 20 games out (or more) from June 24 until everyone mercifully went home.

And if 1954 was some sort of "Introduction to the Show 101" for Killebrew, 1955 was an advanced class in not much. He got into 38 games, went to the plate 89 times, struck out 31 times, and batted .200. Throw out the final month, and his numbers were even worse (.164, three HR, six RBIs). Sure, he was paying attention, thinking along with the managers, getting his work in before the games, and so on. But as far as real situations, trial by fire, and learning by doing, Killebrew barely had a chance. Washington was 5–33 in the games in which he appeared, and he didn't have a single clutch hit to tie or give his club the lead.

The lost season began awkwardly and never got much better. Charlie Dressen had been hired to replace Bucky Harris as manager, and Dressen, though he saw the potential in Killebrew as a big bat someday, grew impatient with the young man's defense. His range, admittedly, wasn't great. Harmon didn't throw the ball as freely and easily as a budding star should have, and the Senators still had it in their heads that somehow he could develop into a solid second baseman rather than a corner infielder or outfielder.

But it didn't help when the 18-year-old, during a workout in spring training at Tinker Field, the organization's ballpark in Orlando, overheard his new manager carping aloud, "How do they expect me to win with guys like Killebrew?" Johnny Pesky, Harmon's baseball roommate, had to calm him down after that one.

Soon thereafter, Dressen instructed a coach named Ellis Clary to hit ground balls to Killebrew by the hundreds. As the earnest but raw fielder sometimes played the ball and other times let the ball play him, Clary coached him hard in long sessions in the hot Florida sun. This supervisor was critical, he was demanding, and he was blunt. "We think you have great potential as a hitter," Clary essentially told him. "Your swing is a little awkward and you go for bad balls, but that should smooth out with experience. You do have power. All we have to do is teach you to field, throw, and run."

Oh, that's all.

* * *

When the Senators broke camp to head north, Dressen assigned Killebrew a new roommate. Pesky was out, and Coach Cookie Lavagetto was in. The idea was that Lavagetto, a former All-Star third baseman with Brooklyn and Pittsburgh before that, would draw the younger man out and keep his mind active even if his body wasn't while he waited his turn. Lavagetto gave Killebrew a baseball rule book to study and frequently quizzed him on game situations and strategy.

Killebrew took some responsibility, too, for keeping the rust off his game while he sat and sat and sat. He developed a routine to stay as ready, and keep his skills as sharp, as he could. "I worked out before every ballgame at home for hours: taking batting practice, fielding practice, and trying to learn a lot of the things that I needed to learn," he said. "But it took my going to the minor leagues before I really learned ... to become a player."

All in due time. There was a bit of business to take care of first if Killebrew was ever going to embark on what would become a legendary career as a slugger. He had to hit one out in a big league game. Killebrew had batted 29 times with one double and four singles combined in 1954 and 1955 when he started at third base on June 24 against Detroit before just 4,188 fans at Griffith Stadium. The Senators already trailed 13–0 in the bottom of the fifth, heading toward an 18–7 spanking, when Killebrew stepped in to face left-hander Billy Hoeft with one out.

The catcher, Frank House—coincidentally a bonus baby himself when he signed with the Tigers back in 1949—decided to give the kid a break. "Kid, we're going to throw you a fastball," House said. Of course, the question was whether Killebrew would believe him or not. Was it a trick? Or a treat?

"I wasn't quite sure," Killer said in an interview nearly 50 years later, "but sure enough, here came a fastball, and I hit it 476'—probably the longest home run I ever hit in Griffith Stadium. I know how far it was because our PR director went out the next day and checked it off to where it hit in the left-field bleachers. Anyway, as I was coming around the bases, I stepped on home plate and Frank House said, 'Kid, that's the last time we're ever going to tell you what's coming.' And sure enough, it was. Nobody ever told me what was coming after that."

While the bonus baby rule assured Killebrew of his spot in the majors for all of 1955, it didn't assure him good times, close friends, or much fun as a young fellow in what clearly was a man's world. Harmon still had his wavy brown locks and a face sporting peach fuzz—many of his teammates were rough-hewn men, tough, their five o'clock shadows showing by noon. His roommate was twice his age and one of his bosses, to boot.

Jim Kaat, the left handed pitcher who would become one of Killebrew's longest-lasting teammates in Washington and Minnesota (1959–73), had a neighbor in Vermont in 2012 who recalled bumping into Killebrew around that time when the Senators were staying in Baltimore. He was in the hotel lobby one day and noticed a young man sitting by himself for quite a while. Finally, Kaat's friend broke the silence, "Are you a ballplayer?" "Yes," the youngster responded, "I'm Harmon Killebrew." At which point the stranger asked for Killebrew's autograph, chatted briefly, and sat back down.

Several minutes later, Killebrew was the one who got up and approached the other man. "I'm going to get some lunch. Want to come along?"

To Kaat, that was an example of the loneliness a bonus baby might feel when he's isolated from his teammates by age, by experience, and by the chance to contribute to the business at hand of winning games. "I experienced that a little bit because I ended up taking [pitcher] Chuck Stobbs' job, who was a veteran lefty with some [friends on the team]," recalled Kaat, who got to the majors at age 20 without going the bonus baby route. "And they were not eager to accept a young player because you didn't have a five-year, multi-million-dollar guaranteed contract. You had 30 days pay and if you got released, that was it—you were out of a job. They were not too pleased to see promising new players come along."

In Killebrew's case, the player bumped off the team when he arrived in 1954 was outfielder Jim Lemon, who was eight years older. Originally signed by Cleveland in 1948, Lemon had yet to establish himself—he had knocked around the minors, clubbing 39 home runs for Oklahoma City in 1950—but his contract had been purchased by Washington just a month before Bluege signed Killebrew. Lemon didn't get his first big break until 1956—as Killebrew became eligible to be farmed out—when he hit 27 home runs and led the AL with 11 triples, batting .271 and slugging .502 for the Senators that season.

In time, Lemon and Killebrew became teammates, a powerful tandem in the batting order, and close friends until Lemon's death in 2006. "He could have had a reaction to that," Harmon said. "But that's not the type of person he [was]."

By the spring of 1956, Killebrew was still learning about himself as a person, as a player, and as a new husband. He and Elaine were married in the off-season, then they turned his trip to Cordoba, Mexico, for winter ball into a makeshift honeymoon.

When Harmon went to spring training this time, there was another notable change in his status. His two years as a bonus baby were up. Nothing would be keeping him in the big leagues besides his performance and the ballclub's needs. The former became an issue as Killebrew appeared in 24 of Washington's first 65 games. The latter was a given for Washington, a franchise of constant and considerable needs at all times. He had started twice at second base, played the field in three more, and otherwise was limited to pinch-hit duty. Or more like pinch outs—he batted .176 in 37 plate appearances with four home runs, one double, and one single along with two walks and 14 strikeouts. Killebrew had a good home run ratio—early success in what would become perhaps his most impressive career category—but bad everything else.

In June, after a series in Cleveland with the Senators due next in Detroit, Killebrew was sitting on the team bus outside Municipal Stadium when Howard Fox, the club's traveling secretary, was called off to take a phone call. When he returned, Fox broke the news to Killebrew that he was heading to the minor leagues. Accounts of that episode say that Harmon stared at Fox for a moment, then quietly exited and searched below with the driver for his bag. Fox had given him train fare for a ticket to Charlotte, the site of Washington's Class A team in the Sally League, so the player began to lug his suitcase up a hill toward the station as the weather took a turn.

"As the thunder rolled over him and the rain fell in torrents, he looked a lonely figure, etched against the dark sky, plodding to the minors," wrote Bob Addie of the *Washington Post*. "There was a silence in the bus because ballplayers understand those things better than outsiders. One fellow in the front seat watched the retreating figure and said, 'He'll be back. The kid's got power.'"

That player happened to be Eddie Yost, who himself would be traded to Detroit one day to open up an everyday position for Killebrew.

"The position for Killebrew is some place where he can play regularly, look at more pitching, and find the spot where his talents are best suited," said Senators boss Calvin Griffith, overriding even Dressen, who liked having Harmon on board if only to pinch hit or plug a hole in late innings.

Killebrew spent the rest of the baseball season in Charlotte. Elaine, expecting their first child, had moved into an apartment in the nation's capital with him but now headed home to Payette. Son Cameron was born in August. Elaine's husband played 70 games in Charlotte, hit

.325 with 15 home runs in 249 at-bats, and earned a late-season call-up to Washington.

He also met a compatriot of sorts in Bob Allison, an outfield prospect in the Washington system who would become Killebrew's roommate in the minors and eventually in the big leagues. A native of Raytown, Missouri, Allison was a strapping fellow—6'3", 205 pounds—who had a Mr. America build, Hollywood good looks, and a football player's aggressiveness whenever he put on a baseball uniform. Infielders and catchers dreaded seeing Allison headed their way on the base paths as he built his reputation for hard slides.

The two soon would combine to give the Senators and later the Twins a powerful 1-2 punch in the lineup; and once the team relocated to Minnesota, the numbers they wore on their backs were changed to reflect it. Killebrew was given No. 3 and Allison No. 4, an intentional nod to those worn by Babe Ruth and Lou Gehrig in their heyday as Yankees sluggers.

Neither fellow was flexing much confidence after 1956, however. Allison had hit .233 at Charlotte with 12 home runs in 344 at-bats. There was another new variable in play in their careers at spring training in 1957—the Senators made another change of managers. Dressen was moved into the front office after managing the season's first 20 games, and Lavagetto was promoted to replace him.

Killebrew didn't seem to mind, and several decades later, the perennial gentleman who seemed to always have kind words for everyone spoke volumes by the praise he did not lavish on Dressen. "Dressen was a different sort," he said euphemistically. "I don't know what to say about Charlie. When he came over to our ballclub we had finished just out of the first division and some of his first comments were, 'I can steal you enough games to put us well up in the first division.' I'll never forget that—and we finished dead last under Dressen. I didn't really dislike him that much; he was all right."

Of Lavagetto, Killebrew recalled, "Cookie was a much better coach than he was a manager. He taught me a lot about playing third base, and I'm so thankful that he was there and I got that kind of experience."

Killebrew and Allison both were farmed out again before spring training in Orlando even ended. This time the destination was Chattanooga in the Class AA Southern Association. Killebrew led that league with 29 home runs, despite playing in one of the biggest parks in baseball, Joe Engel Stadium. He batted .279 with 30 doubles and seven triples. Allison had a more modest season with two homers and a .246 average, but the friendship between him and Harmon deepened. The two also had the bonus of playing for manager Cal Ermer, who would be their skipper a decade later with the Twins.

Ermer was another man helpful to his development, Killebrew said. "Cal really worked with me and helped me, not only with playing third base but also with my hitting. Cal Ermer was just all baseball, 24 hours a day. He was one of the finest men I've ever met." The extra coaching earned Killebrew another September call-up, and he responded by hitting .290 in nine games with a pair of home runs and five RBIs.

* * *

By 1958, Killebrew had serious intentions about sticking in Washington and either grabbing a utility infielder's spot or winning the third base job outright from Yost. Considered the better glove man by far, Yost was famous for his batting eye—from 1948–56, he averaged 119 walks each season, boosting his modest batting average in that span (.258) to a robust .401 on-base percentage. Like Chicago's Nellie Fox, Yost—known by some as "The Walking Man"—was famous for fouling off pitches until he saw one he could drive or the pitcher missed four times. He often would send eight, nine, 10 souvenirs into the stands while waiting for the right pitch. When he retired, only Babe Ruth, Ted Williams, and Mel Ott had amassed more walks. He had some pop in his bat but hit 78 of his 101 home runs with Washington on the road, thanks to the home ballpark's gaping dimensions.

And Griffith loved the guy, reportedly turning down a $200,000 offer from Boston for Yost's contract. "They look at his batting average and think they can swing a deal for him," the owner said in 1954. "I wouldn't swap him for Mickey Mantle straight up."

That's how the deck was stacked against Killebrew in the spring of 1958 when a March afternoon in West Palm Beach dealt him a losing hand.

Harmon had been sent to play in a spring training "B" game that most of the Washington regulars skipped. He even hit a home run that sent the game into extra innings. But in the bottom of the 10th, Kansas City got runners on second and third with two outs. A bouncing ball hit toward Killebrew at third base seemed likely to end the inning—until Killebrew heard shortstop Rocky Bridges yell, "Tag him!" as the Athletics' Hal Smith chugged from second to third. Momentarily frazzled, Killebrew held up on his throw to first, then tried too late to tag Smith and missed. The runner on third crossed the plate to win the game.

In one newspaper account, a Washington sportswriter began his story, "Eddie Yost won the third base job for the Senators today, sitting in Orlando, Florida." Bridges apologized to Killebrew afterward for the bad advice, but that didn't make the story. Although one play in one exhibition game wasn't so almighty crucial to Killebrew's fate that season, it did anchor some opinions about his game and especially his defensive abilities.

He was an afterthought when the Senators began the season. In the first week, Killebrew got into two games as a pinch-hitter and a third in the 10th inning when Lavagetto's options were limited by the extra innings. Then he got the lousy news. Lavagetto told him he would not be staying in Washington. In fact, Killebrew wasn't even staying in the organization, technically. The team was assigning him to Indianapolis, the Class AAA affiliate of the Chicago White Sox. The Senators didn't have a Triple A team at the time although plenty of their fans would have told them to look right there in the Griffith Stadium dugout to find it.

The cumulative effect of Killebrew's trouble getting traction in the big leagues was huge—this was his fifth season out of Payette and he seemed further, not closer, to achieving his goal of major league reliability. He and Elaine were expecting another child. He was off to play for a team in a new city run by an organization that had no vested interest in his success and in a league filled with pitchers strange to him. When he got to Indianapolis, the stress showed up in his game. In 38 games, Killebrew hit only two home runs in 121 at-bats and had 10 RBIs, 37 strikeouts, and 18 walks while batting .215. Or as a wise guy at *The Sporting News* put it, he "failed to hit the size of his hat."

"I was depressed, I'll admit it, by being sent to Indianapolis," Killebrew told *Baseball Digest* the following year. "I was led to believe that I'd have a full crack at third base. They say I wasn't good enough to make the Indianapolis club and maybe I wasn't, considering my mental and physical state. When I joined that club I hadn't played for a month, and it was like spring training all over."

Fighting a serious case of self-doubt, Killebrew reached out to Bluege—increasingly a father figure who plugged the hole left by Clay Killebrew's early death—and told him he was thinking of quitting the game to get a regular job. Bluege, by phone, patiently helped Harmon navigate each crisis that he raised in the conversation.

"Ossie always had words of encouragement for me," Killebrew said. "He was just one of those guys with a good word, and I have to say there are not many of them like that around. I could always go have a conversation with Ossie and walk away feeling better."

How much better? Killebrew was about to find out. Just as he started to find a groove at Indianapolis—that's how he remembered it, anyway—the Senators called to inform him they were moving him again. He was going back to Chattanooga and back to Class AA. The gears of his baseball career were being thrown into reverse. Whatever coping skills Bluege might have taught him were tested almost instantly.

Maybe Killebrew really did cope. Or more likely, maybe he simply played mad. In 86 games back with the Lookouts, he cracked 17 home runs, drove in 54 runs, and batted .308. When he went back to Washington that September and got into 10 games near the end—the Senators finished last again at 61–93—he managed only five hits in 29 trips to the plate with no home runs and 11 strikeouts.

After that, Allison, who had hit .200 in 11 Washington games at the end, went to play winter ball in Cuba. Killebrew headed back to Ontario, Oregon, for a sales job at the gas company. He didn't know it at the time—no one did, with one possible exception—but his days in the minor leagues were over. Killebrew was more concerned that his days in the major leagues might soon be over, too.

Chapter 5

Finally, a Big Leaguer

In later years, Calvin Griffth would become reviled by the fans and players of the baseball team he owned. In Washington, he was known for running a shoestring operation that dwelled a little too contentedly in the American League's basement and worse for yanking the franchise out of town when he got a better deal—financially and literally in greener pastures—in Minnesota.

In Minneapolis, after an extended honeymoon with the public for delivering a baseball team that brought status and strong results, Griffith's reputation returned for squeezing players' salaries—cutting their pay at the slightest downturn in performance—and it hurt him with both constituencies. When free agency arrived in the 1970s, he was ill-equipped to compete, so he let talented players leave or traded them first, stripping the Twins to the bone.

He was ridiculed as a "dinosaur," which actually was pretty accurate if it meant someone who could own and operate a major league franchise as a family business and sole source of income rather than as a marketing tool for some other enterprises or as an expensive hobby for a mega-rich guy sinking in money made elsewhere. Griffith was a baseball man, the 12-year-old bat boy for the Senators' 1924 World Series team, a fellow who learned well from the uncle, Clark Griffith, who took in Calvin and his sister as children and then passed on a ballclub.

Cheap? Foolish at times? Sure. Griffith was mocked for certain insensitivities, even a bit of bigotry. But he grew up in the game and he knew the game, and even near the end—when he tore down Minnesota's roster prior to 1982 and stuffed it with rookies—he wasn't focused only on the bottom line, a payroll that was some fraction of the league average. He was seeding that 60–102 team with young talent that, five years later, would bring the first World Series title to the Upper Midwest.

Later in his life, the harsh feelings toward Griffith mellowed into something more nostalgic. From the time he sold the Twins to billionaire banker Carl Pohlad until his death in 1999, Griffith became something of a mascot for fans, toddling off into his personal sunset as a symbol of baseball days gone by.

In his head, Killebrew saw and knew the same Griffith that everyone else did. But in his heart, he thought of the curmudgeon a little differently. The boss who knew a thing or two about bank accounts always had one with his greatest slugger, dating back to a pivotal—and stressful—time in the Hall of Famer's life.

After bits and pieces of five seasons leading up to 1959, the Senators' bonus baby was barely out of diapers. He had appeared in 113 games, batted .224, hit 11 home runs (but only six doubles), and struck out 93 times. Still just 17 when he signed with and joined the Washington team, he was a few months away from turning 23 when he left Payette for Orlando this time.

Killebrew's budding career as a big leaguer was at a crossroads. Which, in a baseball context, invariably made folks think of the old quote (allegedly) by Yankees catcher Yogi Berra, "When you come to a fork in the road, take it." Harmon was amused by and liked to use that one himself sometimes. But in this case, it was advice worth following. He focused on playing baseball, preparing for the season the best way he knew how. Meanwhile, he got some help from the man upstairs—the rumpled guy in the wrinkled suit, the one whose office overlooked the ballfield.

Griffith had made up his mind. He traded Eddie Yost in December as part of a six-player deal with the Detroit Tigers, giving up one of the game's best table-setting leadoff batters but also opening up the third base spot. Then Griffth told manager Cookie Lavagetto to stick Killebrew at that position and to find room in the outfield for Bob Allison—and to leave them there. Lavagetto had thought about using Reno Bertoia, acquired in the Yost deal, at third, but Griffith nixed that. "He'll cost you a few games because of his fielding," the boss said of Killebrew, "but he's got a chance of becoming a spectacular ballplayer. Let's give the kid a break."

The baseball lifer did as ordered, though at one point that spring Lavagetto reportedly groused about Griffith's demands regarding the Senators' pair of strongboys, "The two of them together aren't worth a bucket of warm spit," he said.

"No one seemed to have faith in Harmon," Herb Heft, the Senators' public relations director, said in the May 1960 issue of *Sport* magazine. "He was a bad fielder, and he struck out too much. But Calvin had the feeling."

Fast-forward to September. Allison played in 150 games that season, started 147 of them (mostly in center field), and wound up as the AL's Rookie of the Year with 30 home runs, 85 RBIs, nine triples, 13 stolen bases, a .261 batting average, and a .482 slugging mark. Killebrew appeared in and started all but one of the Senators' 154 games, playing left field in four, and third base in the rest. He struck out 116 times and batted .242, but, making a real effort now to hone his strike zone, he walked 90 times. That boosted his on-base percentage to .354, while his .516 slugging mark was second only to Detroit's Al Kaline. Killebrew led Washington in nine of 14 offensive categories, including RBIs (105), runs (98), and home runs (42). That total tied him with Cleveland's Rocky Colavito for the league lead. Only Milwaukee third baseman Eddie Mathews (46) and Chicago shortstop Ernie Banks (45) hit more in the NL.

The Senators had punch in their lineup—Jim Lemon hit 33 home runs and Roy Sievers had 21, contributing to the 163 team total (second in the league)—but they ranked next-to-last in scoring runs and last in batting average. About the only thing Washington led the league in was errors (162). The team gave up an average of 4.55 runs and its pitchers walked too many, struck out too few, and had only Camilo Pascual in the regular rotation with an ERA below 4.15. The team again finished last in the standings, and despite an impressive boost in tickets sold, last at the turnstiles, too.

At least fans had the entertainment value of Killebrew's long balls. He officially began his assault on the fences on Opening Day with a two-run shot to deep left off Baltimore's Jack Harshman. (He also botched a routine play at third in the first inning.) But it took a while before he went into full rampage mode—Killebrew was batting just .237 with three home runs at the end of April.

But on May 1 in Detroit, Harmon hit two home runs off future Hall of Famer Jim Bunning in a 10-inning victory. He slammed two more the next day, and in between them he was hit by pitches from Tigers reliever Tom Morgan twice. Killebrew homered again three days later in Chicago, then clubbed two in Yankee Stadium on May 9. His two blasts on May 12 at Griffith Stadium helped Washington catch and beat the Tigers again. On May 17 in the second game of a doubleheader against the White Sox, he hit two more.

In that 17-day stretch in May, Killebrew hit two home runs in a game five times and a total of 11 in 17 games. He added four more before Memorial Day, becoming only the 12th player to hit 15 or more home runs in a calendar month. Detroit's Rudy York had slugged 18 in August 1937, and Babe Ruth managed 17 in September 1927. Killebrew also was the second youngest of those who hit 15, three months older than Joe DiMaggio when the young Yankees star hit 15 in July 1937.

It was exciting stuff, and even President Dwight D. Eisenhower made it out to a game on May 29 to see this "new" sensation. Killebrew hit a home run that day but got a bigger thrill when he swapped autographed baseballs with Eisenhower. The President said he wanted the signed ball for his 11-year-old grandson David—who told Killebrew when they met in 1970, by which time David was married to President Richard Nixon's daughter, Julie, that he still had the keepsake. (Killebrew met seven U.S. presidents.)

By midseason, Killebrew led the majors with 28 home runs and had 70 RBIs. He was named to the American League All-Star team for the first time that summer, playing alongside Ted Williams, Mickey Mantle, Whitey Ford, Yogi Berra, and six other future Hall of Famers, with 10 more on the NL squad. National media descended—there had been few reasons in recent seasons to bother with the Washington club, and now they had one of baseball's best stories. In June, a writer for *Sports Illustrated*—also in its relative infancy—wrote about Killebrew and the Senators in the context of *Damn Yankees*, the popular Broadway musical and movie. The hero of that production was Joe Hardy, a Washington fan who cuts a deal with the Devil to become the best long-ball hitter in the game and help the ballclub win the pennant.

Even Killebrew's teammates and opponents got swept up in the excitement. "You should have seen [Detroit pitcher Ray] Narleski the other night," one Washington player teased him, as quoted in the *Sports Illustrated* story. "He was looking pretty good. Then the Killer swishes his bat once. Bam! I've never seen anybody look as sick as Narleski did."

Senators outfielder Roy Sievers poked through the bat rack before taking cuts in the cage, saying, "Got to get me a Killer model. Where's a Killer model?"

While Killebrew took ground balls during an infield drill, a Tiger player said loudly, "I thought Babe Ruth played the outfield."

Killebrew's nickname was "Killer." Nicknames were still prominent then in sports, used happily by the sporting press in headlines and stories, and Killebrew's name and mammoth clouts lent themselves to a couple that never really suited him. Killer was the obvious one, and strong as he was (5'11" and 200 pounds at that point), he might have looked the part in deeds and in silhouette. But it seemed far too sinister for such a mild-mannered sort. The same with "Harm," which is what most of his family and friends called him anyway. As a shortened name it was fine; as a description of what he did to baseballs and to pitcher's confidence, it was accurate. But the malice inherent in that one felt wrong, too.

Yet the writers and editors—and broadcasters and teammates and fans and just about anyone he might have bumped into on the street—kept using the ill-fitting sobriquets. Killebrew never expressed much preference, but he seemed far more ripe for "Charmin' Harmon," which got a little play in some Twin Cities circles. Then there were the witty things Killebrew heard on occasion from the stands when he struck out or suffered through one of his slumps at the plate, loudmouths cutting loose with a "Harmless Harmon!" jeer.

Killebrew did get more harmless after the All-Star break in 1959. His production at the plate slipped across the board—from a .271 batting average in the first half to .212, from 65 runs to 33, and so on. His home runs and RBIs were cut in half (14 and 35). Pitchers were adjusting their approaches, some pitching him tight and hoping to unsettle him with the occasional knockdown or HBP, others offering up junk to keep the ball off the plate. Killebrew sometimes chased bad pitches out of his strike zone; his discipline was still a work in progress.

The Baltimore Orioles tried a different strategy to thwart Killebrew as a threat—they wanted to make him a defensive liability in hopes of getting him out of the Washington lineup. They began to drop bunts in front of him, beating out three in one game for hits. But when some writers criticized the kid for that, his old pal Ossie Bluege—a former third baseman himself—rushed to Killebrew's defense. "The three that Baltimore got away with couldn't have been handled by anybody," said Bluege, by then comptroller of the Washington team.

Griffith again had Harmon's back, attributing his drop in performance to the attention and distractions coming his way from the media, along with outside interests eager to attach his name to their products or projects. Sometimes it was just fans' curiosity or a call to speak with some Boy Scouts or other groups. There was one day, for example, when Killebrew went to the Pentagon to meet Secretary of Defense Neil McElroy in the morning, then he spoke at a Kiwanis Club luncheon hours later. The next day, he attended a father-son softball game. Somewhere in between, he played baseball.

And he played it rather well, in spite of the dropoff in late summer. Wielding a 33-ounce, 35" bat, Killebrew still wound up hitting one home run for every 13 at-bats in 1959, the best such ratio in the league and a yardstick by which he would be measured more favorably than almost anyone else—both year by year and when his career was done—against the mighty Babe Ruth.

"We could pitch Killebrew high and tight and get him out in 1958," Baltimore catcher Gus Triandos said. "But when we pitched him that way last year, he hit the ball out of sight. Don't ask me about this year. With his strength, he's going to hit a bundle of home runs. And he'll probably get a lot more before he hangs up his uniform for the last time."

Home Run Derby

Home Run Derby made its debut in America's living rooms in the winter between the 1959 and 1960 seasons, bringing the major league's greatest sluggers into focus for Baby Boomers and their growing interest in baseball.

Each week from January 1960 into July, the TV show pitted two power hitters against each other in a precursor and inspiration of the home run hitting contests held during the MLB All-Star break in more recent years. It was filmed at old Wrigley Field in Los Angeles and aired in syndication, produced and hosted by Mark Scott. Early in each episode, Scott explained that Wrigley Field—once the home of the Angels—was chosen because of its symmetrical distances to the left- and right-field fences, thereby assuring fairness for both left- and right-handed hitters.

The rules were basic—each batter would swing for the fences. "It's a home run or nothing here on Home Run Derby," Scott would remind viewers. Anything other than a home run—line drives, ground balls, pop-ups, whiffs—counted as an out. So did called strikes; umpires and catchers were used with two batting-practice quality pitchers (alternating by inning) to assess the offerings and make the conditions as realistic as possible. A batter did not have to swing at any pitch outside his strike zone. Once a player reached three "outs," his half of the inning was over and the other man took his turn.

While one player batted, Scott—a sports broadcaster and sometimes actor in Los Angeles, appearing in a few of his friend Jack Webb's productions—did the play-by-play and chatted with the other contestant from a "booth" set up in foul territory. This went on for nine innings—or extra innings, as needed—with the winner receiving $2,000 and an invitation to return the following week against a new challenger. The weekly runner-up got $1,000. A $500 bonus was paid if a batter hit three home runs in a row with another $500 for a fourth and $1,000 for each subsequent homer. The pitcher who threw the most home run balls also got a bonus.

Nineteen players—nine of them future Hall of Famers—participated, most of them more than once. Henry Aaron appeared seven times, winning on six consecutive shows, and he took home $13,500 as the top money-winner. Mickey Mantle and Willie Mays appeared five times, winning $10,000 and

$8,000, respectively. Jackie Jensen appeared four times, won just twice, but made good on bonuses to earn $8,500.

Killebrew made $6,000 on the show. In episodes 4, 5, and 6, Harmon beat Mantle and Rocky Colavito before losing to Ken Boyer. He returned in episode 20 but lost to Mays. His final home run count: 23. Harmon's pal Bob Allison appeared three times, losing to Aaron, beating Bob Cerv, then losing to Mays. He pocketed $4,000 and hit nine homers. The heaviest hitters in terms of HRD home runs: Mantle (44), Mays (35), Aaron (34), and Jensen (29), thanks to one match in which he beat Ernie Banks 14–11 and a 13–10 loss to Mantle in what proved to be the show's finale.

Harmon's on-air moments with Scott while waiting for another turn at the plate were right in line with his shy public persona, especially at the age of 23. But then, this was baseball in all its black-and-white glory, back in the days of flannel uniforms and natural grass. If any of the sluggers was jaded or sassy, he kept it hidden when the cameras were rolling. (Although Mays got a little cranky about all the talking while he was at the plate.)

A typical exchange while Killebrew and Scott watched Mickey Mantle takes his cuts would be full of pearls such as:

> **Mark Scott:** "That was a tough top-half of the first inning, but there's eight more to go."
> **Killebrew:** "Yeah, that's right, Mark."
> **Scott:** ". . . getting that first one, off the hook now."
> **Killebrew:** "I certainly hope so, Mark."
> **Scott:** "How about that ball, Harmon?"
> **Killebrew:** "Mickey didn't hit that one real good, but with his tremendous power he doesn't have to hit them solid."

Sadly, shortly after the 26th and final episode, Scott, 45, died of a heart attack in Burbank, California. Because the show had been his baby, it was canceled rather than revived with a replacement producer and host. Home Run Derby was perfect for its time, a show that served as a time capsule back to the warm-and-fuzzy Eisenhower years. The faster, flashier, Technicolor 1960s were coming fast.

Word got out—and was confirmed by Reds general manager Gabe Paul—that Cincinnati offered Griffith $500,000 that winter for Killebrew's rights. It was a jaw-dropping offer back when a half-million dollars was big bucks, made to a fellow who probably needed and surely would have liked the money. But the Senators owner turned down Paul. "You can't play $500,000 at third base," he said.

Killebrew's reaction to his apparent value? "It shakes you up." The young third baseman didn't get a cut of the cash he supposedly was worth—or at least, not a very large cut. His salary was bumped from $9,000 to $21,000 for the 1960 season. He wasn't inclined to give any back to cover for his glovework, either, though a wire-service writer in New York had zinged him during the season with this lead: "The most exciting new personality in the major leagues is a young man who plays third base like Pepper Martin and hits the ball the prodigious distance of a Babe Ruth."

"I think I'm learning," Killebrew said, trusting in his approach at third base to knock down balls if needed to make the play. "I know I'm still going to make errors, but I'm covering more ground and my arm is getting stronger. I don't think I'm a bad fielder anymore."

That United Press International story continued on to say, "There hasn't been so much interest in a Washington ballplayer almost since another young feller strode out of Killebrew's native Idaho back in 1907. Tall, gangling feller, that one. Name of Walter Johnson." And it was true. Attendance at Senators games picked up dramatically. They sold 615,372 tickets in 1959, a 29 percent increase from the season before. The following year, the turnstile count would jump another 128,000 as the pieces of a competitive ballclub continued to come together. Washington still ranked last in AL attendance, but the team moved up to fifth in the standings in 1960 with a core of maturing talent and the arrival of catcher Earl Battey, among others.

Killebrew missed games in the spring with a leg injury, reaching the All-Star break with only six home runs and 19 RBIs in 170 at-bats. He picked up his pace from there, however, and finished with 31 homers and 80 RBIs. He hit .298 in the second half to boost his overall batting overage to .276. Allison chipped in only 15 home runs and 69 RBIs, but Jim Lemon came through with 38 and 100, respectively, and the pitchers reduced the staff ERA to 3.77, helping with the 10-game improvement to 73–81.

The moving vans, however, already had been booked. Despite Griffith's assurances to the contrary—he had written in a bylined *Washington Post* piece published on the eve of Opening Day that the Senators "will never leave Washington in my lifetime"—he finally gave in to financial pressures and his wandering eye. He felt the franchise had lost out on California as a lush market when the Giants and the Dodgers had beat him in heading West. Now Griffith had found a golden opportunity—a ready-made major league facility in the suburb of Bloomington, Minnesota—a "compromise" community to quell the forever, cross-river rivalry between Minneapolis and St. Paul. Metropolitan Stadium was sitting there, beckoning to an owner, a shiny, happy place compared to the old joint the Senators called home.

Even Killebrew, who generally liked playing in Washington, enjoyed retelling the joke about a fan calling the ballpark to ask, "'What time is the game?' The voice on the other end said, 'What time can you get here?' That's about the way it was," Harmon chuckled. "There were days when we had just several hundred people come to the games, and that was not good."

The Senators had the worst attendance in the AL for their final six seasons in Washington. They had drawn 1 million fans only once, in 1946 immediately after World War II, and hadn't sniffed that number since. When Killebrew reminisced about the old ballpark later in life, he recalled the smell of bread wafting from the Bond Bread bakery up 7th Street. He also recalled one regular among the spectators who made himself hard to forget. "A Marine who used to take great delight in screaming his lungs out," Killebrew said. "He never actually said anything. He just screamed. They called him 'The Howling Marine.' He got on everybody's nerves."

On the crowded East Coast, the Senators faced competition in and around the D.C. market. Out on the plains in Minnesota, Griffith's team could draw fans not just locally but regionally with North and South Dakota and Iowa as secondary markets. Also, the Twin Cities was a burgeoning metropolitan area, hungry for major league sports and the status it conveyed. The NBA Minneapolis Lakers had just exited for Los Angeles, and Minnesota had only gotten the NFL Vikings a few months earlier as an expansion team. One common refrain whenever public funding was needed for facilities or other expenditures to satisfy the various private sports enterprises was, "Who wants to be a cold Omaha?"

Which is what Minnesota imagined itself to be, until Calvin & Co. came calling. If fans weren't going to come out to see his team, his team was going to go where the (new) fans were.

Chapter 6

North by Northwest

"Strikingly modern," one national magazine called it in 1961, even though it had been completed five years earlier in an attempt to entice one of the Major League Baseball franchises with wanderlust (the New York Giants were the first team targeted). Local boosters raved about its three decks and the "cantilever construction" that got rid of posts and obstructed views. The nothingness of the surrounding area meant elbow room for more than 30,000 fans (bumped over time to more than 46,000) and their 14,000 cars.

Others called it a hodge-podge, a crazy-quilt, a platypus of ballparks, focusing on the haphazard way in which Metropolitan Stadium in Bloomington, Minnesota, came together—piece by piece, an extra deck here, some open grandstands and bleachers there, "temporary" scaffolding that quietly became permanent, and so on.

The good seats didn't extend all the way down the left-field line, yet the section from that foul pole across toward center field was massive (it made more sense when a football gridiron was laid across the outfield on Sundays). There was nothing particularly notable about Met Stadium, no Green Monster, no ivy, and no ornate façade like the cathedral in the Bronx. At best, the ballpark on the prairie could be called endearingly quirky and in time beloved by a generation of Upper Midwest fans whose nostalgia found an extra gear once they were forced to endure a joint known as the Hubert H. Humphrey Metrodome—as plastic a baseball experience as has ever existed.

When the former Washington players—once Senators, suddenly Twins—arrived in the spring of 1961, they simply called Met Stadium "home." This was where boss Calvin Griffith dragged them, and this was where the franchise would stay.

"In the early years before they put a double deck in left field, you could actually stand around the batting cage and see cows grazing out beyond the left-field fence," pitcher Jim Kaat, 21 at the time, said of the relocation. "It was kind of like a little country town. They made everybody feel so comfortable. It was good for guys and their families.... We played in some brutally cold weather early in the year. But as the years went on it was kind of to our advantage because we became accustomed to playing in that kind of stuff."

Harmon Killebrew didn't have that outlook early. He had come through the Twin Cities during his stint with the Indianapolis ballclub in the Class AAA American Association in 1958 and caught an Artic blast of Minnesota weather in what other cities called springtime. "I really took to the warmer weather in Washington and the lifestyle of living in the nation's capital," he recalled some 40 years later. "Plus, we were starting to become a good club, and I thought the fans deserved it after all they had been through. I can't say I was real excited about moving."

Yet Killebrew's concerns melted away more quickly than most winters. "I quickly grew to like it. Pretty much right away I started hitting the ball good, and I loved the fans because they're down-to-earth Midwestern people. They like their baseball, but they're not so rabid like they can be in Fenway Park or in New York. And I had the chance to play with some great guys on some very good teams."

The timing was right for the ballclub, seeded with young stars and with more (especially from its "Cuban connection" scouting system) on the way. The cities of Minneapolis and St. Paul were ready to step up in status. Killebrew—already a gate attraction around the American League for the frequency and scale of his home runs—had a young family ripe for the lifestyle of Minnesota. And he couldn't help but smile when he saw the signs down the left-field line (330') or over toward left-center (402') where most of his mortar blasts would go. The fences at Met Stadium were much more slugger-friendly than the vast expanses at the old Washington Park.

Harmon and his teammates easily slipped into their new baseball identities. They were Twins now, their terms as Senators complete. Griffith wanted to name them the "Twin Cities Twins" to avoid enflaming a fierce Minneapolis–St. Paul rivalry—until the commissioner's office overruled the idea. So the Twins became the first team to be known by the state in which it played rather than a city. Griffith settled for sticking a "TC" as a secondary logo on the players' caps (and maintained thereafter that the initials stood for his sister, Thelma, and himself). The team's primary logo—created by local artist Ray Barton for $15—was a cartoon that showed two large men, representing the market's two minor league clubs prior to 1961—the Minneapolis Millers and the St. Paul Saints. The big guys were shaking hands across the Mississippi River, in essence coming together to root for one Minnesota team.

That first year as a Twin, Killebrew smacked 46 home runs, breaking the franchise record (back through its Washington era) that he had tied in 1959. It's no wonder that more than a few fans mistakenly thought one of the big guys in the logo was a caricature of Killebrew—especially the out-of-towners, who learned of his exploits mostly through morning box scores and faraway late-night radio broadcasts. Killebrew breathed life into the Paul Bunyan tales from North America's more rugged regions, not just with the big numbers he amassed but by the way so many of his home runs soared, high and higher, in immense parabolas whose geometry fascinated even the most reluctant schoolboys.

Fan interest in Killebrew and his team would track his moon shots high and higher during the club's first 10 years in residence, then return to Earth in the following decade-plus. But Opening Day 1961 stood alone, a celebration within the disappointment of a 5–3 Twins loss.

Stadium workers had shoveled snow off the field just a few days before the club arrived after going 5–1 on the road during the season's first week, and pitcher Camilo Pascual had joked, "I never see snow before. Maybe I throw a snowball Opening Day, no?" Killebrew had pulled his right hamstring in Baltimore and would miss the first game in Bloomington. Then there was the crowd—only 24,606 showed up on what proved to be a mild April day. The year before, the then-Senators had drawn 28,327 fans to their season opener. In the moment, the decision to move to Minnesota didn't seem like such a grand idea after all.

Yet there they were and there they played, hoping to mimic Milwaukee's experience from nearly a decade earlier. When the Braves exited Boston in 1953, they immediately became a threat in their new National League digs. Stars such as Eddie Mathews, Warren Spahn, and eventually Henry Aaron averaged 90 victories for their first few seasons there, and at the end of the fifth season they went to and won the World Series. Milwaukee went back in 1958 but lost in seven games.

The Twins began their Minnesota era with similar ambitions, though expectations from outside were more modest. "[The] Twins could do what they couldn't do as Senators last year or any year since 1946: finish in the top half of the American League," *Sports Illustrated*'s baseball preview wrote. "There's a catch, of course. Top half stretches down to fifth place this season." The American League had expanded to 10 teams, adding the Los Angeles Angels and, to placate politicians unhappy with Griffith's move, the "new" Washington Senators.

Killebrew, despite his initial doubts about Minnesota, also felt a responsibility to perform for the club's new fans. They were an eager bunch; home attendance that first season would reach 1,256,723, a half-million more than those who watched the same guys play the year before. Harmon was eager, as well, to be seen from the start as an integral part of the team—at bat and in the field—rather than the prospect who sat on the bench, bounced up and down in the minors, and earned a spot only near the end in Washington.

No one had to wait very long. Killebrew recovered from his hamstring injury, got back into the lineup, and slugged his first home run as a Twin on April 30 off Chicago's Bob Shaw in a 5–3 Minnesota loss. Twenty-six games later, he had 12. The math on a personal level was stunning—he was hitting one out every 9.3 at-bats. But the Twins already had played 41 games, so Killebrew's chances of reaching 50, never mind 60, were slim. He still wound up with a bigger year than the ballclub—the Twins finished 70–90, in seventh place, only a half-game ahead of the expansion Angels but nine-and-a-half games better than the thrown-together bunch that replaced them back in D.C. After their 9–3 start, they had slipped below .500 to stay in late May and lifted their heads above seventh place for just one day in July.

Killebrew achieved career bests to that point in batting average (.288), RBIs (122), hits (156), slugging (.606), total bases (328), and walks (107). His 46 homers—including his only inside-the-park experience—came in 541 at-bats, a rate of one every 11.8 at-bats—which was only good for fourth among AL hitters. Baltimore's Jim Gentile (10.6) was ahead of him in that category, and the leaders were a pair of Yankees known as "the M&M boys." Mickey Mantle hit one out every 9.5 at-bats, and Roger Maris (9.7) was right behind pace, eventually staying healthier in that 1961 season to end their friendly competition and be the one to surpass Babe Ruth's single-season total of 60. Maris hit 61, seven more than Mantle, and by most accounts was irritable at every stage of the record chase.

Maris did bake in an unyielding spotlight that season, but just below the surface there was a power movement afoot in baseball that kept Killebrew in the conversation as a future threat to reach 60. A record 41 players had hit 20 or more homers, and the league turned in a record total number of home runs for the season.

* * *

An easy explanation for the surging home run total was expansion, which threw open the AL's doors to another 20 or so pitchers who would have been minor leaguers in an eight-team league. (The National League was on the verge of doing the same thing, boosting its membership to 10 with new teams in Houston and New York.) There were the usual theories about tightly wound baseballs and advancements in training and equipment. And there was more than a little hand-wringing that the proliferation of the long ball would damage the sport.

"The trouble is, runs have become too cheap," said Frank Lane, general manager of the Kansas City Athletics in 1961. "A guy gets on first base and just stands there, waiting for a home run. It used to be that a hitter was considered a bum if he couldn't hit .300. Today, the highest paid men are the .270 hitters who can belt 35 or 40 homers."

That was a wonderful thing for guys like Killebrew. After the season, in an exhibition home run hitting contest in North Carolina, he picked up an extra $4,000 for a day's work (as the headliner, Roger Maris pocketed $16,000). His boss, Griffith, understood the gate appeal of home runs and the advantage that he might have with the Twins' brawny lineup. Back in June, Griffith had shot down manager Cookie Lavagetto's suggestions to move the Met Stadium fences back for some old-school baseball, and he shot down Lavagetto as manager soon after. "The fans today swoon for the home run," Griffith said. "Why hike distance and cut down on the total? Besides, we hit our share."

Minnesota hit 167 home runs, far behind New York's league-leading 240. Ninety-two of those came at home. Its lineup tilted right—Killebrew, Allison, Lemon, and Battey all hit from that side—so they rarely saw left-handers. But they got the job done.

Killebrew divided his time defensively, playing 119 games at first base (he spent much of 1960 at that spot, too) and 45 at third with a couple in the outfield. Statistically, he hit better that year when he played third than first—.368 with 15 homers vs. .258 with 30 homers, respectively. But Killebrew did like first base because it kept him involved on more plays and put him closer to more players.

"Just a change of the glove from third to first was a big change," he said years later. But the adjustment was worth it. "You had the second baseman and the pitcher to help you on plays, you didn't have to make as many throws, and you got to talk to the players when they'd come down to first base."

He spoke to some of them anyway. "I remember trying to strike up a conversation with Frank Robinson," Killebrew said. "Frank was the most serious player, I think, I can remember playing against over those years. He didn't want to have any conversations with the opponents. He wouldn't even answer me when I talked to him.... Now we've become real good friends. Brooks Robinson, on the other hand, was a very big talker. He'd come down and he'd carry on a conversation with you."

Lavagetto, before he was axed with a 23–36 record in June, had appointed Killebrew team captain. Lavagetto's replacement, Sam Mele, was a coach 14 years older than Harmon who had briefly played alongside the youngster in Indianapolis—one on his way up as a player, the other on his way out. Mele held Killebrew in high regard, too, and illustrated it with a story from September 1961 when pitcher Al Schroll took a no-hitter and a 10–0 lead into the ninth inning thanks in part to Killebrew's home run in the eighth.

"When he came back to the dugout, I said, 'Harmon, I don't want you to feel offended or bad about this, but I'm going to take you out,'" Mele told an interviewer. "I had Joe Altobelli, a real good fielder, and I was going to send him in to help Schroll preserve that no-hitter. Harmon turned to me and said, 'Don't explain anything to me. Go right ahead and send Joe in. I don't think anything of it.' It didn't make any difference, because the first man up in the ninth got a single. But that still makes the point about Harmon."

Mele added, "Last year it was tough on him because he tried so hard to please the fans. He really had pressure on him. You know, pressure limits a player because he can't feel at ease. They were great fans, and he wanted to make a good showing. This year it will be better."

Killebrew, who would work for the Twins and other teams as a broadcaster after his playing days, actually began his radio and television work while still active with the Twins. He had a pregame show on WTCN-TV during the season when the Twins played at home, interviewing teammates and opposing players. In the winter, he did a radio show, writing his own scripts on a typewriter at home. He showed one of them to a sportswriter that winter:

> Every hitter has his own style and stance, but there are six basic "musts" that every good hitter must follow:
>
> Number one...Get a good pitch to hit.
>
> Two...Keep your weight forward on the balls of your feet toward the toes.
>
> Three...Be sure and have full plate coverage.

Four…Develop a level swing.

Five…Keep your head as still as possible.

Six…Be quick with your hands and wrists.

Every one of these six fundamentals is important, and without using all of them a player can never become a good hitter. The question is, how do you become a good hitter? The answer…by using this simple formula and practice, practice, practice.

It wasn't something to quit his day job over, but it wasn't bad for a broadcasting novice.

The 1962 season unofficially began with the birth in February of Harmon's daughter, Shawn. The next eventful news came from Mele, who adapted to the team's acquisition of first baseman Vic Power by moving Killebrew into left field. Power was an excellent defensive player, a live-wire personality who some considered "flashy" in the field for the one-handed way he caught just about everything. Killebrew grabbed yet another glove and logged 151 of his 155 games in the outfield, where he made eight errors, had five assists, and more than made up for any defensive shortcomings when it was his turn at bat.

Killebrew's salary that season was estimated at $34,000—with another $10,000 on the side in endorsements, appearances, and licensing deals. And he earned it by hitting 48 home runs with 126 RBIs and 106 walks to balance his drop in batting average to .243 and his rise in strikeouts to an embarrassing (for him) 142. He hit a skid early and was hitting just .220 in early June when Mele sat him down for four days. Slump management was part of their job requirements, both Killebrew's and his manager's.

"He comes out before games and stays after ballgames to work on his batting," Mele said. "He used to swing at bad balls, and they used to take pitches away from him. He also tried to pull the ball. When he'd start to swing, his head would fly out, sort of like he was looking at left field, and his shoulder would fly out, too. This would cause him to think that outside pitches were bad.

"So I checked with the umpires and they all told me, 'Sam, those pitches were on the plate, maybe 2"–3" in.' He's stopped that and now he's hitting to center and right field—and I tell you, there's no guessing how far the ball will go."

Soon after Killebrew returned to the lineup, he got hot. In one July stretch, he belted seven home runs in seven games. That streak ran right through July 18, when he and the other Twins sluggers unleashed the hounds on Cleveland pitchers Barry Latman and Jim Perry. In the bottom of the first at Met Stadium on a Wednesday afternoon, the first five Twins reached base safely before Allison slammed a Latman pitch over the fence. Then Perry came in and mixed in two singles, two walks, and two outs before facing Killebrew with the bases loaded again. This time it was Harmon's turn to go deep, giving Minnesota a record two grand slams in one inning.

In August, Killebrew turned around a pitch from Detroit's Jim Bunning and sent it onto the roof of the double-decked stands in left field at Tiger Stadium, the ball bouncing out of the park. No one had ever done that. After another brief batting tailspin, Killebrew caught fire late and hit 11 home runs and 21 RBIs in 11 games at the end of September.

With his great power numbers and league-leading RBI total to offset any Griffith grumbles about strikeouts or that 45-point drop in batting average, Killebrew—third in the Most Valuable Player balloting—wrangled $40,000 out of the owner for 1963. The Twins had finished second at 91–71, just five games behind New York, and had drawn more than 1.4 million fans thanks in part to the winning and in part to the home run dramatics.

Killebrew slipped on a soggy field in spring training, hurting his right knee, and it bothered him when the regular season began. He perked up in May—when Minnesota clubbed Cleveland for 12 home runs in a four-game series, Killebrew had a pair—and sent one particular ball in June on a 432' ride into the left-field bleachers. Mele had been making a habit of using rookie outfielder Jimmie Hall—on his way to a 33-homer, 80-RBI season—as a defensive replacement in late innings, lifting Killebrew. At one point, Allison (on his way to 35 home runs) was tied with Killebrew at 25 for the club lead. But Harmon's brawny buddy hit his last of the season on September 10; Harmon cracked eight more in the final 16 games.

None of the other Twins was mixed up about the Idaho guy's value in their lineup. "Harmon gives us class," catcher Earl Battey said in a much-circulated quote. "This team, without Killebrew, is like dressing up for a formal affair with white tie and tails and then wearing muddy shoes."

Killebrew nearly brought Boston's Dick Stuart to tears in their battle for the home run crown. When the teams met in a doubleheader at Fenway Park on September 21, Stuart—who had never led the league in anything good before that season—hit a solo shot off Lee Stange for No. 42. But Killebrew clubbed three in that game and one more in the nightcap to not just catch Stuart but pull ahead by two. Then he added No. 45 the next day, trotting past Stuart right there at first base.

Whatever frustration opponents felt about Killebrew's incorrigible power, the folks back in Bloomington called and raised that with delight. A few years earlier, then-Baltimore manager Paul Richards had said of Killebrew, "The homers he hit against us would be homers in any park—including Yellowstone." And the majesty of Killebrew's blows were matched only by their unpredictability and suddenness, which created a sport within a sport at Met Stadium.

Killebrew's at-bats became mini-events with fans sticking around even in the late innings of lopsided games for a glimpse of what he might do in a final trip to the plate. He and the other Twins muscling up in those years turned batting practice into a must-see event. It was something like the baseball world would see in 1998 with the buzz and bugs-to-a-camp-lantern excitement over Mark McGwire and Sammy Sosa, only this was all natural. Corn fed, maybe, but chemical free.

"I think it's true that the home run hitter holds a special place for fans," Killebrew said. "To me it's the ultimate in baseball—to drive the ball out of the park. Actually, I remember going to other parks, like Fenway, when we had me, Bob Allison, Don Mincher, so many guys who could hit the ball out, and people would give us a standing ovation in batting practice."

Actually, as far as ovations, Killebrew and the Twins hadn't heard anything yet.

Chapter 7

Power on the Plains

From 1961–64, his first four seasons as a Minnesota Twin, burly Bob Allison had clubbed 29, 29, 35, and 32 home runs. He drove in 384 runs, an average of 96 a year, scored 374 runs, had an on-base plus slugging percentage (OPS) of .888, and was walked by opposing pitchers 369 times. An outfielder with a linebacker's aggressiveness, he certainly looked the part of an athletic Alpha dog. On most big league teams, Allison would be the big bopper.

On Harmon Killebrew's team, however, Allison had to be content as Robin to Killebrew's Batman. Killebrew, in those same four seasons, slammed 46, 48, 45, and 49 home runs. He averaged 114 RBIs, scored 362 runs, drew 378 walks, and posted an OPS of .938.

They were brothers in bash, even if they were Twins sluggers from different mothers. Once you got past their right-handedness at the plate and all those biceps, they didn't have much in common, although they roomed together for most of their time as teammates.

"We are different, and we've had different problems [in the game]," Killebrew said in an interview back then. "We have never really given each other much advice, although we talk baseball a lot. Bob always is on the go. He's got to be playing cards, going some place, meeting someone, or doing something. I would just as soon read, watch television, or something like that."

"Harmon has that graceful fast swing," Allison said. "He swings up at the ball just a little bit and hits those high homers. He has had that swing ever since I have known him. And he has worked harder to improve it than he has worked on anything else. It's more compact now, and he's hitting more consistently than I have ever seen him. I swing down at the ball, and I'm more of a line-drive hitter. I have never been as much of a long-ball hitter as Harmon. I had played more football than baseball before I signed my first pro contract. So I've had to learn to swing."

That stuff Ted Williams used to say about the difficulty faced by a ballplayer at the plate—round ball, round bat, trying to hit it square—spawned an industry of hitting coaches over baseball's most recent half-century or so. And from the teachings of Charley Lau and Walt Hriniak to those of Rudy Jaramillo, Jeff Pentland, and Kevin Long, there are about as many schools of thought on the proper stances, grips, and weight shifts as there are fellows to tout them.

The Minnesota Twins of the early-to-mid 1960s kept things simple for their pupils, enrolling them all in just one hitting school—the school of hard knocks. Lesson No. 1: See the ball? Crush the ball. Lesson No. 2: Follow lesson No. 1.

In their first four years in Minnesota, the Twins were a ballclub built for the wide open spaces and rawboned living of the Upper Midwest. They averaged 200 homers annually—199.5 to be exact. Their hitters produced 28 seasons of double-digit home runs, 13 seasons of hitting 20 or more, seven instances of at least 30, and Killebrew's aforementioned four times above 40. If the Yankees were known as the Bronx Bombers, the Twins were every bit the Minnesota Maulers. Other aspects of the game sometimes were left wanting, but they sure could hit.

And they only *made* it look easy.

"I'm not so sure that ballplayers who are called natural hitters really are natural hitters," Killebrew said around that time. "Hitting is not something a person learns to do and then never forgets, like riding a bicycle. Instead, it's a constant challenge.... Nobody does this consistently well without working at it all the time. Making contact with the baseball is something I think about constantly. The game of baseball is a child's game against a demanding background of higher competition. It's adult work—a job."

Some adults punch clocks, some adults punch singles up the middle. Then there was Killebrew, who gave up all that Punch and Judy stuff after a conversation early in his career with Pirates slugger Ralph Kiner. Kiner was all over the younger man with that "singles hitters drive Fords, home run hitters drive Cadillacs" stuff. He told Killebrew that if he really wanted to put his innate power to use, he would move up in the batter's box and pull the ball toward left field as often as he could. To heck with a gaudy but anemic, batting average.

Killebrew wasn't one of those men who went through life craving and chasing power. He had it, and he spent most of his 22 major league seasons channeling it in an appropriate yet intimidating manner.

"It's something you either have or you don't," he said. "I watch the ball all the time I can see it in the pitcher's hand. I see it when it leaves his hand. That's when I pick it up. But if the pitcher is one of those herky-jerky guys, I try to pick the ball up at a spot out in front of him."

Once Killebrew got locked in, all hell could break loose. Some power hitters used to claim they never hit home runs when they tried to. Harmon said he hit a lot of them when he was trying to.

"I don't try to just meet the ball. I try to hit the ball *hard*," the slugger said. "I don't believe in that idea of just meet the ball and the home runs will take care of themselves. I don't try for a home run every time up, but I do try to hit the ball hard. That's what I mean—you try to hit the ball hard, *then* the home runs will take care of themselves."

Strikeouts were considered to be inevitable by-products of such an all-in approach. Killebrew struck out 1,699 times, a total that ranked second only to Mickey Mantle (1,710) when he retired and is still ranked 24th in 2012. He had seven seasons of 100 or more strikeouts with probably four or more that would have pushed into triple digits if he had been healthy all year. His batting stroke wasn't as long as some writers described it—a short, fast hack with lots of torque was more like it—but he did have to commit early and committing early can mean strikeouts.

"Timing is everything in this game," Allison told *The Sporting News* in August 1964. "Harmon has that big swing. And if his timing is off, he gets into a slump. When you are hurt, it throws your timing off. It's harder for a man with thick muscles to play this game anyway than it is for a guy like Tony Oliva, who has those long, slim muscles."

Timing was what opponents went after according to Johnny Sain, a renowned pitching coach who worked both for and against the Twins at various times. "You don't challenge him right away," Sain said. "You must constantly change pitches. You try to finesse him—anything to upset his timing."

There wasn't much to upset Killebrew as the 1964 season began. He had undergone surgery in December on the sore knee he'd hurt in spring training, but his rehab seemed to be going well. Away from the field, he and Elaine were busy with their four children—daughter Kathy had arrived in October.

The mood changed when Killebrew got to Orlando. His knee was more trouble than he had anticipated; adhesions made it painful for him on the bases, in the field, and even at the plate. Once the season began, the Twins sputtered through an early 4–8 stretch that dipped them below .500 in the first week of May where Harmon was batting a puny .187 with four homers, 14 hits, and 17 strikeouts.

Some of the heat was off Killebrew, however, thanks to the arrival of Tony Oliva, the latest product of the franchise's fabled "Cuban connection" dating back decades to a friendship between Calvin Griffith and talent scout Joe Cambria. Oliva was raw and often needed pitcher Camilo Pascual to serve as interpreter for manager Sam Mele, but the lean, smiling outfielder earned a starting spot that spring and began to tear up AL pitching with one of the most astounding Rookie of the Year performances ever.

Oliva hit .323 to win the first of his three batting titles, and he led the league in hits (217), runs (109), doubles (43), and total bases (374) while adding 32 home runs, 94 RBIs, nine triples, and 12 stolen bases. He made it to the All-Star Game at Shea Stadium that July and wound up fourth in Most Valuable Player balloting. Best of all, as a left-handed bat, Oliva, Jimmie Hall, and Don Mincher were a terrific complement in the lineup to Killebrew, Allison, Rich Rollins, and Earl Battey, preventing opponents from loading up with either lefty or righty pitchers.

"He was a Rod Carew–type hitter with power," Killebrew said of Oliva, with whom he would team for years in a K-O punch. "He hit the ball all over the ballpark and was the best off-speed hitter I've ever seen. You could throw him 99 fastballs and one change-up, and he would crush [the change-up]."

A good example of the Twins' L-R-L-R nightmares for pitchers came on May 2 with both the team and Harmon (.161, two homers) sputtering. They were in Kansas City and needed a solo blast in the ninth by the slumping Killebrew gave them a 3–2 lead before the Athletics scored a run in the bottom half, pushing the game into extra innings. Baseball legend has it that Charlie Finley, the Athletics' irascible owner, called in from out of town and got his team's PR man, Jim Schaaf, on the phone just as Oliva was digging in to lead off the 11th inning.

The Twins' right fielder drove Dan Pfister's pitch over the fence in right, and Schaaf dutifully reported that bit of bad news to the boss. Allison stepped up and did the same but to left. Finley's mood worsened. Then it was Hall sending Pfister's offering out to right and the pitcher himself off to the showers. While Schaaf tried to soothe his boss after Minnesota's three consecutive home runs, Athletics manager Eddie Lopat called for reliever Vern Handrahan. This time it was Killebrew's turn to go yard.

"Killebrew's home run was too much for Finley," Twins popular play-by-play man Herb Carneal claimed later. "He was so convinced that Schaaf was pulling his leg that he fired him over the phone."

In spite of that drama, Killebrew still wasn't right and made sure to let Mele know it, even apologizing for his sub-par play. The manager scoffed at that—no apologies necessary for Harmon—but he did opt for an approach that had worked so well in June 1962 when his slugger was mired in a similar slump. Mele gave him four games and five days off, time to work out the kinks in his swing away from the pressure of live competition.

"When I get in a slump, every pitch seems to be a borderline case—either a close ball or a strike," Killebrew said. "I swing at the bad pitches, and the ones I let go by are called strikes.... You've got to correct your problems as soon as possible. If you keep going on, 0-for-4, 0-for-4, you keep doing the same thing over and over. It takes you a week or maybe a month to figure out what you're doing wrong. But if you know yourself in a given situation, this is the biggest thing you can know."

Be ready, as Baltimore manager Hank Bauer said during Killebrew's slump. "At least once a game you get your pitch," the former Yankees outfielder said. "When you do, don't foul it off because you might not get it back again."

Harmon stepped back into the box on May 14 against Chicago left-hander Gary Peters, the AL's top rookie in 1963, and sent Peters' fastball into the left-field bleachers. In the next 16 days, Killebrew would add nine more home runs. One of those came on May 24 when he mashed a 471' drive off Milt Pappas over the hedge in left-center field at Baltimore's Memorial Stadium It was one of the longest shots in that park's history. By the end of July, Killebrew had batted .331 with 32 homers in a 10-week tear.

"His home runs were spectacular," Orioles third baseman Brooks Robinson, whose glove work earned the same level of professional awe from Killebrew, said after both of their careers had ended. "He hit [68] against us, and I got tired of seeing him run around third base. He had the nicest, sweetest stroke you would want to see for a home run hitter. He just rested his bat on his shoulder, just took it back and—wham! No extra motion, no hitch or anything. He just muscled it out."

Pitcher Jim "Mudcat" Grant arrived in June in a trade from Cleveland and knew what he was in for—a whole lot of brawny run support. "When I was traded to the Twins, it was like going to heaven," Grant said, "because I knew [Harmon] was going to hit a lot of home runs, some with men on, and he as going to put some runs up on the scoreboard for me."

August began with renewed buzz about Killebrew's home run pace and his chances of chasing down the single-season record of 60 set by Babe Ruth in 1927 and topped by Roger Maris with 61 in 1961. Hitting one out every 10.1 at-bats through July, Harmon had 36 homers with 58 games remaining. Ruth, by comparison, had 33 at the same point in 1927. Maris already had 40 in his big year.

Killebrew's pace slackened during the final two months—for Ruthian ambitions, anyway. He hit 13 homers in his final 215 at-bats and just four in his last 26 games, batting just .216. He had plenty of chances at that one extra dinger to reach 50, a milestone that would elude him in his career, but he managed only one home run in his final 48 at-bats. "I think I put more pressure on myself than the pitchers put on me," Harmon said. "In those days, 50 home runs was kind of a magical number."

The Twins tailed off, too, going 9–15 from Labor Day to slip and stay below .500, finishing 20 games behind the Yankees. Minnesota led the league not only in homers (221) and runs (749) but in slugging (.427) and OPS (.749), as well. But the pitching staff ranked at or below the AL average in most categories, and the Twins made the second-most errors.

An indication of the team's all-or-nothing approach came in a comparison of close and blowout games. When the difference in runs was a robust five or more, the Twins were fine, assembling a 24–14 record. But in one-run decisions, their record was 28–38. And perhaps the biggest disappointment of 1964 was that they were 40–41 at Met Stadium—their home-field advantage of the past two seasons (93–69 in Bloomington) had vanished. The only other teams that were below .500 at home that summer were Washington and Kansas City, and they each lost 100 games or more. The home runs were great, but the losing made Twins baseball a little less fun for local fans.

One happy memory from the season came in May when the Twins were in New York for a two-game series. That spring, an eight-year-old boy named Jack Guiney had suffered burns over 50 percent of his body when the garments he wore as an altar boy at his Brooklyn church caught fire as he was lighting candles. He lay bandaged in a hospital for weeks, his family cheering him with talk of and updates on Jack's favorite baseball player—Harmon Killebrew. Mike Guiney eventually contacted the Twins, wondering if the slugger might be able to drop by his son's room. And so he did on the morning of May 20, an autographed baseball in hand.

It sounds like a scene from a schmaltzy 1950s movie, something to be parodied a couple decades later, but the following did happen. The bandaged boy talked some baseball with his hero, and Killebrew told him that the next time he came to town when Jack got well, he would bring him to Yankee Stadium to meet the other Twins. Guiney said he would watch that day's game on television and then Harmon said, "Maybe I'll hit you a couple."

Whoa. Not just one? A couple? Even for a sizzling Killebrew, that would be a tough order, certain to disappoint a sick young boy. So in the first inning, with one on, one out, and three Minnesota runs already in, Killebrew chased Ralph Terry with a two-run homer to left. He singled in the fourth, struck out in the sixth, and went to the plate in the eighth with the Twins up 6–2 for what likely would be his final time on that trip. Yankees reliever Steve Hamilton always tried to work Killebrew low and away, offering nothing he could pull with his power stroke.

So Killebrew went down and drove Hamilton's pitch over the wall in right, where Ruth had dumped so many before him. Forty-seven years later, Guiney—by then 55 years old and living in nearby Queens—told a Minneapolis newspaper that the experience, the visit and the day "lifted my spirits. I watched the whole game from my hospital bed. I was shocked." Guiney was listening to the radio in May 2011 when he heard Killebrew was sick. "I said a little prayer when I heard that," he said.

Killebrew's place in Guiney's heart, even for a New York kid, was understandable. He had just won his third consecutive home run title (and to prove it, in January at a banquet in Baltimore, he was presented with a $2,000 jeweled Sultan of Swat crown). No one else in the American League, and only Willie Mays, who had hit 47 homers for the San Francisco Giants in the NL, had even reached 40 that season. When the 1965 season began, Harmon had already hit 272 in 995 games (261 in his six seasons as a regular).

At a similar place in his career—through the season in which he turned 28—the great Ruth had hit 238 homers in 947 games, with 218 in the five seasons since he switched from pitcher to outfielder. Ruth did have Killebrew beat in an even more important category, appearing in six World Series to Killebrew's none. That needed to change, as far as Harmon was concerned. After two seasons with 91 victories and his first taste of the first division, as they called it back then, this season of slippage back to sub-.500 and a sixth-place finish was unacceptable.

That's the attitude Killebrew and the rest of his crew took to Orlando in the spring of 1965. In a few months, the Beatles would drop *Help!*—their fifth album and second movie—on the American scene. The Minnesota Twins were going to have to help themselves.

Chapter 8

Close but Not Quite

Sam Mele knew the Twins needed something different. All those home runs and nothing to show for them besides a tie for sixth place wasn't going to cut it.

The Twins manager had been paying attention in October when the St. Louis Cardinals had made life tough on the aging yet mighty New York Yankees in the World Series. The Cardinals, whose 109 home runs in the regular season ranked 15th among the 20 big league teams, hit only five more—half of what New York belted—in their seven-game Series. But St. Louis had twice the fun, playing a peskier, more aggressive style that years later would get referred to as "small ball." It wasn't that the Cardinals stole bases—leadoff man Lou Brock, who had pilfered 43 during the year, didn't try even once—as much as it was sending runners, pushing from first to third, daring to take the extra base.

Two complete-game victories by Series MVP Bob Gibson in Games 5 and 7 didn't hurt, either. But Mele liked the other stuff, too—the attitude, the mindset—and made a few mental notes. If St. Louis could end New York's domination in the World Series playing that way, maybe the Twins could borrow from it to combat the Yankees' reign of terror—five straight pennants, 15 of the last 18, 22 of the last 29—in the American League.

So at Tinker Field the following spring, Mele put a little giddy-up in his players' git-along. Rather than allow hitters to amble around the base paths after their turns in the batting cage, he mandated that they sprint to first base. Then, at the crack of the bat by the next man, they would take off for third, regardless of where the ball was hit. The Twins were about to become practitioners of the hit-and-run in ways not seen up to that point in Minnesota. The thinking wormed its way into the club's culture, and people started to notice before anyone even left Florida.

"After a while," Boston outfielder Carl Yastrzemski said, "you found them forcing you into fielding mistakes because you were rushing."

Or as Twins shortstop Zoilo Versalles, destined for big things that season, told *Sports Illustrated*, "If you get to one base and you can see the ball on the ground in the outfield, run like hell to the next base."

Mele wasn't sure how challenging it would be to convince the Twins' heavy lifters to wait on fewer pitches and be ready to swing with runners in motion. He wasn't even inclined to ask Killebrew, given the respect he had for him and the results Killebrew already was giving the ballclub. But Harmon was a team guy first. He noticed what was happening around him anyway and even sought out teammate-turned-hitting coach Jim Lemon to make sure Mele asked the same of him as the others. "Tell Sam I would like to hit with runners going once in a while," he told Lemon.

As the saying goes, to whom much is given, much is required.

Killebrew's salary had reached $50,000, the fattest in franchise history—the average American worker made $6,450 then, and a typical U.S. house cost about twice that. But this was back in the days before guaranteed, multi-year contracts; any dip in performance could and usually would be held against a player when it came time to sign another one-year deal. Calvin Griffith, the Twins owner, never hesitated to pounce on those dips—though it also was common for him to reach an agreement quickly with Killebrew each winter, then use that as a ceiling to shoot down the other players' demands, "Why, if Killebrew's fine making [fill in the blank], who are you to ask for so much?"

There were other things at risk, too, including individual goals such as those home run titles and the just-below-the-surface Ruth chase that might be harder to achieve with an alteration to his proven style. Killebrew's hitting wasn't broken, so did he and Mele really want to "fix" it? Killebrew seemed to not even hesitate. The man who never bunted in 22 big league seasons was ready to sacrifice.

"From the conversations I had last summer and last winter," Killebrew said deep into the 1965 season, "I knew the club wanted me to cut down on my strikeouts. I struck out 135 times last year. Of course, I've tried to cut down on them before. Never could do it. But I set out this year with the purpose of hitting the ball more often."

Mele wondered if Killebrew could "hit .300" by putting the ball in play more often. Never mind that his on-base percentage of .377 ranked eighth in the league in 1964. Most folks didn't follow on-base or any of the advanced metrics so common a few decades later. "I don't think so," Harmon told him, "because I can't run well enough to run out any infield hits. I could cut down on my swing. But would that help the club?"

Mele answered, "You can cut down on your strikeouts but hitting the ball more often. And if you hit the ball more often, you will get your home runs anyway."

There was one more area where Killebrew wound up sacrificing—the other half of his game. Mele had come to camp ready to move his most valuable performer from the outfield, where he had spent most of the previous three seasons, to first base. It was yet another adjustment foisted on a premium player, but Mele had a trade-off in mind—he would assure Killebrew that there would be no more shifting around. It was hardly a company secret, for instance, when Killebrew at a winter baseball dinner in New Hampshire had admitted, "I really hate to bounce back and forth from one position to another. It's this jumping around that really bothers me."

It was a great plan with lousy execution. Right before the end of spring training, Don Mincher—the other first baseman on the roster—went public with a request to be traded. He felt he had not received, and would not get, enough playing time with Killebrew in at first. A tall left-handed batter from Huntsville, Alabama, Mincher was feeling a little of the Eddie Yost-logjam that Killebrew had endured in Washington. Acquired with Earl Battey from Chicago, Mincher had spent five seasons with the Senators/Twins without getting 300 at-bats in a season. He wanted to build on a solid 1964 showing and not go backward. "I wish they would trade me," Mincher said. "I'm no more ready to play now than I was the first day of spring training."

So Harmon stepped up again, freeing Mele from his agreement. "I'll play another position so Mincher can play first base, if it will help," he said.

Mincher stayed put and got into 128 games, up from 120 the year before. He hit .251 in 346 at-bats with 22 homers and 65 RBIs and, partly because he was the last left-handed bat in the usual lineup, he led the league with 15 intentional walks. Rich Rollins played third against lefties, made 140 appearances, hit .249, was the Twin's best bunter, and had a stellar season in the field. Killebrew wound up juggling gloves again with about 60 percent of his defensive work at first base, a third of the year at third, and a pair of games in left field.

No one could quibble with the results, though. Minnesota went 8–3 in April and 19–12 in May. (Harmon squeezed in a quick trip to Payette after his and Elaine's fifth child, Erin, was born). A week into June, the Twins were 31–15. Their home runs were headed south from 221 to just 150, but most other categories were pointing north. Mudcat Grant, Jim Kaat, and Jim Perry combined that season to go 51–25 with a 2.96 ERA. In keeping with the hit-and-run tactics of the hitters, new pitching coach Johnny Sain even had the pitchers working more quickly. During the best (21–7, 3.30 ERA) of his 14 major league seasons, Grant said, "With the kind of stuff I've got, it isn't worth thinking about what you're doing."

The Twins outscored opponents by an average of 1.1 runs, almost double second-place Chicago's 0.6 differential. The Twins took 13-of-18 games against New York and 11-of-18 from the White Sox. They went a combined 32–4 against Boston and Washington. As for those problem "splits" from 1964, this time Minnesota was 30–22 in one-run games and as successful at Met Stadium (51–30) as it was on the road (51–30).

There were other terrific individual performances that season, as well. Versalles was named AL Most Valuable Player after having a monster year at the plate by shortstop standards of the time—a .273 batting average, 19 home runs, 77 RBIs, 27 steals, and the league lead in doubles (45), triples (12), runs (126), and total bases (308)—and Gold Glove work in the field. Oliva won his second batting title (.321), topped AL hitters in hits (185), and received the one first-place MVP vote that Versalles with 19 votes didn't. Bob Allison and Jimmie Hall hit 23 and 20 home runs, respectively.

Mele made sure to credit Killebrew, drawing a line straight back to his willingness to put the team ahead of his own preferences. The manager called it "an inspiration to every player."

Killebrew wasn't exactly a mascot, of course. Through August 2, the big man had 22 home runs and 70 RBIs, and even if his home run frequency was down to one every 16.5 at-bats, his batting average was at .278, his on-base at .393, and his OPS a nice round .900. Killebrew had managed to hit a couple long balls that endured, too.

The first came in July at the end of a four-game series against New York immediately before the All-Star Game—which, to the Twin Cities' excitement, would be played right there at Met Stadium. The Twins technically had more to fear from Cleveland, Baltimore, Chicago, and Detroit when that weekend began; those clubs were bunched closely behind Minnesota, within 6.5 games of the AL lead. The Yankees were 12.5 back—but because of their pedigree and history, they still were seen as potential trouble.

The Twins won the first two games then dropped the nightcap of Saturday's doubleheader. Come Sunday, a 4–4 tie turned into a 5–4 New York lead in the ninth after errors by Rollins and Twins pitcher Jerry Fosnow. In the bottom of the inning, with Rollins on first and two out, they were down to their last strike when Killebrew lashed Pete Mikkelsen's 3–2 fastball over the left-field fence for a walk-off homer long before anyone thought to call them that. It was considered the most dramatic home run in Twins history until Kirby Puckett ended Game 6 of the 1991 World Series with his Metrodome blast.

"I remember that home run like it was yesterday," Kaat said later. "Harmon fouled a bunch of pitches off.... We had our lead back, a little breathing room. Then we gradually increased it, and it became apparent the Yankees weren't the Yankees any more and they fell 15, 16 games out of first. But I didn't realize going into that season that we had that good a team."

Killebrew's next big fly was more for show and civic pride. A number of national media members already were in town for the Yankees series since they could stick around for the All-Star Game two days later. The assemblage of talent was staggering: 12 future Hall of Famers on the visiting NL squad, and five more on the AL.

Roberto Clemente, Frank Robinson, and Billy Williams were *back-up* outfielders that day, playing behind Willie Mays, Henry Aaron, and Willie Stargell. Juan Marichal started for the senior circuit, got relief assistance from Don Drysdale and Sandy Koufax, and then—good Lord!—watched Bob Gibson pick up the save in a 6–5 victory.

The NL jumped out front early to 5–0. But it was 5–3 when Killebrew faced Cincinnati's Jim Maloney in the fifth with Brooks Robinson on base, and his shot to deep left-center—to a deafening cheer, according to those in the ballpark—tied it for a spell. The Twins had six All-Stars on the roster—including Versalles, Oliva, Hall, Grant, and Battey—but there was no doubt which local hero was the most beloved that day.

Killebrew managed to take one more for the team that summer. He had already driven in the tying or winning run seven times in 1965 when his season very nearly ended. He was playing first base on August 2 when Baltimore's Russ Snyder hit a slow roller to Rollins at third. The infielder's throw was up the line, and Killebrew reached to grab it as the ball and Snyder arrived at the same time. The collision made grown men wince, dislocated Harmon's left elbow, and felt even worse than it sounded.

"It felt like it broke my arm off," Killebrew recalled. "I was afraid to look at my arm." The team physician on duty was a general practitioner, not an orthopedic specialist, and his first instinct was to simply snap the arm back into its socket. "As it turned out," Killebrew learned later, "that was the best thing that ever happened to me because it wasn't broke, and the quicker he got it back into place the better."

Still, his prognosis was bleak and the timing seemed horrible. The Twins clearly were the class of the American League. Long-term, Killebrew worried about his arm, how it would respond to rehab and recovery, and any effect the elbow injury might have on his ability to hit, either with power or at all. Short-term, however, his fear centered on the World Series and the prospect of being cruelly cheated out of what he and so many other players dreamed about.

The pain was severe, the worst Killebrew had experienced to that point. He missed Minnesota's next 48 games. He and the team's trainer, George "Doc" Lentz, stayed diligent with therapy, and the Twins stayed comfortably afloat in the standings. On September 21, aching to ready himself for the Series that was surely coming, Killebrew suited up, went 0-for-4 with a walk in a loss to Baltimore, and was delighted that his elbow held up for three fly outs and a grounder. Five days later in Washington, he went 0-for-3 and that was marvelous, too—the Twins clinched the franchise's first pennant in 32 years that afternoon.

Down the stretch, in 10 final games, Killebrew's numbers weren't much—he hit .184, homered three times, and drove in five runs. But like *Seinfeld*'s George Costanza, he was back, baby. And the Twins were viewed by many as favorites in facing the Los Angeles Dodgers. A preview in *Sports Illustrated* described Killebrew's team this way: "What the Twins have is a rare blend of power, speed, and pitching that is almost un-American; they are a National League–type ballclub with a quality of daring that just might blow the 1965 World Series apart."

Well, not exactly. The Twins did grab a 2–0 lead at home in the best-of-seven championship by beating the Dodgers' Hall of Fame pitching tandem, sinking Drysdale first for an 8–2 victory and Koufax next (he had flipped starts with Drysdale to observe the Jewish holiday of Yom Kippur) in Game 2, 5–1. In that one, Allison played his way into Twins lore with a fifth inning, streaking, diving, and sliding catch into the left-field corner at Met Stadium to rob L.A.'s Jim Lefebvre of what surely would have been a run-scoring double—and possibly a game-changing extra-base hit. From his position at third base, Killebrew considered his roommate's play "the greatest catch I've ever seen."

Harmon went 3-for-6 with a run, one RBI, and two walks in the two victories and wondered privately if this was going to be easier than they expected. "We thought, 'Gosh, we may have a chance to sweep the Series,'" he said.

Or not. The Dodgers' ballpark, known as Chavez Ravine, was uncomfortable for the Twins; the infield was harder, the distances to the outfield fences were greater, and the results were daunting. In the three games in Los Angeles, the Twins were outscored 18–2, with both of their runs coming in a 7–2 loss in Game 4 as solo home runs by Killebrew and Oliva. The only real highlight from a Killebrew point of view was the fact that Elaine, through mutual friends, had met actress Rosalind Russell during the stay and had her seats upgraded for the third game there. So she had a better view when the Twins managed only four hits and a walk against Koufax, sending only 29 batters to the plate thanks to three double-plays turned by the Dodgers.

Back home, down 3–2, the Twins got a big-game effort from Grant, who battled both the National League champs and a fierce cold, beating them 5–1 to force Game 7. The personable pitcher went the distance, gave up six hits, struck out five, walked none, and had Twins fans believing again after hitting reliever Howie Reed's pitch to him to deep left-center for a three-run homer. But Game 7 meant Koufax again, and even on two days' rest, the Dodgers' left-hander meant trouble for Minnesota.

The Twins' only real chance in the game came in the bottom of the fifth inning, trailing 2–0, when they had two men on with one out. Versalles' chopper toward third was gloved by L.A.'s Jim Gilliam, his momentum taking him right to the base for an easy force out. Koufax got Joe Nossek to ground out and wound up retiring 14 of the final 15 men he faced. Killebrew's line-drive single with one down in the ninth twice brought the tying run to the plate, but Battey struck out looking and Allison struck out swinging—then slammed his bat hard into the dirt in frustration.

Killebrew eased the moment a little bit, saying, "I told Bob after the game, 'If you had swung at the ball as hard as you swung at the ground, we might have won the game.'" Killebrew considered Koufax's work that day—heavy on fastballs, good for 10 strikeouts, three hits, and three walks—"the greatest pitching performance I've ever seen." Harmon batted .286 in the Series with six hits, six walks, and that one home run. He looked forward to his next shot at October baseball, which he eventually tasted twice more—but never again in the World Series.

* * *

The AL pennant that the Twins raised before the home opener in 1966 was the only one Minnesota would win for 22 years, at which time Killebrew was a color analyst on their televised games. The expectations by both the ballclub and its fans were quite different from that, naturally, and the season had its share of highlights, most notably Kaat's stellar 25–13 season. The rangy left-hander had a 2.75 ERA and led the American League with 41 starts, 19 complete games, 304⅔ innings, a ratio of 1.6 walks per nine innings, and 3.73 strikeouts per walk. He won the fifth of his 16 Gold Gloves as arguably the greatest fielding pitcher in baseball history and even drove in 13 runs that season, hitting a pair of homers and batting .195. It was his misfortune, alas, to do all this in the final season before the AL and NL began presenting separate Cy Young Awards to their top pitchers.

Koufax won the last combined honor by going 27–9 with a 1.73 ERA and 317 strikeouts in his farewell season.

Killebrew marveled at Koufax's greatness. But he was pretty happy, too, with the left-handed ace of Minnesota's staff, not just for his pitching skill but for his tenacity. "I remember playing first base one night," Killebrew reminisced years later, "and Jim took a one-hop line drive in the mouth. The ball ricocheted over to Rich Rollins at third. Rich fielded the ball, threw it to first base for the final out of the inning. Like I always did, I looked at the ball to see if there were any scuff marks or anything. I looked at the ball, and there were Jim's teeth—part of his teeth—in the ball. Of course, I gave him the ball."

There were lowlights and disappointments for the Twins in 1966, too. Versalles had a contract squabble and was looking like a one-season wonder. Battey was in decline, and Hall would find himself used more and more as a platoon player, his production dropping off. After a sweep of Kansas City to start the season, Minnesota lost seven of its next eight, settling quickly into sixth place and watching the Baltimore Orioles' taillights grow smaller. Even at 28–28 halfway through June, the Twins were 10 games out, stuck in fifth place while losing ground to Brooks Robinson, Frank Robinson, Boog Powell, and a couple of young pitchers, Dave McNally and Jim Palmer, both of whom soon would become dominant members of baseball's best rotation.

Any shot at getting back into the race fizzled in a five-game series at Baltimore at the start of July. With doubleheaders Friday and Saturday and a single game Sunday, Minnesota allowed only 19 runs but scored just 10 and was swept. Instead of cutting the Orioles' lead into single digits, the Twins left town 19 games back. That was their low point—by going 54–30 after July 3, the Twins were 8.5 games better than the next-best team. But Baltimore cruised to a 42–38 mark over the same period and still ended up 97–63 to Minnesota's second-place 89–73.

Killebrew hit 39 home runs, drove in 110 runs, had a line of .281/.391/.538, banged out a career-best 27 doubles, kept his strikeouts in double digits again (98), and led the AL with 103 walks, 18 intentional. He was on the move again in the field, logging 42 games at first base, 107 at third, and 18 in left field. His team's strong second half surely had much to do with this. Harmon had 17 homers, 47 RBIs, and a .264 average in 85 games before the All-Star break and 22, 62, and .300 after the break. He placed fourth in MVP balloting, but the top three spots all went to Orioles—Frank Robinson, Brooks Robinson, and Boog Powell—and Frank Robinson was a runaway choice as baseball's first Triple Crown winner in a decade with 49 homers, 122 RBIs, and a .316 batting average.

* * *

For 1967, owner Calvin Griffith—though cranky enough over a Twins payroll that featured Killebrew ($60,000), Kaat ($54,000), Oliva ($40,000), and Versalles ($38,000) among its top earners—added a couple more big paychecks by acquiring pitcher Dean Chance ($47,500) in a trade with California and reliever Ron Kline ($35,000) in a deal the next day with Washington. Gone in the exchanges were Don Mincher, Jimmie Hall, Camilo Pascual, and infielder Bernie Allen. But Mele was eager to bolster the staff and felt the team's farm system could plug any holes opened by the trades.

The most promising newbie was Rod Carew, a second baseman born in Panama who signed in 1964 and spent the 1966 season in the Class A Carolina League. The left-handed spray hitter not only leaped over the next two minor league levels, he showed enough, fast enough, to start at second base on the AL All-Star team and earn Rookie of the Year honors with a .292 average, seven triples, and eight home runs in 137 games.

The season began with a whimper, the Twins going 5–10 in April and spinning their wheels at 25–25 in early June. Kaat, in particular among the pitchers, was not healthy and thus ineffective, dropping seven of his first eight decisions to that point and lugging around a bloated 6.00 ERA. Oliva was battling injuries, too, and he was hitting

.237 through those 50 games with just one home run and 15 RBIs. There was only so much Killebrew's big numbers (14 homers, 40 RBIs, and a .290 batting average) after perking up in May, could do.

They couldn't save Mele's job, not after Griffith got it into his head that a change was needed. Mele was still in charge on June 3 when Killebrew launched the longest home run ever hit at Metropolitan Stadium, a blast off California Angels pitcher Lew Burdette that, after some initial miscalculations, was properly estimated at 520'. Amazed by the strength required to deposit the ball in the upper deck of the left-field pavilion, the Twins seized the moment by marking the seat struck by the ball. Years later, with the ballpark gone and the Mall of America shopping center in its place, a lone red seat was affixed to the wall high above an indoor amusement park at approximately the same spot where the Killer's blast landed.

The next day, Killebrew cranked another one, maybe even harder, off Angels pitcher Jack Sanford that bounced off the facing of the upper deck in left. Afterward, he was promptly asked by sportswriters to explain these ZIP code–challenging home runs.

"Well, I had been sharing an apartment with [hitting coach] Jim Lemon until my family moved here for the summer from Ontario [Oregon]," Killebrew said when asked about the record distance. "Jim's a pretty good chef and did a fair job of cooking, but he couldn't seem to open up a carton of eggs without frying the whole dozen. Elaine got here from Ontario a couple of days ago, and since she's been around to cook, I've been on a home run diet."

Then Killebrew stopped teasing and attributed the big hits to the warmer temperatures finally descending on the Twin Cities.

Mele got roughed up even worse than the California pitchers on June 9, the day Griffith finally did fire him. His replacement, Cal Ermer, was called up from the Class AAA Denver team. Whether it was Ermer's style, strategy and rules, a few Twins getting healthier at the right time, or some combination, Minnesota responded and played with pennant fever the rest of the way.

Kaat went 15–6 with a 2.11 ERA after the managerial change. Oliva was back, too, for the season's final two-thirds and produced 16 HR, 67 RBIs, 28 doubles, 132 hits, and a .303 average. Chance went 11–11 under Ermer, but his outings were strong down the stretch—a 2.78 ERA, .237 opponents' batting average, 11 complete games, and 139 strikeouts to 35 walks in 181 innings all on his way to a 20–14 record. As for Killebrew, he was Mr. Consistency in 1967; he produced at the same rate over the final 112 games as he had through the first 50.

After a momentary dip to 26–27 as Ermer moved in, the Twins went 65–44 the rest of the way. They moved into first place by beating the White Sox on August 13 and, after going 10–6 on a grueling 16-game road trip, still held a share of first place with Boston. Chicago sat one game back, and Detroit was behind by one and a half games. Ten days later, the four teams were in a virtual tie for first place.

During the season's final five weeks, six teams—the four mentioned above plus California and Baltimore—all played at a .529 clip or better, all clumped within two-and-a-half games through that stretch. Heading into the last series, a two-gamer at Boston, Minnesota held a one-game edge over both the Red Sox and the Tigers. The White Sox were two back. Detroit had a pair of doubleheaders vs. the Angels to navigate and split the four games. What went on at Fenway, though, packed the real drama and soon enough brought tears to the Twins.

They needed to win one. They got neither. Kaat had a 1–0 lead on Saturday but suffered a torn elbow tendon, gave way to the bullpen, and watched Yastrzemski lead Boston back for a 6–4 victory. Yaz and Harmon each hit their 44th home runs that day, maintaining their tie for the AL lead and allowing the Boston outfielder to win a slightly asterisked Triple Crown (with 121 RBIs and a .326 average).

In the finale, Chance's 2–0 lead vanished on a two-run single by Yastrzemski in the sixth. That inning ran on, with the Red Sox scoring three more thanks to a pair of wild pitches by Twins' reliever Al Worthington and an error by Killebrew. In the eighth, Minnesota's hopes died when Allison, after a run-scoring single made it 5–3, got thrown out badly by Yaz while trying to hustle to second base.

After losing the pennant to Boston at the end, it didn't make the Twins feel any better to know that they actually beat the Red Sox head-to-head that season, 11–7. The Twins also bested Detroit, 10–8. They just hadn't taken care of business as thoroughly against some of the AL's weaker clubs.

Killebrew still had reasons for optimism. He had played 162 and 163 games the past two seasons, and he had no injuries serious enough to cost him games. He went into the off-season with 380 home runs at age 31. Ruth, at the same age, had hit 356. With the sort of good health Killebrew had been enjoying, it's no wonder he looked forward to the next season.

Turns out it wasn't only the Boston Red Sox dreaming the Impossible Dream that fall.

Chapter 9

MVP

If not for 1968, there might have been no 1969 for Harmon Killebrew. More precisely, if not for the hobbling, if not actually crippling, injury that Killebrew suffered on what should have been a breezy, happy July evening in Houston, he might never have responded with the most productive, most prodigious, most decorated season of his long and power-packed career.

Fear, pain, and desperation can be great motivators sometimes.

From the start, Killebrew's injury at the 1968 All-Star Game was an accident waiting to happen. The first man to be named to All-Star teams at three positions—let's face it, his bat got him in each time, regardless of where the Twins happened to be using him—Killebrew was back at first base for the American League. The Houston ballpark, obviously, was hermetically sealed; no rain, no outside elements at all, got under that roof. The dirt around the bases was trucked in, and it wasn't like the real stuff at other parks. It was more fine. Less firm.

So when Killebrew reached out, low, lower, extending his left arm and leg for a throw from Angels shortstop Jim Fregosi in the third inning in hopes of nabbing St. Louis' Curt Flood, the soil did not hold.

The Twins slugger lost what little bit of leverage and balance he had as his lead foot gave way. Killebrew would take a little pride later from still gloving the ball—Flood was out—but at that point, so was the big man, who had folded over his left leg in a complete split.

This wasn't Baryshnikov at a ballgame. Killebrew wasn't built to bend that way, and his left hamstring took the brunt of it, and a piece of bone pulled away from his pelvis, as well. "I heard it split like a rubber band," he said later. Twins owner Calvin Griffith, down in the visitors' clubhouse with his guy afterward, reportedly muttered something along the lines of, "Nothing's going right this year."

The 1968 season already was rough enough on guys like Killebrew. "The Year of the Pitcher" they called it, even as it was happening. There were 339 shutouts thrown that year and 82 games that—just like the All-Star Game—ended in a 1–0 score. Carl Yastrzemski won the AL batting crown with a .301 average, the only man to crack .300. Detroit's Denny McLain won 31 games as the Tigers won the pennant. Over in the NL, Bob Gibson's ERA shrunk to 1.12, the lowest ever by a pitcher with more than 300 innings.

Killebrew was good enough to be an All-Star in spite of his meager first-half stats—13 home runs, 34 RBIs, a .204 average—and Minnesota's mediocre play (39–42). But a bad season for him suddenly had gotten worse. Forget about hunting down the pennant that had eluded him and his teammates in 1967. Killebrew poured his worries into the possibility that, at the still-young-enough age of 32, his playing days might be done.

During the next seven weeks, he followed the orders of his doctors. And trainers. And coaches. He got treatment, did his rehab work, stretched, and strengthened. By September 1, he was healed enough to test the leg, walking to the plate with no small measure of doubt as a pinch-hitter with two outs, no one on, in the ninth inning. His club trailed Chicago 5–3, so those in the crowd of 16,373 at the Met who hadn't already gone home stood to cheer. But this drama, facing White Sox knuckleballer Wilbur Wood, was all about Killebrew and his future. He turned on Wood's second flutterer and sent it out way faster, over the fence in left.

Killebrew managed to play 20 games, spot duty, that September, hitting three more homers while batting .257. Then he was off to Oregon again for a winter of walking, hunting, weights, and even some running as he regained full strength in that left leg. "A blessing in disguise," he later called the All-Star injury, for it set him up for arguably the best individual season in Minnesota history, certainly then, and maybe even now.

To be fair, he did get a little help. Baseball expanded again, adding two new teams in each league, and the leagues themselves each split into two divisions of six. The Twins were put in the AL West along with both expansion clubs, Kansas City and Seattle. The game's rulebook was tweaked, and the pitching mound was lowered from 15″ to 10″. The strike zone shrank a little, too (allowing for individual umps' preferences). Baseball already was getting grief as the NFL's slow, stodgy, less sexy sibling. Well, by God, there was going to be hitting in 1969.

* * *

The Twins, already well-equipped for that, added a hungry, aggressive manager in Billy Martin, the former infielder and coach who had lusted for the chance under both Sam Mele and Cal Ermer. Martin was high-maintenance. "Like sitting on a keg of dynamite," Griffith would say when he fired Martin four days after the season ended. Martin got his greatest notoriety that summer when he beat down pitcher Dave Boswell one night outside a Detroit sports bar. But for that single season, the future foil of Yankee owner George Steinbrenner grabbed the Twin Cities' attention with a hustling ballclub while leaning on and respecting the No. 1 slugger in his midst.

Killebrew was back healthy and strong, hitting .309 with four homers and 17 RBIs in the first month. He had help, too. Minnesota had two 20-game winners on its pitching staff that year, Boswell and Jim Perry, and a bullpen ace in Ron Perranoski. But their lineup was a lumber company about to lead the AL in runs and average, finish second in OPS, and finish fourth in both home runs and stolen bases. Cesar Tovar, the pesky leadoff man, scored 99 runs, had 45 steals, and even hit 11 homers. Rod Carew won his first batting title (.332) and stole home seven times. Tony Oliva batted .309, scored 97 runs, and drove in 101 runs. Killebrew's biggest problem on days he batted clean-up was finding enough men left on base to drive home—though, in reality, that wasn't a problem at all. He amassed 140 RBIs in 1969 and matched his personal high of 49 home runs.

The field of MVP candidates was a crowded one that season. Reggie Jackson, in his pre-Mr. October days, had emerged as a young slugger in Oakland. Frank Howard, the Senators' towering (6'8") and powerful left fielder, was known variously as the "Washington Monument," the "Capital Punisher," or just plain "Hondo". Baltimore's Boog Powell was set up much like Harmon, batting in the sweet spot of the Orioles' order behind terrific table-setters. Then there was Denny McLain, the 1968 AL MVP who was back for one more stellar season. When asked for his strategy when facing either Killebrew or Howard, the usually cocky Detroit right-hander had said, "Prayer for the most part."

True to his nature, Killebrew saw another blessing in disguise in the number of great seasons played out in 1969. "I think the closeness of this thing is good for [all] of us. Of course, you're always trying to do your best, but this way you're more conscious of it."

One blessing undisguised was Baltimore's spot over in the AL East. The Orioles were a machine that season, headed to 109 victories (12 more than the Twins) while shredding the stronger of the two divisions. If it was going to take a side door for the Twins to reach the postseason for a second time—the division championship series were born that year, inserted between the end of the regular season and the World Series—so be it.

One early highlight for Killebrew was his third home run, on April 27 in Chicago off Gary Peters—it was the 400th of his career, coming barely 10 years after he cracked Washington's lineup to stay in 1959. He would have had it in 1968 if not for the Astrodome setback, but his wife, Elaine, was looking forward that night. "Harmon's going to hit 600," she said excitedly. "I won't let him quit until he does."

Various parts of Killebrew's best season were chronicled inadvertently by a budding author on the major league scene—former Yankees pitcher Jim Bouton, now laboring for the expansion club in Seattle while keeping a diary that would become *Ball Four*, a blockbuster, comical "tell-all." Its irreverence, while rattling both baseball big-wigs and Bouton's peers, was irresistible. A series of entries from July veered into Killebrew territory:

> July 11 / Minneapolis
>
> When Dick Baney went into the game to throw his first major league pitch, everybody in the bullpen moved out to the fence to watch him. We wanted to see how he'd do against the Brew, which is what we call Harmon Killebrew. Inside I still think of him as the Fat Kid, which is what Fritz Peterson over at the Yankees always called him. I'd say, "How'd you do, Fritz?" and he'd answer, "the Fat Kid hit a double with the bases loaded." Well, the first time the Fat Kid faced Dick Baney, he hit the second pitch 407' into the left-field seats. After the game I was shaving next to Baney. "Welcome to the club," I said. "You lost your virginity tonight."
>
> July 18 /
>
> In a couple of days two men are going to land on the moon. How the hell can I be nervous about starting a baseball game? Even if it is against the Fat Kid and his wrecking crew.

July 19 /

[Bouton had crashed in a rare start, lasting only $3\frac{2}{3}$ innings against the Twins.]

When my boy Mike was still a baby and he cried, I'd say to him, "Harmon Killebrew's little boy doesn't cry." Now I wonder if Harmon Killebrew ever thinks of crying.

July 26 /

It's still hard to get used to playing baseball again after the All-Star break. Three days off reminds you how much tension you live under playing baseball every day. During the break, Harmon Killebrew can't get you. Reggie Jackson can't get you. It's peaceful…

Bouton explained his many references to the Twins slugger in a magazine piece the following spring. "It was a crime for any pitcher to have to face a slugger, especially one as tough as the Fat Kid, in that Seattle ballpark," he said. "Instead of going into the trainer after a game, you'd go in and have a half hour with the club psychiatrist. It was a really tiny park."

Asked what emotions run through a pitcher when he stares in at Killebrew, the writing righty said, "Mainly fear. Two kinds of fear: fear for your life and limbs should he hit a line drive back at you, and fear of losing your ballgame should he hit one out of the park."

Charlie Manuel, who would go on to greater baseball glory some four decades later as the manager of the Philadelphia Phillies, was an outfield prospect in 1969 just getting his taste of the big league scene. In spring training, he showed up to find his locker between Bob Allison's and Killebrew's.

"He was very impressive," Manuel said in July 2011. "I used to take him for granted because he hit so many—really, 49 home runs is a lot of home runs. It was almost like you expected him to hit one every night. Seriously. But in 1969, I can tell you this, since I've been in baseball, I've never seen anybody hit that many *clutch* home runs in the latter part of the game. And I've had some great hitters. And I don't know for sure, but I want to say that he hit 11 off Oakland—check his numbers on Fingers that year."

Killebrew knocked around A's reliever Rollie Fingers for three homers and a .600 average (6-of-10). In fact, he did hit 11 home runs against Oakland, driving home 34 runs with a .435 average and 16 walks in 18 games. The Twins went 13–5 against Jackson's and Fingers' team, accounting for most of their nine-game final margin over the second-place A's.

Phil Roof, later a Twins teammate and Killebrew friend, was Oakland's catcher that season, calling the pitches for a young staff. "I stuck out a lot of long fingers, believe me. We had Jim Nash, Catfish [Hunter], Lew Krausse, Vida Blue, 'Blue Moon' Odom, Chuck Dobson—we had a lot of guys who threw hard early. So we may get Harmon the first at-bat, but after that it was a different story. He would tune up—if you lost a little bit on location or a little bit of velocity, he would crush you, big time.... And you know what else he did? Of all the players that I played against, in the seventh, eighth, and ninth innings, if his team needed a run, he got the most RBI singles of any hitter I've ever been around. He was able to do something, make an adjustment on his swing, and put the ball in play, and he got lots and lots of RBI singles. We just couldn't get him out in that situation."

Some went to extremes to try. A few desperate managers set up with their second basemen on the shortstop side of that bag, packing Killebrew's "pull" side with fielders. Given the slugger's lack of foot speed, if he started poking balls through the right side, there was always a chance the right fielder might throw him out at first.

"Sort of the reverse [Ted] Williams shift," Chicago's Eddie Stanky said before one series. "I know it's not original, but Harmon has to think a bit when he sees that alignment. If he decides to go for right field, that would take away his home run threat."

After Killebrew drove a pitch from Baltimore's Jim Hardin into the right-field corner for a double in an early August meeting, Orioles manager Earl Weaver said, "I like him hitting to right. Hell, I'll take a double from him anytime. The big thing is not to challenge him. You challenge a [Rod] Carew maybe because he can't hurt you as much, though he has other things going for him once he gets on. But with nobody on in a tight ballgame, you work on Killebrew."

A number of pitchers felt that changing speeds was the best option against him, in hopes of messing with his timing. So New York reliever Steve Hamilton decided to *really* change speeds. Ahead in the count 1–2 and sick of getting "crushed pretty good" by Killebrew, Hamilton chose to rainbow in his "Folly Floater," a blooper pitch with zero *oomph* on it.

"He took his stride," Hamilton recalled the following spring, "and simply froze with his bat in the same position, his body in the same position, and the ball forever and ever drifting down toward the plate. Finally, it dropped over and the umpire called it strike three. It was the first strikeout ever racked up by the Folly Floater.... He dropped his bat on the plate and gave me the weirdest look, a kind of what-in-the-world-was-that look. Every time he sees me now, he asks, 'What was that pitch?' I suspect he's trying to set me up to throw another so he can really crack it."

Killebrew got his share of chances overall, playing in 162 games, a victory in itself considering his injury history. Martin moved him from third to first in the field and up (third) or down (fourth) in the order based on the other team's pitcher—he would flip-flop the left-handed swinger Oliva in the lineup and use Rich Reese, Rick Renick, or Graig Nettles in an infield platoon. But the feisty manager rarely even lifted Killebrew for a pinch runner and obviously never asked him to bunt

Killebrew arrived in Washington in 1954 as a 17-year-old "bonus baby," with the Senators projecting him as a power-hitting second baseman.
(Photo courtesy of the Minnesota Twins)

Killebrew met President Eisenhower before the start of a May 1959 game against Boston. He and the President exchanged autographed baseballs.
(Photo courtesy of the Minnesota Twins)

Eventually, Killebrew's swing led the Twins to win the 1965 World Series.
(Photo courtesy of the Minnesota Twins)

Harmon Killebrew, fan favorite. (Photo courtesy of the Minnesota Twins)

Killebrew watches one of his long flies in 1974, his final season in a Twins uniform. (Photo courtesy of the Minnesota Twins)

A humble guy with a good sense of humor, Killebrew always was more relaxed behind the camera than in front of it. (Photo courtesy of the Minnesota Twins)

Killebrew was a willing signer of autographs and encouraged later generations of Twins players to sign their names so fans could read and appreciate them. (Photo courtesy of the Minnesota Twins)

AL president Joe Cronin, a Hall of Famer and former Senators star himself, presents Killebrew with the 1969 AL Most Valuable Player award.
(Photo courtesy of the Minnesota Twins)

Bob Allison, Tony Oliva, and Harmon Killebrew—the Twins' heavy hitters—posing together at Metropolitan Stadium. (Photo courtesy of the Minnesota Twins)

The hard-swinging statue of Harmon Killebrew was unveiled near Target Field in Minneapolis, Minnesota, on April 3, 2010 with the Hall of Famer in attendance. (Photo courtesy of the Minnesota Twins)

Harmon Killebrew (center) and Rod Carew (right), two of Minnesota's former Most Valuable Players, present catcher Joe Mauer with the 2009 AL MVP award in April 2010. (Photo courtesy of the Minnesota Twins)

Killebrew is introduced as a member of the 50 Greatest Twins honorary team at Target Field in September 2010. (Photo courtesy of the Minnesota Twins)

(obvious, because Harmon made it through 22 seasons without every laying one down).

He had honed his batting eye by this point, forcing pitchers either to put him on base via walks or give him something to swing at. Killebrew was walked 145 times, 20 of them intentionally. "We always thought that we could probably have a better chance of getting the next guy out," Roof said. "We didn't feel it hurt us as much by walking him. And we did that frequently."

* * *

By the end of August, the MVP competition was tight. Killebrew had 38 home runs, 116 RBIs, and a .272 average. Oakland's Jackson was in front with 45 homers, 105 RBIs, and he was hitting .281. Howard's numbers with a month to go were 42 homers, 97 RBIs, and a .309 average. McLain, despite his 21–6 mark and 2.74 ERA, wasn't going to swipe the position player's trophy this time. And Boog Powell out in Baltimore was pushing Killebrew with 113 RBIs, along with 33 homers and a .311 average. Or maybe Killebrew was pushing Powell.

"He needs to be pushed once in a while," Orioles catcher Clay Dalrymple said, claiming the intensity of the 1969 MVP chase was good for his roommate. "Killebrew keeps looking over his shoulder to see what Powell is doing, and Boog is awfully good coming at somebody. If this thing is close at the end of the season, watch Boog go after it. He'll take extra batting practice. But if he's leading by 15 or 20, he might just stop."

Powell "stopped" when Killebrew tore through September with 11 more home runs and 24 RBIs. That included a game on September 7—a 16–4 rout of Oakland—in which he drove in seven runs in the first two innings. (Powell drove in eight the entire month.) The Twins followed their best player's lead, going 18–13 down the stretch, all the while making sure that Killebrew's RBI quest wasn't some lonely pursuit. After one game in which Carew, casually rounding third, got thrown out at the plate, Martin walked the second baseman over to Killebrew's locker. "I want you to apologize to Harmon," the manager told Carew. "You might have cost him the RBI title."

Not to worry. About the only thing that didn't go Killebrew's way that season was the ruling on a ball he hit in Fenway Park. "I hit one just over the wall to right center, and it hit a seat and fell back on the field," he said. "The umpire didn't see it and ruled it a hit. The outfielder didn't even go after it." Had that one counted, he finally would have reached that magic number of 50 home runs in a season.

Still, Killebrew's stats line was magical enough, maybe the best ever by a Twin. As mentioned in a previous chapter, Twins shortstop Zoilo Versalles had a lightning-in-a-bottle season in 1965, reaching career highs across the board—plate appearances, at-bats, runs, hits, doubles, triples, RBIs, steals, walks, strikeouts, on-base percentage, slugging, OPS, and total bases. He was an All-Star, a Gold Glove winner, and a runaway as AL MVP as Minnesota went 102–60 and made it to the World Series.

Eight years after Killebrew's big season, Carew won the AL MVP at the peak of his Hall of Fame powers. He flirted with a .400 batting average that summer before settling at .388 with a .449 on-base percentage and 1.019 OPS. Carew rapped 239 hits, scored 128 runs, and had 16 triples—all tops in the league—while hitting 14 homers and driving in 100 runs.

First baseman Justin Morneau was named 2006 AL Most Valuable Player after hitting .321 with 34 home runs and 130 RBIs. Morneau scored 97 runs, walked 53 times, struck out 93 times, and had a .559 slugging average and a .934 OPS. The native of New Westminster in Canada's British Columbia helped Minnesota reach an AL division series against Oakland, where it dropped three straight games.

And three years later, Twins catcher Joe Mauer became the fifth MVP of the franchise's Minnesota era. The local hero won his third batting title in 2009 with a career-best .365 average and his second Gold Glove behind the plate. He had 28 home runs, drove in 96, scored 94, walked 76 times, and topped the AL in on-base (.444), slugging (.587), and OPS (1.031). That Twins team also made it to the postseason—and was swept by the Yankees.

Killebrew's MVP season ended in a sweep, as well, with the Orioles taking three in the best-of-five ALCS and pouncing on Martin's stubborn decision to start journeyman Bob Miller in Game 3 rather than Jim Kaat. It was rumored to be an I'll-show-you-who's-boss move against Griffith, and as the last straw in a tumultuous season, the decision probably cost Martin his job.

The phone call with the MVP news came to the Killebrew's home in Oregon in November after the Twins' elimination. Sports columnist Jim Murray of the *Los Angeles Times* wrote a syndicated piece on the player's outstanding season, lavishing praise on Killebrew as the "MVP every year."

> He is kind to animals—and people. He is a country boy who never raises his voice. He is a man of monumental strength who uses it only to hit baseballs. He's so humble you'd think they platooned him. He blushes. He never argues with the umpire or fights the manager. He shows up for 8 p.m. games at 3 in the afternoon. He hangs in there on pitches that rip buttons off his shirt. He's as popular as Santa Claus, as taken-for-granted as electricity, as cheerful as a Kansas picnic, as temperamental as a penitential monk. His language could be used in the Vatican. If they had a category for 25 all-time "nicest," he would be so far out in front that whoever was second would be in a monastery.

Did Murray happen to mention "gracious" in there? That's how Killebrew reacted the next time he saw Boog Powell, whose consolation prize from the MVP race was a trip to the World Series against the Amazin' Mets.

"'Killer' was the most favorite opponent I played against," the big Baltimore first baseman recalled. "The absolute nicest man, the finest gentleman I think I ever met on or off the field—he and Brooks Robinson. Killer never had anything bad to say about anybody. With the game on the line, I hated to see him up there.

"One of the nicest things that happened to me in baseball was after the '69 season. I had a heck of a year, but Harmon was the MVP. The next year, on the first day of spring training, Harmon came to me and told me I probably should have won it. Which is really a pretty cool thing to say. Then I won it that year."

Chapter 10

Facing the Killer

Dave DeBusschere was one of professional basketball's all-time bests. A 6'6", 230-pound forward who averaged 16.1 points and 11.0 rebounds in 12 NBA seasons, DeBusschere went to eight All-Star Games as a member of the Detroit Pistons and the New York Knicks. He was a defensive terror, making the league's all-defensive team the first six years after the NBA created that honor. After serving as the Pistons' player coach from the tender ages of 24 to 26—the youngest coach in NBA history thanks to a desperate owner—DeBusschere was traded to New York where he won two championships with the Knicks while playing on a team considered one of the most selfless and artistic in league history.

His retired jersey hangs in the rafters of Madison Square Garden. The native of Detroit was inducted into basketball's Hall of Fame in 1983, served as Knicks general manager when they drafted franchise center Patrick Ewing, and was the last commissioner of the old American Basketball Association. In 1996, DeBusschere (who died at age 62 in 2003) was voted as one of the 50 Greatest Players of the NBA's first half-century.

And he owed it all to the subject of this book.

Before Bo Jackson and Deion Sanders became known as marvelous, multi-sport athletes, there was DeBusschere. And only a few others were like him. DeBusschere was one of just 10 men (as of 2011) who were gifted and driven enough to play in both Major League Baseball and the NBA. Like most of them, he was a pitcher—a lanky right-handed reliever/spot starter signed out of the University of Detroit by the White Sox in April 1962 for a $75,000 bonus.

That summer, a wild-armed DeBusschere pitched in 12 games for Chicago, giving up just five hits in 18 innings, striking out eight but walking 23 of the 82 batters he faced. That fall, he reported for his second rookie season with the Detroit Pistons—he had been a "territorial pick" back when the NBA did that sort of thing to capitalize on a college kid's regional popularity. DeBusschere earned his $15,000 hoops salary, giving the Pistons 12.7 points and 8.7 rebounds while playing all 80 games. Then it was back to baseball; this time, he went 3–4 with a 3.09 ERA in 24 appearances, yielding 80 hits in 84.1 innings with 53 strikeouts and 34 walks.

DeBusschere never pitched again in the big leagues, pursuing and reaching his athletic destiny in the other sport. For the next four decades, whenever someone asked, he had a two-word explanation for his permanent switch to basketball, "Harmon Killebrew."

In his two MLB seasons, DeBusschere faced 132 different batters a total of 447 times, according to the website Baseball-Reference.com. Killebrew had four of them—home run, walk, strikeout (looking), and home run, in that order. That's a .667 batting average, 2.667 slugging percentage, and 3.417 OPS. The Twins slugger welcomed DeBusschere the only time he saw him in 1962 with a two-run clout in Minnesota's 8–4 victory at Met Stadium on June 10. He said bye-bye (though neither knew it at the time) a year and 10 days later, again in

Bloomington, with a solo shot in the fifth inning of the Twins' 9–4 victory.

Those other 131 guys, in their 443 plate appearances, took DeBusschere deep only eight times.

"I've got a better chance against [Wilt] Chamberlain," DeBusschere told reporters after leaving baseball for good (he actually stuck around with Class AAA Indianapolis, going 30–20 with a 3.77 ERA in 1964 and 1965). "Wilt's a lot bigger, but Harmon might have been stronger."

We only know all this, of course, because DeBusschere went on to a famous second career. There's no telling how many pitchers—wannabes or almost-dones—Killebrew chased into other professions through the years.

The 500 Home Run Club is a book from a handful of *Sport* magazine issues as well as an assortment of other sources in books, publications, and newspapers that were published deep into Harmon's career and more recently. The following pages offer a sampling of thoughts from people in baseball on what it was like facing "the Killer." To them, that nickname seemed a lot less ironic and a lot more appropriate when they were the ones standing 60' 6" away, hoping to get Killebrew before he got them:

Rollie Fingers, Hall of Fame reliever

(Killebrew went 10-for-29, .345 average with 4 HR, 8 RBIs, 9 SO, 6 BB)

"Harmon Killebrew gave me more fits than anyone. He was a fastball hitter and had a short, quick stroke. He could turn real quick and was strong enough to hit it out. In 1969, I was a rookie, just a young kid, and I kept trying to run fastballs in on his hands and he just kept hitting them. In his first nine at-bats against me, he hit four homers, two doubles, and a single. I finally figured out I'd better either pitch him out and away or, maybe even better, walk him."

Hal Newhouser, Hall of Fame starter

(Never actually faced Killebrew)

"Nobody ever hit a ball over the left-field [stands at old Tiger Stadium] in Detroit, you know, because it's got two decks there. I was scouting and sitting with the umpires before a game and one said, 'Hal, look at that guy. This is the new power hitter in the major leagues—a guy named Killebrew. He really has some kind of power. If anybody is going to hit a ball out of this park, it's going to be Killebrew.' I sort of laughed and said to myself, 'I don't think anybody can do it.' By gosh, about the sixth or seventh inning, he hit one over the roof."

Mel Parnell, Boston starter

(Killebrew went 0-for-1, with 1 BB)

"Harmon had a little bit of an upward stroke. And making contact, he would get backspin on the ball and it would really carry. He always seemed to get the bottom part of the ball."

Lew Burdette, California reliever

(Killebrew went 1-for-6, .167 average with 1 HR, 3 RBIs, 1 SO)

"I was practicing my knuckleball, trying to come up with a new pitch. And I threw Harmon one. He swung and missed. So I threw him another one. The wind was blowing out, and he hit a towering fly ball. It was the one where they painted the seat and put a plaque on it. You should have heard Jack Sanford. He was cracking up in the dugout. He yelled, 'Nice going, Lew—you just gave up the longest homer in the history of the park.' The next day Harmon hit one off Sanford in the upper deck just three rows below mine. I wish I could tell you what I told him."

Milt Pappas, Baltimore/Cincinnati/Atlanta/Chicago Cubs starter

(Killebrew went 19-for-87, .218 average with 5 HR, 16 RBIs, 22 SO, 9 BB, 2 SF)

"Making a mistake to Harmon was death. The last one he hit off me was a dandy. He dropped his bat and watched it sail out of the park. As he was rounding the bases, I told him if he ever did that again and tried to show me up, I would drill him. The next time up, I drilled him."

Jim Lonborg, Boston/Milwaukee/Philadelphia starter

(Killebrew went 14-for-29, .483 average with 6 HR, 12 RBIs, 7 SO, 6 BB)

"Harmon was probably the best fastball mistake hitter I ever saw."

Ryne Duren, New York Yankees/Los Angeles/Philadelphia/ Cincinnati/Washington reliever

(Killebrew went 3-for-15, .200 average with 2 HR, 2 RBIs, 7 SO, 1 BB, 1 HBP)

"He remembers me every time the weather changes—I hit him in the elbow and dislocated it. He hit two off me in Minneapolis in one game—one of them almost went out of old Met Stadium."

Jim Palmer, Hall of Fame starter

(Killebrew went 8-for-60, .133 average with 4 HR, 8 RBIs, 20 SO, 13 BB)

"When you're a starter and out there facing him four times, well, first of all, you don't throw as hard in the ninth inning as you do in the first and, anyway, if you keep pitching him the same way every time he'll adjust and murder you. There are some hitters who you can keep pitching inside, inside, inside and they don't adjust. But with Harmon . . . all of a sudden he's looking for the ball there and he hits it out of the park. . . . Dave Boswell was with the Twins and he hurt his arm and came to us. And he came in one night and it's a tie ball game, and he gets two quick strikes on Harmon. And he looks over at Brooks Robinson and says,

'Double heat'—you know, a really good fastball—and he threw him a good fastball, and Harmon hits it into the upper deck in left field."

Bert Blyleven, Hall of Fame starter

(Never faced longtime Twins teammate)

"It was a thrill for me as a rookie to be on the same team with Harmon—the classiest guy I ever met, along with Willie Stargell. He had that short, compact swing that could lift a ball out of any ballpark. It was great pitching and knowing that, with him in the lineup, you just tried to hold them to a run or two, knowing Harmon could get that many with just one swing."

Mel Stottlemyre, New York Yankees starter

(Killebrew went 24-for-89, .270 average with 5 HR, 13 RBIs, 7 SO, 10 BB)

"When I first came up, I thought of him as only a slugger, the type of hitter who would hit the ball out of the park if he got his pitch but the kind you could get out if you pitched him right. I always felt that if you got ahead of him you could make him chase bad breaking pitches. But now he lays off them and makes you throw strikes. I don't know how he made the change, but I sure wish he hadn't. Now there's no one single way to pitch him. You have to change patterns, either every time or every other time. He's simply a good hitter now, one who will come up with a decent average as well as hit his 40 to 50 home runs."

Earl Wilson, Boston/Detroit starter

(Killebrew went 20-for-73, .274 average with 9 HR, 20 RBIs, 25 SO, 22 BB)

"To tell you the truth, if I knew how to pitch to him, I'd do it. He hits me pretty hard, so I guess I'm doing something wrong. Maybe you want to talk to someone else."

Mickey Lolich, Detroit starter

(Killebrew went 20-for-100, .200 average with 6 HR, 19 RBIs, 24 SO, 13 BB)

"A lot of your home run hitters lay back for the fastball, and if they get the breaking pitch, they're way out in front. It gives you a way to pitch to them. But Harmon stays back real good. He waits and hits the breaking ball, which really makes him tough. And me being a left-hander makes it easier for him because everything I throw is coming in to him. He doesn't have to go out and get it.... And even if you fool him, he can still get enough wood on the ball to hit it out."

Gaylord Perry, Hall of Fame starter

(Killebrew went 3-for-20, .150 average with 1 HR, 3 RBIs, 6 SO)

"Pitchers just kept challenging him. Most didn't realize he was a tremendous off-speed hitter. You try to curve him and make him look bad, and he would hit a home run."

Rich "Goose" Gossage, Hall of Fame reliever

(Killebrew went 1-for-8, .125 average with 2 RBIs, 3 SO, 4 BB)

"He's the ultimate professional, the consummate pro.... He was a very humble person. I didn't pitch to him in his prime, but he still struck the fear of God in you."

Jim Bunning, Hall of Fame starter

(Killebrew went 13-for-68, .191 average with 5 HR, 8 RBIs, 16 SO, 15 BB)

"When he came into the league, he was a low fastball hitter, so he was easy to pitch to. Then all of a sudden, when he started hitting all those home runs, where we were pitching him became his power. We started pitching him up, and he started hitting that pitch. After that, it seemed we didn't know what to do with him. He made himself a great hitter because he overcame his weaknesses. Somebody taught him how to hit the high fastball."

Dean Chance, California/Minnesota/Cleveland/Detroit starter
(Killebrew went 14-for-61, .230 average with 4 HR, 8 RBIs, 18 SO, 8 BB)
"I was 2–0 on him one night, and I threw him a fastball. The home run he hit on that pitch was hit so hard that no one in the stands even yelled."

Mel Nelson, California/Minnesota/St. Louis reliever
(Killebrew went 1-for-1, 1.000 average with 1 BB)
"Harmon ranks up there with the best. He didn't hit for an average like Ted Williams, yet as a person he was near the top. He was strong and had arms like big irons. He could catch the ball. It was fun to have Harmon as a teammate. It wasn't fun to pitch against him. When he hit the ball, it would go. You could watch it go far into the night."

Tom Hall, Minnesota/Cincinnati/New York Mets reliever
(Never faced former Twins teammate)
"When I think of home runs, I think of Hank Aaron and Harmon Killebrew. I don't think of Barry Bonds and Mark McGwire."

Steve Hamilton, Cleveland/Washington/New York Yankees/ Chicago White Sox/San Francisco/Chicago Cubs reliever
(Killebrew went 3-for-13, .231 average with 2 HR, 3 RBIs, 4 SO, 3 BB)
"He could overpower your best pitch. I tried to work him low and away—I figured it was a ground ball at worst. But Killebrew went out after the down-and-out pitch and hit it over the right-field fence. That's what I call overpowering the ball.... Something else I've noticed is that he [had] a rare ability to be able to hold up in the middle of his swing, which helps him a lot in not chasing bad pitches. I think a lot of times

the umpires don't call it on him because he's Harmon Killebrew, but maybe I feel that way just because I'm a pitcher."

Dave Leonhard, Baltimore reliever

(Killebrew went 0-for-3, .000 average with 1 SO, 1 BB)

"It never leaves your mind that he's liable to crunch one. As a general rule, never throw him a fastball. But if you have to, make it a fastball on the fists, where you can get him on a strikeout or a double-play grounder. He is so strong he can reach out over the plate and still hit the ball into the center-field bleachers."

Jim Bouton, New York Yankees/Seattle/Houston starter

(Killebrew went 16-of–53, .302 average with 2 HR, 10 RBIs, 13 SO, 6 BB)

"He hit an infield pop off me once with men on base that was so damned high everyone would have scored, including him, had it fallen safely. It wasn't an easy play. I mean, the wind was blowing a little and that ball went up and out of sight. It comes down pretty fast. It was like a Mantle pop-up. Only Killebrew and Mantle could hit them that high."

Gary Peters, Chicago White Sox/Boston starter

(Killebrew went 15-of-57, .263 average with 6 HR, 15 RBI, 10 SO, 28 BB)

"I'm going to pitch him fastballs inside. You can pitch Harmon all over, but you can't get the fastball out over the plate. That's the pitch he loses. If I throw my slider soft, he'll usually handle that pitch, too. Throw everything hard—that's what I'll try to do."

Tommy John, Cleveland/Chicago White Sox/Los Angeles/ New York Yankees/California/Oakland starter

(Killebrew went 16-of-58, .276 average with 6 HR, 11 RBIs, 8 SO, 16 BB)

"I'd rather not [pitch to him], but [manager Eddie] Stanky says I can't walk him four times to get to Oliva. There is no way I can overpower

Harmon like Gary [Peters] did last night. I just haven't got that hard fastball. I've got to be cagey. Keep moving the ball around.... Even when [Frank] Robinson and [Al] Kaline are healthy, I think Killebrew is the single most dangerous hitter in our league. He has the perfect batting stance. You look down at him, and there's no place to throw the ball."

* * *

Let the record show, too, that Killebrew faced 606 pitchers across his 9,833 career plate appearances. Many of those hurlers disliked the duty. None of them relished it, even if they began to think they had figured out the bopper.

Jim Bouton, better known after 1970 as the author of *Ball Four* than for his 62–63 record during 10 seasons in the big leagues, was told once that Tommy John in his Chicago days had identified a weakness in Killebrew's hitting. John described it like this, "It's a guy with a real, real good fastball like a [Sam] McDowell who can throw it by him upstairs."

Great, Bouton thought. "That information does guys like me a lot of good," he said sarcastically. "Sam McDowell can strike Harmon Killebrew out up high? Okay, that's fine. The rest of us have to work the ball around and change speeds." McDowell was called "Sudden Sam" for his blistering velocity and led the AL in strikeouts five times in six seasons from 1965 to 1970. Twice he whiffed more than 300 hitters.

Bouton recalled a Yankees pitcher's meeting before one Minnesota–New York series and how much time got used up scouting Killebrew. "First someone would say, 'High ball.' But someone else would reply, 'No, no, no, he hits that into the seats,'" the pitcher said. "Then someone would say, 'Well, pitch away from him,' but someone else would say, 'Yeah, but he goes to right.' Then someone would say 'Pitch him low,' but someone else would say, 'He'll knock your leg off.' So finally we'd all say, 'Pitch around him.'

"Which was fine until you came to Oliva."

And for what it was worth, McDowell didn't have it as good against Killebrew as Tommy John might have thought. Yes, he did hold the slugger to a .211 average, three home runs, 25 strikeouts, and 12 walks in 90 confrontations. But like a lot of guys, he remembered the ones that stung, like the day McDowell fell behind in the count 3–1 and decided to mix in a change-up. "Up until that point, I hadn't thrown him any change-ups in a long time—I think I had pitched four games against the Twins [in 1969] without throwing him a change-up. So there was reason to think it would work. It didn't—he hit my change-up into the upper deck in left field."

Fritz Peterson received credit in Bouton's book for hanging that snarky nickname—the Fat Kid—on Killebrew, and it was easy to see why. Harmon hit him at a .324 clip over the course of 10 seasons with two home runs, 12 RBIs, eight walks, and only five strikeouts. So when the Yankees left-hander compared him with another AL slugger in 1970, his teasing still dripped with frustration. "He's not as scary to look at up there as Frank Howard, but he's just as dangerous," Peterson said. "You know that he doesn't swing at any bad pitches, so if you're in a position where you can't walk him, you're usually in trouble. See, he's got a small strike zone because he's little and fat and ... no, I'm only kidding. He's squat but he's all muscle.

"Anyway, I haven't found any weaknesses. Harmon's soft-spoken, minds his business, is short and fat and one heck of a hitter."

No one, though, topped journeyman left-hander George Brunet in the professional respect department. In 15 major league seasons pitching for nine teams—he also spent parts of 15 seasons in the minors across 10 leagues—Brunet faced 26 Hall of Famers (not counting those inducted as a pitcher or a manager) and dreaded Killebrew above all others. How do we know? In 63 plate appearances, Brunet walked him 22 times, more than twice what he issued to any of the rest. Six of those were intentional; many more were semi-intentional.

Killebrew homered off Brunet four times, same as Frank Robinson, and batted only .250. Yet Brunet wanted nothing to do with him. In a game in June 1966 in Minnesota, the flaky 31-year-old went the distance in a 7–2 victory. But he walked Killebrew four times, three of them intentionally, before risking a fly out to center that ended the game.

"We're here at the Met, two outs, nobody on in the first, and Brunet is looking at me, shaking his head toward first," former Twins manager Bill Rigney, then with the Angels, once told the *Minneapolis Star Tribune*. "I figure it out—he wants to walk [Killebrew]. I run out there and say, 'If you're going to walk him, George, at least make it look good.'"

Chapter 11

500

If he said it once, Harmon Killebrew said it a hundred times, at banquets, to sportswriters, in front of civic groups, with a microphone in front of him, or when meeting with a Boy Scout troop. "I hear hitters say they never hit a home run when they were trying to. And I never did believe that because I hit a lot of them when I was trying to."

Or not.

Killebrew had hit memorable home runs before. There were the two in the summer of 1965 vs. the Yankees, the homer in the All-Star Game, his World Series blast off Don Drysdale, and naturally his first ever against Detroit's Billy Hoeft.

He had hit massive home runs before. There were the Howitzers in back-to-back games in 1967 off Lew Burdette and Jack Sanford, shots onto and over the roofs in Detroit and Chicago, beyond the hedge in Baltimore, all the way back to that 435′ eye-opener into the beet field in Payette that got this whole thing started.

And obviously, Killebrew had hit milestone home runs before. Take your pick: No. 100 vs. Early Wynn in Chicago in 1961; No. 200

vs. Washington's Jim Duckworth in 1963; or No. 300 vs. Bob Friend in New York in 1966. No particular problems with any of them.

That's why things took an awkward turn with the one home run that, try as he might, Harmon could not hit—two of them, actually—in a new and somewhat embarrassing experience for the big man in the summer of 1971. It took him seven weeks to go from No. 498 to No. 500, the longest such dry spell of his career that didn't involve an off-season, a major injury, or a trip to the minor leagues. Quite unexpectedly, a guy who was used to having folks pull out tape-measures for his home runs was at risk of someone setting up a sun dial to clock him.

It had never gone that way before. No. 400 came and went smoothly enough in 1969—off White Sox pitcher Gary Peters on April 27 at Comiskey Park. That one and the other 48 Killebrew hit in his most marvelous MVP season took him past a different sort of milestone. Twins owner Calvin Griffith ponied up $120,000 for his third baseman/first baseman's services for 1970. A report in *The Sporting News* estimated that Killebrew had signed for $95,000 and thus had to wait another year to become the Twins' first $100,000 player. But in an interview for the Hall of Fame long after Killebrew retired, he cited the $120,000 figure and called it "the most money I ever made in baseball."

While Killebrew targeted the likes of Stan Musial (475) and Lou Gehrig (493), the Twins got busy with another successful season on the field, in the standings, and at the turnstiles. They went 98–64 in 1970, won the American League's West division again, and topped 1 million in attendance for the 10th consecutive year since leaving Washington for the Upper Midwest.

Those broad strokes, it should be noted, didn't capture some of the inside-baseball changes from one postseason-bound season to the next for Minnesota. Billy Martin, the eager, abrasive manager who had given the Twins an edge in 1969 only to suffer for it in his relationship with Griffith, was gone. In his place was Bill Rigney, well-liked and a solid baseball man but more of a hand-wringer and a finger-pointer than the aggressive, pugnacious Martin. In 1970, the Twins had the AL Cy Young winner in steady vet Jim Perry and the second- and third-place finishers in MVP balloting—Tony Oliva and Killebrew, respectively. But with Martin gone, intangibles were missing, too.

Minnesota base runners, for instance, were less daring. With Rigney's 30, only leadoff man Cesar Tovar had more than five steals. The hitters slipped to fifth in the league in home runs and scored 46 fewer runs than the previous season—due at least partly to second baseman Rod Carew's serious knee injury suffered in June while turning a double play in Milwaukee. The defending batting champ would return at the very end of the season for a handful of pinch-hit appearances but go hitless right through another ALCS sweep by Baltimore. Killebrew's road roommate since their Washington days, Bob Allison, retired that off-season, and it would be another 17 years before the Twins played any more serious October baseball.

* * *

It would be nice to say that the club's fortunes perked up in 1971, but they did not. Things became considerably worse for the ballclub—a plummet to 74–86, a decline so severe that it was a wonder Rigney's job survived another winter after that. The team's power flickered and then went on battery backup—the Twins hit just 116 home runs, about half what they and their fans were used to from the brawny 1960s. They were bland in a lot of ways, finishing fifth in the AL in runs and total bases, ninth in walks, and near the bottom in ERA and most other pitching categories. Minnesota ranked seventh in errors while turning fewer double plays than all but one opponent.

Attendance dropped below the 1 million mark for the first time, a 25 percent drop of more than 300,000 tickets sold, and was headed toward a free-fall that would last for years to come.

Killebrew was productive in 1970—a .271 average, 41 home runs, 113 RBIs, 128 walks, his 10th year as an All-Star—but he hit a curious skid late in the season, hitting only three homers in 37 games after August 22. He had some serious business awaiting in 1971, milestones, ghosts and legends to chase down, and the heightened focus on the Twins' biggest star and his mighty march toward No. 500 figured to offer some fan appeal that the ballclub itself could not.

If only the pressure of it all hadn't put the "Bataan" in Killebrew's bat. His mighty march became more of a slog as he neared the important numbers. Had home runs been water, he and half of the state's fabled 10,000 lakes would have run dry waiting for Harmon to replenish them. He hit No. 498, a two-run shot off Oakland's Daryl Patterson and his 11th of the season, on June 22 in a 10–1 victory at the Met. And then ... crickets. He wouldn't hit another homer for more than a month. Although Killebrew shrugged off suggestions that he was feeling the urgency to reach and surpass the target in front of him, others weren't so sure.

"The guy is human," said Rigney, his manager. "Only nine players in the history of baseball have hit 500 homers, so it's not something a man can take lightly. It's there; he can't ignore it. It's on his mind, and it could be affecting his swing."

Henry Aaron knew what his friend was facing. Back in May 1970, Aaron bore down on and finally got his 3,000th hit. Fourteen months later, he was moving ever closer to Babe Ruth's all-time mark of 714 home runs. So he knew something about the challenges of crossing thresholds.

"When you get it, you are relieved," Aaron said. "You know you can hit, and you know you will get it, but everybody wants to know when. If you have a couple of bad days, you just wish you could get it over so everyone would leave you alone."

Killebrew's lone respite that summer came in Detroit on July 13 in what would be his final All-Star Game appearance. That night, six future Hall of Famers—Roberto Clemente, Johnny Bench, Frank Robinson, Reggie Jackson, Hank Aaron, and Killebrew—crashed home runs, with Jackson's rocketing off a transformer on the right-field roof in the AL's 6–4 victory. Harmon's homer went out to left field into the wind off the Cubs' Ferguson Jenkins.

The game's aftermath was almost as memorable for Killebrew. "After the game," he said, "they come in to tell me, 'You won the MVP award for the game. The commissioner wants to award you the trophy on television.' So I went out, I was standing in front of the cameras on the field next to the commissioner. All of a sudden, before the lights came on, they said, 'No, no, no, it's not you. It's Frank Robinson!'"

Killebrew was quickly moved out of the camera shot. "That was a big thrill—but kind of one of my most embarrassing moments," he said.

It was good practice, actually. Because the homer against the National League didn't count toward Killebrew's career total, he and his fans went back to waiting. Finally, on July 25 against Boston, he slammed No. 499 at home, a three-run job off former teammate Luis Tiant in a 6–2 Twins loss.

But that would be Killebrew's only home run in a stretch of 112 at-bats—a little odd for someone used to cranking one every 14 or 15 times he stepped to the plate. Yes, he had some aches and pains in that stretch—seven weeks, 36 games—but nothing that was going to buy him much sympathy or time.

"I don't think the pitchers are doing anything different to try and get me out," he told reporters at Yankee Stadium during the drought. "I'm not doing anything different, either."

Typically, Killebrew was distinctive at the plate in how still he became in preparation for receiving a pitch. He would give his bat one swing between pitches, then pull it back and rest it on his shoulder. As the pitcher began his delivery, Killebrew's hands would cock upward. "I try to stay as calm and relaxed as I can," he explained in one *Sports Illustrated* story. "It helps me concentrate, which I think is the most important thing about hitting."

It wasn't helping him at the moment, however, and behind Killebrew's placid expression and words, his mind was racing. It didn't help that everyone had an opinion, including Twins owner Calvin Griffith, who was never shy about sharing. "Harmon went into a big slump... and nobody can tell me that it wasn't because of the pressure," the boss said. "Harmon had to be thinking about that. It is only natural that a man thinks about it, especially since everyone is talking about it."

It didn't help that the Twins marketing folks arranged for a commemorative mug promotion and scheduled it for July 6, by which time they assumed Killebrew would have hit his number. The mugs wound up being distributed without a date on them, providing a tangible reminder to the player and everyone else of what hadn't happened. This was starting to feel a little like Early Wynn's anguished quest for victory No. 300, when the Hall of Fame hurler (and future Twins pitching coach) needed an extra winter to get it. Wynn won just once in the final eight starts of his 300–244 career.

"After getting 500, I think there won't be any pressure on me any more," Killebrew said. "I'll be satisfied with whatever else I reach."

Little did he or anyone else know that after becoming the 10th player to hit 500 homers, he would need maybe 90 minutes to get No. 501. Killebrew's homers tended to come in bunches. On August 10, 1971, Killebrew drove a breaking ball from Baltimore's Mike Cuellar over the fence for a solo shot in the first inning. In the sixth, he got

Cuellar again, this time for two runs. Afterward, Killebrew got the red-carpet treatment—make that the white-towel treatment, as a path of them led from the clubhouse door to his locker. Waiting on ice from Griffith was a bottle of grape juice and a champagne glass. The Met Stadium crowd that night was a modest 15,881—a big drop from the 26,687 who came out on July 6 for the homerless mugs.

Photos of Killebrew after the game, holding up two baseballs marked "500" and "501," preserved the achievement, but it was hard to discern whether the slugger was showing more joy or relief. "I'm glad that's over with," Harmon said, finally acknowledging the mounting pressure. "People keep asking you when you will hit it, and you try harder."

And wouldn't you know it, as soon as the pressure was turned off Killebrew had one of the most prolific stretches of his career. During the final quarter or so of the 1971 season, he hit 14 home runs in 147 at-bats with 42 RBIs, 37 walks, and a .958 OPS, wrapping up his season with a .254 average, 28 home runs, 119 RBIs, and 114 walks.

* * *

Killebrew wasn't done adding to his totals or launching some mortar blasts for sheer entertainment value. But this is a good place to consider some of his home run quirks and fun facts:

- The home plate umpire for home run No. 500 was Bill Kunkel, who pitched briefly in the American League with Kansas City and New York and gave up three home runs to Killebrew in five at-bats.
- By the end of Killebrew's career, nearly three-quarters of his plate appearances (7,182) had come against right-handed pitchers, the remainder (2,651) against southpaws. The R-L breakdown of his home runs was almost perfectly in sync with that (422–151).
- Killebrew hit home runs off 271 pitchers, including 12 Hall of Famers. Earl Wilson took the most abuse, giving up nine.

Killebrew went deep in 18 different AL parks during his career, and his 393 home runs in the decade of the 1960s were the most in baseball.

- He was one of only three players (as of 2011) who hit at least 100 home runs at three different defensive positions—third base, first base, and left field.
- The largest share of his homers were hit at Met Stadium (246). His other home park, Griffith Stadium, absorbed 41. After that, Fenway Park (37), Tiger Stadium (35), and Cleveland's Municipal Stadium (33) were his favorite spots.
- He hit three homers in a game only once—against Boston on September 21, 1963—and legged out an inside-the-park homer only once. He hit two in a game 45 times. He hit 277 solo shots, and 296 came with at least one runner on base.
- Killebrew's lifetime rate of one home run for every 14.22 at-bats ranked third when he retired, behind only Babe Ruth (11.76) and Ralph Kiner (14.11). The order was the same when calculated by plate appearances: Ruth (14.86), Kiner (16.95), and Killebrew (17.16).
- The physics professor who had created the Twins' home run chart for Met Stadium was asked to recalculate the distances based on how far the balls would have traveled and landed if unimpeded, as opposed to the places where they actually hit something. That's how Killebrew's blast off Burdette in 1967 went from a more mortal—and wrong—435' initially to 520'.
- From the moment he hit homer No. 532 off Oakland's Ken Holtzman on July 28, 1972, and passed Hall of Fame slugger Jimmie Foxx, Killebrew ranked No. 1 among right-handed hitters in AL history. His reign lasted 37 years, until the Yankees' Alex Rodriguez passed him. (Three of Foxx's lifetime total 534 homers came in a brief stint with the Chicago Cubs in 1942.)

- He had eight seasons of 40 or more home runs, something only Ruth (11) before him had accomplished and only Rodriguez and Barry Bonds since. (Heading into 2012, Albert Pujols had six.) Killebrew led his league six times—only Ruth (12), Mike Schmidt (8), and Kiner (7) did it more often.
- At 35 years, 51 days when he hit his 500th, Killebrew was 230 days older than Babe Ruth when Ruth hit that mark. As of spring 2012, he still ranked as the fifth youngest of the 25 men who have gotten there. Only these four—Jimmie Foxx (32 years, 337 days), Willie Mays (34 years, 130 days), Henry Aaron (34 years, 159 days), and Ruth (34 years, 186 days)—were younger.
- Killebrew also got there in the second-fewest official at-bats (6,671), which was 870 more than the Babe but 403 fewer than Foxx, 629 fewer than Mantle, 862 fewer than Mays, 1,941 fewer than Aaron, and 2,578 fewer than Mel Ott, among others.
- Killebrew hit 475 home runs as a Twins player. His first 84 came as a Senator, the final 14 as a Royal. His career stretched from Ted Williams to Mike Schmidt with legendary sluggers in between.

"Sure, it would be a great time to hit, and the money is unbelievable," Killebrew said later in life, during what would become known as baseball's steroid era. "But I am very happy to have played when I did. I call it the golden years of baseball. Look at the great players—Ted Williams, Frank Robinson, Mickey Mantle, Willie Mays, Hank Aaron, Willie McCovey, Ernie Banks, Stan Musial. To just be a part of that time is special to me."

Robinson hit his 500th home run a month after Killebrew. Coincidentally, he also hit two on the same day—though with a twist. In the first inning of the first game of Baltimore's home doubleheader against Detroit on September 13, Robinson hit No. 499 of his Hall of Fame career off the Tigers' Mike Kilkenny to spark a 9–1 victory. Six hours later, in the ninth inning of the nightcap, he hit No. 500 near the end of a 10–5 Orioles loss. That was only the second time that two players had reached 500 home runs in the same season. In 1967, Mickey Mantle and Eddie Mathews did it two months apart with the Yankees and the Astros, respectively.

Speaking of Robinson, it's worth noting that members of baseball's 500 home run club have come in a wide range of shapes and sizes, with equal variance in their styles. Ruth, of course, was XXL in appearance and in deeds. The wrists brigade included lithe hitters such as Henry Aaron, Ernie Banks, and Robinson. Mantle was a Hollywood casting agent's ideal of a baseball slugger, except for his knees in late career. Willie Mays nearly overshadowed the damage he did with a bat in his hands with the havoc he created on the bases and the theatrics he displayed in center field. Ted Williams was long and lean with a precision strike zone, and he was arguably the greatest all-around hitter in history.

Killebrew in person never was as physically imposing as his numbers, his trajectories, or even his distinctive name would have suggested.

"I have that same feeling when I see guys like him or Hank Aaron, compared to the sluggers we have today," said Paul Molitor, a Killebrew fan growing up in St. Paul in the 1960s and '70s. Molitor, the great infielder/designated hitter for Milwaukee, Toronto, and Minnesota, was nine years old when the Twins played in the 1965 World Series. Killebrew was the player he imitated at the plate, the one whose No. 3 he wanted to wear in Little League. In time, Molitor would join his boyhood idol in the Hall of Fame and even forge a strong friendship with him.

"McGwire, Sosa, Bonds, whatever your feelings about them, there is just a totally different physicality," Molitor told ESPN.com upon

Killebrew's passing in May 2011. "And it adds to the lore of Harmon as a hitter. He was known for his towering home runs—it seemed like he didn't hit many low line drives—and he hit them so high and far the ball looked more like a Titleist than a Rawlings."

Again, he wasn't 6'6" and 275 pounds. Killebrew was 6' and 210 pounds. He was solid, thick, stocky even, and strong, built more like a bull or a rhino than some sort of Hercules. "One of the nicknames Harmon had in the clubhouse, from my roommate Bill Pleis, was 'the Panzer,'" said Twins pitcher Jim Kaat, Killebrew's teammate for nearly 15 years in Minnesota and Washington. "He was built like a tank."

Kaat said that only two sluggers in his day consistently stopped other players in their tracks with the sound and scope of their blasts: Mantle and Killebrew. Both had recognizable home run trots, with Killebrew—somewhat unexpectedly—contributing one showbiz element so rampant today among big hitters. He routinely would admire his own handiwork as it soared toward distant bleachers, fences, and walls. You might not think of Killebrew as a precursor for Reggie Jackson, Rickey Henderson, Barry Bonds, and others, but the nature of his home runs—so high that they either were gone or likely fly outs—made it natural for him to pause and peek.

"He was so consistent in his routine," Kaat said. "He would look at it for just a second or two, drop the bat, you could almost mimic his trot, like you could Mantle. Then when he got about three steps from the dugout, he would take out his soft cap, take off the helmet, and make the quickest switch you'd ever see." Killebrew had thinning hair as a young man, eventually going mostly bald but for a fringe.

He was hit by pitches 48 times, but Kaat didn't think any were aimed as retaliation for his tiny bit of gawking. "No, because it was such a routine," Kaat said. "He didn't do it like he was trying to attract attention to himself or show up the pitcher. You know, he hit these moon shots.... Some hitters when they hit them have to run hard because they don't know if it's going out or it's going to be a double. But when he hit them, it was pretty evident that thing was gone. That's why it was part of his trot—a couple of slow steps, and he'd look at it and he'd go."

Chapter 12

Coach? Who, Me?

Harmon Clayton Killebrew Jr. turned 36 soon after the 1972 baseball season began—sooner than usual, since the game's first labor strike by the players' association shaved eight games off the schedule—and the fun factor was fading fast. "The last couple of years I spent in Minnesota were kind of tough for me," Killebrew said. "I had some physical injuries, my knees were starting to get real bad, and I wasn't playing as much as I would have liked to have played. And our club wasn't winning so much in those days. So it was a little frustrating."

Attendance was down, now about 60 percent from what it had been at the peak of the Twins' popularity just five seasons before. After 10 consecutive seasons of topping the 1 million mark, a big deal in the sport's economics of the time, Minnesota was two years into a stretch of falling short of the mark 11 times in the next 13 seasons. Among American League clubs, attendance slipped to fifth, then seventh, then 10th, and finally to last in Killebrew's last four seasons in Minnesota. No wonder rumors began to waft that owner Calvin Griffith might be thinking about relocating the franchise—again.

Oakland, an AL West neighbor, had established itself as Minnesota's better, winning 101 games in 1971 and headed toward three straight World Series crowns from 1972–74. Minnesota, with finishes of 77–77, 81–81, and 82–80 in those years, couldn't keep up. The A's—owned by Charlie Finley, managed by Dick Williams and Alvin Dark, and dominated by strong personalities such as Reggie Jackson, Sal Bando, and Rollie Fingers—were a ballclub for the modern age, with loud green-and-gold uniforms, white spikes, moustaches, and shaggy hair all around. The Twins, by comparison, seemed to be all black and white and sepia tones with a touch of gray.

The irksome part for Killebrew and for so many outstanding athletes is that they get smarter about their pursuits at the same time their skills go dull or slip away. Harmon had honed and polished his strike zone into a thing of beauty, trusting himself only to offer at the pitches that dared enter into it. That drastically cut back on his weaknesses at the plate. When he veered into a slump, he knew better than ever why and what he had to do to pull himself out. It was the actual pulling that got tricky. Timing, bat speed, eyesight, concentration, quick-twitch fibers—all those things were headed in the opposite direction.

From July 23 to July 30 in 1972, Killebrew cranked five home runs in six days, as good a home run streak as he'd ever had. He drove in eight runs and batted .368 for a pretty good week. *Sports Illustrated* sent a writer out but, oops, too late—over the next *month*, Harmon hit three home runs, had eight RBIs, and batted just .206. "I asked Ralph Kiner once how long you can stay in the groove," Killebrew said. "And he said, 'Not many games.'"

Sports analysts would later refer to it as being "in the zone," but to Killebrew and others of his generation, they knew it as a groove, a feeling that was elusive and tantalizing and seemed at times to toy with good hitters. Describing it wasn't any easier than bottling it. "You wait better when you have the good feeling," Killebrew said. "You feel like you can wait a long time on a pitch and still get your weight completely behind it. Then, when the perfect timing slips and the ball starts beating the bat to that good leverage point, sometimes you try to quicken yourself up with your body. Then you get yourself into trouble."

Got all that?

Maybe a better way to describe the task Killebrew faced nearly 10,000 times in the big leagues, each time he dug in with a bat in his hands to face a determined fellow glaring at him from 20 yards away, came from *Sports Illustrated*'s Roy Blount Jr. "People tend not to appreciate how resistant a thrown baseball can be," Blount wrote. "It comes in not only as a hopping, sinking, sailing, or hooking will-o'-the-wisp but also as a ramming line of force. Killebrew is the kind of hitter who can pick a fastball off his chin, or chest, or wrists, and jerk it out of a stadium. This is comparable to picking off a runaway outboard motor and in the same motion heaving it up a flight of stairs."

Killebrew in '72—there actually were some bumper stickers like that in the Twin Cities in the Presidential election year—appeared in 139 games, hit 26 home runs, and drove in just 74 runs, his lowest total for a full season. He didn't have any serious injuries, just a continued accumulation of a career's worth. When he got his contract for 1973, a $110,000 salary, it included "contingencies" for bonus pay if the ballclub topped 1.1 million in attendance and if Harmon appeared in a specified number of games. Well, it didn't and he didn't.

The Twins drew 907,499 through the turnstiles, and Killebrew played in just 69 games, his fewest since being farmed out to Indianapolis and Chattanooga in 1958. Rod Carew won another batting title, Bert Blyleven won 20 games, Tony Oliva got revived thanks to the American League's new designated hitter rule (DH)... and Killebrew wound up sidelined when he tore knee cartilage in June and underwent surgery in July. He had hit three home runs before he got hurt, then two more when he returned for 12 games in September. That gave him five in 248 at-bats in 1973—one every 49.6 at-bats for a pace that was more Baby Ruth than Babe Ruth. On a more positive note, what had been a section of 83rd Street in Bloomington leading to Met Stadium was named "Killebrew Drive" in his honor. Always eager to please in such public venues, Killebrew said he had never taken that particular street to work but would adjust his route.

* * *

The arrival of the DH rule so deep into Killebrew's career sparked some debate for and about the slugger. Killebrew didn't become an All-Star and eventual Hall of Famer with his glove—could he have done it without one altogether? Had he been born 15 or 20 years later, Killebrew almost certainly would have been slotted into someone's lineup as a DH and left there. He never would have gotten jerked around from third to left field to first base or made to feel like a utility infielder when he was moved to minimize his exposure on defense or to accommodate someone else on the team's roster. If it wasn't Reno Bertoia at third, it was Rich Rollins or Frank Quilici. If it wasn't Don Mincher at first base, it was Rich Reese or Vic Power.

It was hard to know if Killebrew became more irritated at being moved around or if he just got more comfortable talking about it later in his career. The switching from one spot one day to another the next was the most irritating part. It "bugged" him, he admitted, to be "catalogued as a bad defensive player." "I really worked at [it] but that label always stuck with me," Killebrew said. "I don't know how I could have changed it. I could have refused to go to several different positions.... But I always thought that if you could help the ballclub any way you could, then that's what you did." He never did use it as an excuse for any failings on offense, however.

Billy Martin, the Twins manager in 1969 who kept Killebrew in the lineup by moving him around other platoon players, addressed the topic testily that summer with a writer from *Sport* magazine. "Harmon plays a very good third base and a good first base, which may surprise a lot of people. He's not just a swinger of the bat."

Pitcher Jim Kaat, who won 16 Gold Gloves to Killebrew's none, said he was fine with the slugger's glove work behind him. "Harm had the ability to do a decent job at three positions," Kaat said. "He was not a defensive liability. He just didn't have the range and speed that a lot of players had because he was heavy-legged. He had a lot of—and this is before you had strength and flexibility coaches—little injuries. But if the ball was hit to him, he had good hands and a good throwing motion."

To his credit, Killebrew was a man who knew his limitations, both in the field and on the bases. "I used to run better before I hurt my legs, too," he said once. "How fast am I going from home to first? Oh, about 14 seconds flat."

All things considered, Killebrew would have been a logical choice at DH starting in 1973. A number of hard-hitting but defensively challenged—or just aging—players settled into the role to milk their careers, such as Frank Howard, Orlando Cepeda, Frank Robinson, Gates Brown, Tommy Davis, and Tony Oliva. Critics were abuzz over what began as an experiment and has lasted now for 40 years, and it was such a novel approach to old-fashioned, two-way baseball that not everyone knew what to make of it.

"It wasn't appealing to me at first because I always felt there were two parts to the game," Killebrew told a Boise reporter during his surgery layoff in 1973. "I like to be involved in the whole ball game. But I can see it can be advantageous to a player to stay a few years longer. Especially fellows like Oliva who couldn't play if it wasn't for the rule."

There was that issue, as well. The Twin's DH job was taken. Oliva had undergone five knee operations and wasn't capable of playing the field. He never put on a glove in a game his final four seasons. But he was solid at DH, stroking the first home run ever hit by a player in that position and batting .291 with 16 homers and 92 RBIs in 1973. The next season, he went .285 with 13 homers and 57 RBIs. He handled the DH chores in 254 games those two years; Killebrew got his turn 66 times. Even with his assorted ailments—bum leg, bad shoulder, sprained right big toe, varicose veins—he could amble around better than Tony O.

Early in the 1974 season, the Braves' Henry Aaron grabbed the world's attention by catching and passing Babe Ruth with home run No. 715, giving the 40-year-old outfielder baseball's all-time record. Later that summer, Harmon Killebrew was given a Harmon Killebrew Day at owner Calvin Griffith's insistence, finally selling the 38-year-old slugger on the idea because of the charitable contributions that would be made. The Met Stadium crowd of 27,363 saw him single twice and score the decisive run in Minnesota's 5–4 victory.

Mostly, Minnesotans saw an old friend and by now an ordinary player with a famous name. Killebrew's numbers in what was his 21st season since leaving Payette were down—a .222 average with 13 home runs and 54 RBIs in 122 games—but they actually had begun their descent much earlier.

Remember that home run on August 22, 1970, his 38th that year? Remember how he hit only three more in the Twins' final 40 games? Using that date as a turning point, the statistics break down like this—from his first game in the big leagues to that point, Killebrew hit 484 home runs, had 1,244 RBIs, rapped 1,640 hits, and batted 6,204 times—representing about three quarters of his AL production. That can be pro-rated to a 162-game "average" season of 43 HR, 111 RBIs, and a .264 average.

From that point on—ages 34 to 39, including the 1975 season in Kansas City—he had 89 HR, 340 RBIs, 446 hits, and 1,943 at-bats.

The 162-game average for those stats: 23 HR, 89 RBIs, and a .230 average.

Obviously, there was a laundry list of reasons for a decline, some were natural for any player at that stage, while others were specific to Killebrew's injuries and unavailability. No matter, by 1974, he essentially was one-half of one-half of a player. That is, Killebrew and Oliva shared the DH role to a great degree, contributing little (Harmon) or nothing (Tony) in the field. Once one of baseball's great 1-2 punches, they now teamed up for numbers that either man used to get alone. In tandem, they finished with 26 HR, 111 RBIs, 71 runs, and 205 hits ... but of course, they used 792 at-bats between them. And they made approximately $200,000 combined.

"Instead of just one designated hitter, the Twins are paying two," wrote *New York Daily News* baseball scribe Red Foley in November 1974. "And according to Calvin's son, Clark, who serves as vice president, secretary, and treasurer, an agonizing decision is going to have to be made.... It's unrealistic that the Twins should carry two such players. Though both have contributed immensely in the past, baseball is a what-have-you-done-for-me-lately business. And soon, either Killebrew or Oliva is going to find that out."

Off the field, mind you, Killebrew was as valuable as ever to the organization. He was a mentor in the clubhouse to younger players on baseball, life in the Twin Cities, even media training—hearing one of his vanilla exchanges with the writers or TV guys was like a crash course in *Bull Durham* cliché-spewing. It wasn't that Killebrew was a dull guy—he was actually witty, with a dry sense of humor—but he kept his shields up much of the time. "I've seen a lot of players hurt by what they said," he once confided. "[Roger] Maris was hurt. He said things he didn't mean, or he didn't think they'd get printed. So I guess I'm wary of saying the wrong things because the spotlight is on me."

He was an elder statesman who made several exotic, baseball-related trips in the off-seasons, going to Alaska in 1964, to Vietnam in 1966 to visit U.S. troops there, and to Japan in 1969 for some major league diplomacy—and to sell a few "Harmon Killebrew Power-Stride Batting Trainers," intended for young sluggers everywhere.

While there, Killebrew met Sadaharu Oh, the famous power Japanese hitter who hit 868 home runs. "I asked him his philosophy of hitting," Killebrew said. "He said eat, drink, sleep—he said *shreep*—and practice. He took a bat home after every game, whether he went 0-for-4 or 4-for-4, and swung it a thousand times. I was pretty dedicated, but I doubt I would do that after going 4-for-4. I told Ted Williams that—I thought *he* was the most dedicated player I ever saw—and he did not make any comment at all."

Killebrew still was popular with the fans, of course, obliging autograph and snapshot requests and as down to Earth as any star athlete ever. Sharon Lawrence—sister of Mark Heleker, the Payette High principal who started Killebrew Day back there—was married and living in Washington, D.C., in 1973 and drove to Baltimore to catch a Twins visit. She went early ("It was my first major league game.") and from her seat near the visitors dugout, she noticed Killebrew on the steps.

"I hollered 'Harm! Harm!' a couple of times," she recalled. "He walked over and I yelled, 'I'm from Payette' and he kept coming with a big smile on his face. I told him who I was, and he asked about my father and other news from Payette, signed some programs for me [I didn't ask!] and soon a coach walked over and said it was time to get back to warm-ups. A very magical time for me!"

Then there was Killebrew the teammate and pal. "I played against him for a number of years, played with him for five, and he was just a joyful human being," catcher Phil Roof said in 2012. "I was just glad to be associated with him. A quiet individual, but one-on-one you had a good conversation with him. He could talk about anything, was always reassuring to young guys, and—with me being traded over there—he welcomed me with open arms."

Roof, 40 years after he was a guest on Killebrew's TV show, still raved about the microwave oven he got as a gift. "It lasted maybe 20 years," he said. "Me having a wife and four kids, Harmon knew I could use that."

There was the day on the road when Killebrew called Roof in the hotel and told him to come up to his room. "So I came up to his room and when I looked around, he had two bowls of ice cream, three scoops in each one. And I said, 'Harmon, you're treating me like a major leaguer.' But he said, 'No, there's something else I brought you up here for. Look around.'

"Well, I looked around and looked around, and hell, I couldn't tell him anything but ice cream. And next thing you know, he took his index finger and he pointed to his head. A friend of his out of Chicago gave him a nice toupee and he had it on. I told him, 'Harmon, you look good in that.' But he said, 'It's too much work. I'd have to do too many things to keep it going. I'm not going through that.'

"I laughed," Roof said. "But I was mad at myself because I didn't recognize it. Once I put my eyes on the ice cream, I didn't know anything else."

Kaat told an ice cream story about Killebrew at the slugger's memorial service at Target Field in May 2011—about a botched room-service order one night that left Kaat with three big bowls of ice cream, and Harmon's eagerness to help with it—and he told it again in a later interview. "I don't know if it was a Mormon tradition or if it was about abstinence or what, but I know Harmon didn't eat a lot of dessert at home," the pitcher said.

His wife Elaine used to bake him pizzas as a reward for home runs when they were a young couple in their Washington days. But she watched Harmon's diet pretty closely later in his career. So while Jim Bouton was writing about Mickey Mantle and the other Yankees carousing with cocktails and "baseball Annies" [groupies], a lot of the racy stuff about Killebrew centered on his ice cream habit. His Royals teammates at the end of his career remembered his invitations to "go get a milkshake." His brother Bob talked about a particular ice-cream shop in Germany that Killebrew couldn't walk past.

Killebrew wore other hats over his thick head of scalp: husband, father, neighbor, role model away from the ball park, leader, and anchor when he was there. "In his productive years, he was our lifeblood," said Frank Quilici, first Killebrew's teammate and backup, then later his manager. "It was inspiring for me just to replace him in the lineup for defense. Now to see him struggling is heartbreaking."

Pitcher Jim Perry, a teammate for 10 seasons, said, "He was a really good guy to have on the team because the guys really looked up to him. It's nice [for someone] to be in the Hall of Fame, but it's about the off-the-field stuff, too. He wasn't just a great player, he was a great leader."

How good of a guy was Killebrew on the field? He played 2,435 games in the majors and never got ejected. He did, however, get *rejected*. It happened over the winter after the 1974 season. He had been at Met Stadium filming a commercial at the park when Griffith sent word for him to come up to the office when he was done.

"It was about the time of the year that contracts were tendered to the players, so I thought rather than him sending it to me, he would probably want me to come up and sign my contract," Killebrew said years later. "And boy, was I wrong. That was the furthest thing from his mind."

Griffith had been appreciative of Killebrew as the franchise's ready-made star when the club relocated to Minnesota. His wholesomeness held extra appeal for straight-laced fans in the Upper Midwest, and he was a family man, non-threatening, with a blocky build and a pleasant face. “He kept us in business,” the owner said midway through that final season together. “When we first arrived in Minnesota, Harmon and Bob Allison were our stars and our gate attractions. Everyone likes long-ball hitters, and with them we had a home run derby.”

Still, Griffith’s instincts as a businessman were as sharp as Killebrew’s swing. He almost couldn’t help himself when there was a nickel to be squeezed. A year earlier, the owner’s brainstorm had been to ask Killebrew to report to spring training without a contract at all. “If we saw that he could play, that he could help the club, he could sign then.”

Mostly, Griffith was chafing at baseball’s labor deal at the time, which limited pay cuts to a maximum 20 percent without the player’s cooperation. He wanted to get Killebrew’s salary down more than that. “Frank Howard was making $140,000 [with Washington/Texas], but he agreed to play with Detroit last season for about $60,000,” Griffith told Twin Cities baseball writers. “That’s still a lot of money.”

Killebrew didn’t go for that one, finally signing for $80,000 (one source reported $90,000). So a year later, Griffith was going to offer his former MVP and 11-time All-Star a deal to be a player-coach for $52,000, dodging the pay-cut rule by adding the coaching duties. Or he was prepared to see if Killebrew wanted to go back to the minor leagues as manager of the franchise’s Class AAA affiliate in Tacoma.

Killebrew didn’t like either option. He wanted to play. He figured he had one, maybe two years left and had recently told the beat writers, “The No. 1 thing I still want to do is play with the Twins next season.”

Griffith’s response? The owner heard what he wanted to hear. Killebrew recalled, “He said, ‘Well, that’s fine if you’d like to do that. You’re welcome to call any other club or talk to any other ballclub that you’d like to.’”

Insult? Shock? Yes, both of those. After absorbing them, Killebrew did speak to several teams and came back with an offer from Kansas

City. He had hit it off with the team's owner, Ewing Kauffman. He knew of the Royals' manager, Jack McKeon, from crossing paths in the Senators/Twins organization; McKeon had played, then managed in the club's minor leagues. "They were Midwestern-type people, and I was from a small town in Idaho and had been playing in Minnesota," Killebrew said. "I thought Kansas City would fit my personality."

Killebrew was given his release on January 16, 1975. Eight days later, he signed with the Royals for an estimated $70,000. And he began to think that maybe Kaat had been right all along.

Kaat had always battled Griffith more directly at contract time. "I was kind of stubborn and had my squabbles with Calvin every time, and Harmon was Mr. Nice Guy," the pitcher recalled. "I used to tell Harmon that Calvin was taking advantage of him—I'm sure he took care of him in decent fashion, but you know he didn't overpay him. Calvin would make a concerted effort to get Harmon signed, and then when the rest of us came in and started arguing about contracts, he said, 'Well, I got Killebrew signed already. He didn't give me any trouble.'

"Harmon would say, 'Jim, if you'd be a little more pleasant with Mr. Griffith, when your career is over he'll take care of you.' And I'd say, 'Harm, when you quit hitting the ball over the wall, they won't know how to spell your name.' I think I saw him in spring training the next year and I said, 'The Cardinals made a vice president out of [Stan] Musial, and the Twins wanted you to go to Triple A.' I really thought that was disrespectful."

When Kaat had wrist trouble in August 1973, after holding out that spring in pursuit of a three-year deal worth $60,000 per season, the Twins pounced, cutting him loose. He signed with Chicago, reunited with old pitching coach Johnny Sain, and won 21 games for the White Sox in 1974 and 20 in 1975. He pitched another 10 years overall, until age 44, chewing up 1,516 innings, going 93–78, striking out 610, throwing 47 more complete games, and getting 12 saves all after the Twins figured him for done.

Killebrew had never played hard ball over money—he was slow to mail back his contract a time or two, but he never staged a protracted holdout to turn the screws on Griffith. But 16 months after Kaat's dismissal, it was Killebrew's turn. The rough draft of the Twins' press release on Killebrew's exit read in part:

> ...Mr. Griffith agreed to Killebrew's request but expressed sincere regret at his leaving the Twins' organization. "Harmon has been with the Twins for the past 14 years and before that he was with the Washington Senators," Mr. Griffith said. "I'm tremendously indebted to him for all he's meant to our organization and to our area, and I wish him every success in his new association with the Kansas City club. I would have been very happy had he accepted the contract offer we made to him recently, but I'm sure he is convinced in his own mind that he is acting in the best interests of his family and his career."

It was over. That meant Killebrew never had a last home run, last hit, last game, last play, last at-bat as a Twins player—not that anyone knew about in advance, anyway. All of it had to be retrofitted to the butt end of the team's lackluster season.

On September 10, Killebrew played the field for the final time, shifting from designated hitter to first base in the 15th inning against Chicago in a game the Twins won in the bottom of the inning. He went 0-for-5 with a pair of walks and one putout.

On September 11, he pinch hit for Oliva in the eighth inning, stayed on as the DH, and hit a two-run shot off Oakland's Darold Knowles in the bottom of the 10th inning for a 5–3 victory. It was his final home run for the franchise.

On October 1, Killebrew played his last full game with the Twins, going hitless in four at-bats as the DH, walking and scoring a run.

On October 2, Killebrew stepped to the plate against a Texas Rangers' right-hander named Steve Foucault, pinch-hitting for Larry Hisle. In the ninth inning, with two down, no one on base, and the Twins trailing 2–1, Foucault struck out Killebrew looking.

The announced crowd that day: 2,570. And the greatest player in franchise history exited with the bat on his shoulder.

Chapter 13

Royal Blues

George Brett was a Southern California kid of a certain generation, raised in a baseball family with older brothers in the game—all four of Jack and Ethel's sons played professionally—and one in particular, Ken, was considered by some scouts to be one of the most talented prospects ever. They had started out East and moved West, like the team they followed once they got there, the Dodgers.

By 1967, when George was 14 years old, he watched his 19-year-old brother pitch for the Boston Red Sox in the World Series, the youngest pitcher to work in the Fall Classic. But two years earlier when they both were still at home in El Segundo, it was the L.A. Dodgers vs. the Minnesota Twins that brought a fellow named Harmon Killebrew into focus.

"Growing up in Los Angeles and watching that World Series between the Twins and the Dodgers, and [Sandy] Koufax and [Don] Drysdale and Harmon... so obviously I knew who Harmon was by then," George Brett said in January 2012. The Brett family was fine with the outcome that October, L.A. scratching back from its 0–2 start to win the Series in seven games.

Ken Brett would face Killebrew seven times from 1970 to 1972 and get the better of that matchup. The Twins slugger walked three times, struck out once, and went 1-for-4 with no home runs or RBIs. In 1973, Ken was off to the National League, but it was George's turn to cross paths with Killebrew. Just 20, the kid was a late-season call-up by the Kansas City Royals and although they didn't play in the same game, George noticed the veteran on the field beforehand. His reaction was the same as a lot of folks when they saw Killebrew in person for the first time.

"You'd have thought he'd be 6'3", 210 pounds, built like one of these tremendous *athletes*," Brett said. "But that wasn't him. It's like the first time I saw Yogi Berra, I couldn't believe it. What he'd done [in the game]? And now when I see Yogi, he's shrunk another 5" and he's *really* small."

George Brett and Killebrew went about their business in the AL West in 1974, with the Royals third baseman placing third in Rookie of the Year balloting behind Mike Hargrove and Bucky Dent, and the Twins first baseman/DH winding down at age 38. Then Brett showed up at Terry Park in Ft. Myers, Florida, for spring training in 1975, and there he was—Killebrew.

"Obviously, I didn't go up to him and just start shooting the shit with him, you know," Brett said some 37 years later. "I knew who Harmon was but had never said two words to him then, just admired the way he played the game, admired the things he had accomplished, even though he was near the end of the line. And then it was a real treat, not only for myself but for a lot of members on the Kansas City Royals when he came over and played his last year with us. Then I got to know him extremely well."

A lot of people forget that Johnny Unitas, the legendary NFL Baltimore Colts quarterback, played his final days with the San Diego

Chargers in 1973, his helmet adorned with lightning bolts instead of that iconic Colts horseshoe. It was that way, too, with Bobby Orr, the game-changing Hall of Fame defenseman for the NHL Boston Bruins, who finished his career limping and frustrated with the rival Chicago Blackhawks. It went that way, too, for Joe Namath in 1977, about as far away from Broadway as he could get, backing up Pat Haden for the Los Angeles Rams, throwing three touchdowns and five interceptions and getting sacked seven last times.

And frankly, why shouldn't people forget, given how little those star players, heroes even, resembled their past selves? No one thinks of Michael Jordan as a Wizard any more than they think of Joe Montana as a Chief or Henry Aaron as a Brewer, no matter what their stats were or how much they claimed to enjoy those out-of-whack final laps. And no one thinks of Harmon Killebrew as a Royal, particularly because of the stats and how little he wound up enjoying it.

"I didn't understand it," Brett said. "Why would a guy play his whole career in one town and then come all the way over to K.C. for one last year? The only thing I could think of was that Harmon wanted to play one more year and Calvin probably said, 'Well, we don't want you, we're only going to pay you this…' And Harmon probably got more money to come to the Royals, but he thought he could play one more year, too. Be productive, and do something you love to do."

There had been reports that the Texas Rangers were in the hunt for Killebrew, too, though both sides eventually backed away from the other. Texas chose not to meet Killebrew's price of $80,000 for one year, and Arlington Stadium didn't strike Harmon as the best place to add to his home run count.

The Royals had a park with dimensions more friendly to Killebrew's style of power hitting and were eager to add a right-handed bat to an already solid lineup. "Harmon gives us home run and RBI potential to go with Hal McRae, Amos Otis, and John Mayberry,"

Kansas City general manager Joe Burke said. "If we have three guys like Otis, McRae, and Killebrew, it will be pretty tough to pitch around Mayberry." Mayberry, in fact, had the best year of his career that season—34 HR, 106 RBIs, 119 walks, .963 OPS—and finished second to Boston rookie Fred Lynn in MVP balloting. Of course, Mayberry's play made for only rare opportunities for Harmon at first base (he got into six games at the position, Mayberry played 131).

If home run immortality had been Killebrew's only motivation, the season in K.C. hardly would have been worth it—from No. 559, where he started, to No. 573, where he finished; he passed no one on the all-time list. But then, he might have figured he'd hit more than 14. Or stick around more than one season. Besides, the money was still good—not just the contract but other perks and pension benefits—and Harmon did make some new friends, get a different look around the American League, and so on. Brett wasn't the only one who suspected that going out on his own terms, rather than Calvin Griffith's, played a role, too.

Killebrew met and quickly came to like Royals owner Ewing Kauffman. But it became clear just as quickly that there was a disconnect in their respective visions of the season. "It was the longest season of my life," Killebrew said when it was over. "I thought I was going there to be the full-time DH. But [manager] Jack McKeon had other ideas. He platooned me as a DH, and he also wanted me to play some first base. That artificial turf destroyed what was left of my knees."

Killebrew ended up splitting the DH role with Tony Solaita, whose story was as interesting in some ways as that of the Hall of Fame slugger. Solaita, whose actual first name was Tolia, was the first major league player to be born and raised in American Samoa. His family moved to Hawaii and then to California when his father, Tulafono, joined the Marines. Solaita became pals with future Cardinal Ken Reitz, joining him in youth baseball. The Yankees scouted and signed Solaita out of high school and briefly considered him as Mickey Mantle's heir apparent. In 1968, in the Class A Carolina League, he hit 51 home runs (two in the playoffs) and was named Topps Minor League Player of the Year. But he got buried and didn't surface for good until McKeon, who had managed Solaita the year he hit 51, brought him to the Royals before the 1974 season.

After the 1979 season, Solaita chose to play in Japan, landing a four-year deal and averaging about 40 home runs per year for the Nippon Ham Fighters. In time, he returned to his homeland, Samoa, but in February 1990, Solaita was shot and killed by a rival in a land dispute there.

A 6', 210-pounder, Solaita turned 28 in 1975, and from the left side he clubbed 16 home runs in 231 at-bats—the second-best ratio (14.4) in the majors behind Dave Kingman (13.9). Killebrew, who knew a little about home run ratios, hit 14 in 312 at-bats. He and Solaita combined to drive in 88 runs, and although both craved the other's plate appearances, they became good friends. Brett said it was routine for all three of them to head to the clubhouse sauna after home games, unwinding and telling stories.

Killebrew's season broke down like this: 10 home runs, 33 RBIs before the All-Star break, then only four homers and 11 RBIs after the break in about half as many plate appearances. He served 92 games as a DH and pinch-hit 19 times. In certain situations, he still could dial up his concentration and performance—he batted .273 with two homers and 17 RBIs when at the plate with two outs and runners in scoring position. But platooning meant too many idle days in the dugout, and Killebrew believed that the lack of continuity dulled his stroke.

"In retrospect, if I had stayed in Minnesota playing on grass and dirt, I probably could have played that season and another year," he said at one point. Maybe not if he'd spent half his time or more coaching.

The challenges started coming from the start. On Opening Day in Anaheim, he struck out four times against one pitcher in a game for the first time ever. The fact that it was Nolan Ryan—against whom Killebrew batted .185 through the years, striking out 11 times in 37 plate appearances—didn't lessen the sting much for him. "Not a very good way to start off an experience with a new ballclub," he said.

One thing Killebrew did not have to worry about was acceptance from teammates. He wasn't the player he had been—Killebrew in 1975 was a little thicker, a tad slower, a bit more gray around the fringe. But he had taken teams places and done things in baseball that the Royals could only dream about. Their days as an AL force were ahead of them; in its first six seasons from 1969–74, Kansas City topped .500 only twice, finishing second both times. Beginning in 1976 and through the next 10 seasons, the Royals would win the AL West six times and place second three times. They made it to the World Series in 1980 and lost in six games to Philadelphia, then made it back in 1985 and beat St. Louis in seven games.

Killebrew, in that way, was part of the Royals' prep work for excellence. No other member of the 500 Home Run Club ever played for Kansas City, before or since. Among Hall of Famers, period, Brett is the real deal of course, and Orlando Cepeda (1974) and Gaylord Perry (1983) had cameos in K.C. on their way out. But that has been it. In terms of credibility and baseball wisdom, Harmon Killebrew was a big name and a big help.

"Just watching Harmon, how he did his daily routine, how hard he worked, how mentally prepared he was, all those things, I think, paid dividends for the Royals," Brett said. "Maybe he was the stepping stone. 'Okay, let's bring in this veteran-type guy.' Maybe Joe Burke—who was this real mild-mannered man, same personality as Harmon basically, very calm—said, 'We need somebody who's been there, done that on our team for a year, who can show these guys what it's like. Don't get too excited when things go good, don't get too down when things go bad.' That was Harmon Killebrew for us."

Never to his knowledge, Brett said, did any of the Royals' young guys—out of cockiness or ignorance—wonder something like, "What's up with the old dude?" Nor did they question his value during Harmon's rather quiet second half. "No, when he came over he was such a big star, everybody looked forward to it and appreciated the fact that we were going to play with a future Hall of Famer," the third baseman said. "I didn't know what my career was going to be, and I was in awe of him. If Harmon Killebrew would have told me to do something, I would have done it. I think everybody knew he'd played on championship teams and y'know, 'Hey, he can teach us a lot of things. Let's just watch him.'"

Frank White, for example, would become the greatest second baseman in Royals history, with eight Gold Gloves and five All-Star selections, and have his uniform No. 20 retired by the franchise in 1995. But at the time, he was a 24-year-old backup infielder and part of his job then was to be a sponge for whatever he could learn from a veteran with experience. "He was just a nice guy, a real professional guy," White said of Harmon. "I remember he and [catcher] Fran Healy used to hang out together after games, and they'd go get milkshakes every day. Just a pretty clean-cut guy. For a young guy, being around a veteran, he was an outstanding guy to ask for help, and he really helped me a lot."

Pitcher Bob McClure, 23, a rookie left-hander who was still getting out major league hitters at age 41 in 1993, got a dose of baseball medicine advice from Killebrew. "One day he said, 'Bobby, come over here for a second.' So I went over and he was real nice. He said, 'The first thing I want to suggest to you is never go into the training room.' This is 1975, and I really didn't understand what he was saying, because in the minor leagues, there really weren't any training rooms. So I asked, 'Why's that?'

"He said, 'Well, if you're in the training room and the trainer's working on you and the manager sees you and then you don't pitch well and somebody's pitching really good at Triple A, there's a good chance they'll bring him up and you may never get your job back.' So back then, if I needed to put ice on my arm or something, I'd do it back in the hotel room. I remember not going in the training room for quite a few years."

McClure, who became a pitching coach for Colorado, Kansas City, and most recently Boston, added, "He used to ask me all the time, 'Hey, c'mon kid, let's go out and have a milkshake.' He was very kindhearted, and I was a little bit in awe of him."

Brett's admiration grew later when he was "the old guy," still at it at age 39 or 40, trying to maintain the routines and find the discipline to hang to, the stuff he could control even when his skills began to erode. He'd had a resurgent season in 1990 when he was 37, winning his third batting title and leading the league with 45 doubles. Then he got married. Then he and his wife had a child.

"All of a sudden, if I had to leave for the ballpark at 2:00, I'd lay down at 1:00 and say, 'I'm going to take an hour nap.' Then it would be an hour-and-a-half nap, a two-hour nap," Brett said. "Instead of getting there at 2:00, now I'm showing up at 3:00, 3:30.... The Royals offered me another contract to play [at 41], but you know what? I didn't feel like I was the player that I once was, and I lost the respect for the game. I used to pride myself on being the first one in the locker room.... It was tough to beat Harmon there when he was on our team. And he'd always be the last one to leave."

* * *

Killebrew was far away from Elaine, the five kids, and the friends with whom he would normally go through a season. That changed in early May when the Royals traveled to the Twin Cities for a three-game weekend series against his old club. A mere 2,946 fans showed up for the opener, a game in which Killebrew batted clean-up and went hitless in four trips with a pair of walks before being lifted for a pinch runner. The next game, Solaita was K.C.'s designated hitter against Bert Blyleven, the in-his-prime pitcher, so Killebrew did not face Blyleven in their one season as opponents, although Blyleven started four times vs. the Royals.

The Sunday finale of that series, May 4, had been promoted as Harmon Killebrew Day, a move by wily ol' Calvin Griffith to make a few more bucks off the All-Star slugger even after his departure. It didn't goose the gate that much—the announced crowd was 14,805 with sparsely populated sections of stands in the background of photographs of Killebrew and the Twins' officials. It was jarring for many of those in the park, that day or for any of his games in 1975, to see his familiar form wearing those Kansas City powder blues—double-knit uniforms of that era already were enough like pajamas, but the Royals' road garb looked one step up from Dr. Denton's. Fortunately, the famous No. 3 that Griffith and the Twins retired that afternoon was Killebrew's old classic Minnesota shirt.

Showing a real flair for the dramatic, Killebrew slammed a two-run homer in the first inning off Minnesota starter Vic Albury. In the fifth, showing no flair for the dramatic whatsoever, reliever Jim Hughes plunked Killebrew with a pitch. Hughes then struck him out in the seventh and ninth innings.

By June, Killebrew still had high hopes, still had specific goals—such as chasing down the guy in front of him on that list of baseball's all-time power brokers. "I guess that I would like to finish fourth on the all-time list behind Hank Aaron, Babe Ruth, and Willie Mays," he told *The Sporting News*. "Frank Robinson is ahead of me right now, but I don't think Frank will get to bat as much as I will this year, and I think I'll be able to overtake him." Let the record show that Robinson began the 1975 season with 574 home runs—one more than Killebrew would have at retirement—and had added four by the start of June. He hit nine in 1975 overall and three more in 1976, all while managing the Cleveland club.

Killebrew also told the weekly sports newspaper that in his estimation he had at least three more years as a player. "I feel the best I have, physically, in the past few years," he said. "As to the future, I would like to stay in baseball in some capacity, but I'll have to wait and see."

In July, however, Killebrew pulled a muscle in his right thigh and missed time. He was the eighth oldest player in the major leagues that summer, a bookend to his arrival in June 1954 when he joined the Senators in Chicago as a bonus baby at age 17.

None of this was lost on Killebrew. "There wasn't a player in the league who was there when I first started," he said about 1975. But then, he had known he was getting old for a while. If it wasn't the growth and development of his children or the arrival of disco music, it was occasionally bumping into young players in the league who were the offspring of guys Harmon had played against—like Jim Hegan's son, Mike, and Gus Bell's kid, Buddy.

Killebrew made his last appearance as a player at Met Stadium on September 18, 1975. And as the Royals DH, he deposited one more baseball where he had sent so many before it, into the left-field bleachers. It was a solo shot off the Twins' Eddie Bane, the left-hander Griffith had used as a gate attraction straight from college in 1973, and it put the Royals up 2–0 in a game they would win 4–3. Killebrew walked to lead off the seventh inning, and then he was lifted for pinch-runner Rodney Scott, who scored in K.C.'s game-winning rally.

In four more games, Killebrew managed just one single in 10 at-bats, dipping his average to .199. His final run, his final RBI, and the last home run of his marvelous career came in that farewell at the Met.

* * *

Later in life, some of Killebrew's comments made it sound as if he missed his youth, which had left him even before he left the ballfield. "If I had a time machine, I think I'd try to go back to where I was the best in my life physically. Don't ask me when that is—I would guess sometime in the 1960s." He also said, "If I could change anything about my life, I'd make me younger. You know what Stan Musial said: 'Old age is not for sissies.'"

But he had nothing to regret or apologize for, as far as teammates such as George Brett were concerned. When the former Royals star was deep into his career but not quite at the end, Brett casually said in an interview that he didn't want to go out "like Harmon Killebrew." The comment got back to Killebrew, hurt his feelings, and embarrassed Brett until they got a chance to talk.

"I didn't mean that as a slap to him," Brett said. "I just remembered this guy that was a really, really, really good ballplayer when I was a kid, and when I got the chance to play with him, he wasn't a very good ballplayer anymore. He wasn't the Harmon Killebrew that I remember. Harmon said, 'George, some day I'm going to tell you'—he said this at the Hall of Fame one year—'I'm going to tell you why I played one more year.' And he never did.

"But I could have thrown in any 40-year old guy that ever played the game for 20 years and was a Hall of Fame player. I felt bad because I think Harmon felt slighted by what I said. And I didn't mean any disrespect. You know what? The game gets tougher. The older you get, the harder it gets. I know when I was 40, I wasn't the player I was when I was 25, 26, 27. But you know, you continued to play and do the best you could."

Killebrew had a moment late in that season—literally in the September of his years as a player—that was as telling to him then as it is poignant to everyone else today. He was signing autographs near the dugout at Anaheim Stadium. "There was a big kid and a little kid there," he remembered. "I was signing a ball for the big kid, and I saw the little kid next to him kind of punch him and say, 'Who is that guy?' The big kid said, 'That's Killebrew.' The little kid said, 'Well, is he any good?' And the big kid turns to him and says, 'He used to be.'

"I mean, kids tell it like it is, and he was right. It was time for me to quit."

Chapter 14

After the Game

When Killebrew realized he was done as a major league ballplayer, he shifted to Plan B. He had no idea that over the next three decades or so he would have to go deep into the alphabet—Plan C, Plan D, and beyond—to sort out and survive the chapters still facing him. "See the ball, hit the ball" worked in baseball beyond his wildest dreams. But real life was not quite that simple.

"So I got on a plane, flew back to Minnesota, went in to Mr. Griffith and told him I wanted to manage his ballclub," Killebrew recalled much later of his initial steps into athletic retirement. The Twins had fired Frank Quilici, his old teammate and manager, after a 76–83 finish in 1975. Unfortunately for Killebrew, Quilici set a precedent that owner Calvin Griffith wasn't interested in following. The boss told his former slugger that, nope, he wouldn't be hiring any more managers who did not have minor league experience. Instead of hiring the man who once was his franchise's biggest star, Griffith brought in Gene Mauch, who at age 50 had already logged 16 seasons as a big league manager in Philadelphia and Montreal.

It was a reasonable enough decision, but it seemed to some from the outside to be tinged with a little spite. Griffith, some folks recalled, had told reporters upon Killebrew's departure for Kansas City, "I won't say that I'd never have a job as manager or coach if he should ask me in the future. But I made no commitment along those lines. It has been my policy that once a player leaves us, he's gone from the organization unless we want him back."

The owner and the slugger had more in common at that point in their lives than they might have realized. Just as Griffith struggled with the advent of free agency in baseball, pricing him out of the market for top talent and shifting power to the athletes and their agents, so did Killebrew struggle for a time with his personal free agency out of baseball. He played in a time when baseball salaries weren't quite the Powerball jackpots they became later; his top salary of about $120,000 would have been worth about four times that in 2011 dollars but not 100 times that—or, if he were paid like Albert Pujols, 200 times that—by recent MLB standards.

Killebrew wasn't yet 40. He had a life to live and a living to make.

"Those of us who played in that era weren't going to be self-sufficient from [what we earned in] the game," said Jerry Kramer, the great Green Bay Packers lineman who grew up in Sandpoint, Idaho. He was the same age as Killebrew, one of the state's all-time sports stars, and a good friend once the two men got to know each other through golf tournaments in the 1970s and '80s. Kramer's even-shorter football career ended in 1968, a few months before Killebrew's MVP season in Minnesota. Kramer got a jump on retirement by authoring the best-selling sports book *Instant Replay* with Dick Schaap, then he did some TV work for CBS, had speaking engagements, and developed other business interests. "We knew we were going to have to do something else," Kramer said.

Killebrew made his retirement official in March 1976 at a news conference in Boise. "It has been a difficult decision for me to make," he said. "I haven't been looking forward to it with a great deal of anticipation.... I love baseball. It's difficult to give it up."

Jim Poore, a sportswriter from the *Idaho Statesman* in Boise, soon visited Killebrew at the family home outside Ontario overlooking the Snake River and the Oregon Slopes. The newness of his post-playing life amused Killebrew, but the elephant was already in the room. There was a void that needed filling up, and soon. "I think it's easier for me this year, because I did spend that time last year in Kansas City," Killebrew said. "But still, it's a tough thing because I played for so many years and all of a sudden not to play... it's going to feel real strange for a while. I was telling my wife the other day it's the first time in 23 years I've been home on this particular date."

Killebrew signed on with the Twins to do color analyst work on the team's television broadcasts—there had been some changes in the booth, and Griffith had lent Killebrew a hand after all. Of the 50 or so games, only a handful were home games, so Killebrew commuted from Oregon to wherever the club happened to be. And despite playing in 2,435 games at baseball's highest level, Killebrew—along with Quilici, who was joining the Twins' legendary radio voice, Herb Carneal, that season—had to learn how to keep score. He learned an unorthodox system with pens of multiple colors from friend Bob Prince.

"I thought sitting behind a microphone describing what happened on the field would be easy," Killebrew said. "But it's not as easy as it looks. I had a pregame show as a player that I could prepare for. But you can't prepare for games because you never know what to expect."

Joe Boyle, the play-by-play man working with him said, "Harmon works hard. He may have been a baseball superstar, but he doesn't treat this job like a superstar.... A lot of people told me it would be tough working with Harmon because he was not an outgoing type of person. But he's surprised the hell out of me."

He had two stints with the Twins, at WTCN-TV from 1976–78, then with KMSP-TV and TwinsVision from 1984–88. During that second one, Killebrew got to call games and interview players—and suffered no small amount of champagne damage to the wardrobe—when the 1987 Minnesota team won the World Series, beating St. Louis in seven games. He was only 13 years removed from his own days as a Twins player, and there were a few familiar faces around (Bert Blyleven as a starting pitcher, Tony Oliva as a coach) to make the vicarious thrills special. You can find clips on YouTube of Killebrew interviewing the winners, and he seems as happy as any of them.

In the middle of his first stay in the Twins booth, a shot at the type of job Griffith had denied him came along. In June 1977, Texas Rangers owner Brad Corbett approached Killebrew about managing that ballclub. Frank Lucchesi had been fired with a 31–31 record. Seven games passed on the Rangers' schedule, with coaches filling in, while Corbett nailed down a replacement, as Killebrew considered the offer.

Finally, he declined, telling Corbett he was happy with what he was doing and preferred not to be pulled away from family and his budding business interests. "That [managing] was the furthest thing from my mind," he said. "A few years ago, I thought what I really wanted to do was manage a ballclub. But I got it out of my system, out of my mind. But to get hit with it, it really threw me a little bit. It's quite a thing to be offered a thing like that after not managing at all. And to be offered a club that's a contender, it's pretty nice." Corbett wound up hiring Baltimore coach Billy Hunter on a three-year, $250,000 contract.

Killebrew worked as a color commentator in Oakland from 1979–82, adding duties in 1981 as a batting instructor in spring training and in the A's farm system. In 1983, he shifted farther south as part of the California Angels' TV crew. He also found time for other pursuits—some financial, some social, some charitable.

There was Killebrew Motors, an auto dealership he opened for business in Ontario, Oregon, across the river from his hometown of Payette. Harmon Killebrew Enterprises, based in Salt Lake City, was best known for marketing his Power-Stride batting trainer contraption. He studied for and got into the insurance business, with an assist from the Idaho legislature when it approved a bill permitting an out-of-stater to sell such products, as long as the principal place of business was within state lines. Killebrew commuted to the insurance and financial-planning company in Boise, where he was a partner with Idaho congressman Ralph Harding.

Killebrew and Harding were instrumental in creating and growing the Danny Thompson Memorial golf tournament, in honor of the Twins shortstop who played four seasons in the big leagues while slowly dying from leukemia. Diagnosed in 1973 as part of a routine spring training physical, Thompson's illness—chronic granulocytic leukemia—was deemed fatal by specialists at the Mayo Clinic, yet they would allow him to continue playing baseball. Despite the toll his treatments and his plight took on Thompson physically, mentally, and emotionally, he was able to play 406 games and bat .242 after his diagnosis—he even got included in the trade that sent Blyleven to Texas for shortstop Roy Smalley in June 1976.

Six months later, at age 29, Thompson was dead.

"Danny was just a great kid," Killebrew said years later. "I remember wanting to go see him when he was up at the Mayo Clinic [in Rochester, Minnesota]. His wife said, 'No, Harmon, Danny doesn't want anyone to see him like this.' I went to his funeral in his hometown of Capron, Oklahoma. It was so large they had to have it in a high school gymnasium."

In 1977, Killebrew and Harding came up with the charity golf tournament to help the shortstop's widow and two children and eventually to raise money for cancer research. The event in Sun Valley,

Idaho, became a highlight of Killebrew's year and despite his quiet nature much of the time, he wasn't shy about encouraging his friends in the sports world to participate. The tournament continued even after Harmon's own passing from cancer in 2011; by 2012, after 36 years, it was reported to have raised more than $11 million.

Kramer, one of the early invitees, found himself enjoying Killebrew's company so much, and vice versa, that they would call each other for casual golf when they happened to be in town together. "He called me 'Geraldine.' I called him 'Harmonious,'" said Kramer, best known for his block to spring quarterback Bart Starr on the goal line in the famous Green Bay–Dallas "Ice Bowl" for the 1967 NFL championship. "Just a sweet man. A good man. A solid man. He didn't tell dirty jokes. He didn't make loud noises. And always pleasant, always nice words and a smile."

* * *

Killebrew's sense of humor was on full display—and maybe put to the test a little—in 1986 when he was featured for an entire hour on *Late Night With David Letterman,* the then-NBC show that defined everything "hip" in pop culture at the time. Killebrew had been scheduled to appear in November 1985 on Film Festival night, appearing in one of several short films commissioned by the *Late Night* show, along with Bette Midler, Michael Keaton, and others. Harmon's got bumped for time, however, so to make it up to him, Letterman arranged to devote a whole show to the former Twins star.

What resulted on February 11, 1986, was a Bizarro World version of the old *This Is Your Life* series from the 1950s, dripping with Letterman irony. There was an opening segment in which Harmon hit a fungo "into the audience," with the sound of a woman screaming in pain. There were guest visits by Bob Allison and Jim Kaat, old Washington and Minnesota teammates. Modern artist

LeRoy Neiman was backstage painting a Killebrew montage while the show unspooled (asked if he'd give the piece to Harmon when done, Neiman deadpanned, "No!"). Country singer Charley Pride called in to sing to Killebrew over the phone.

But wait, it got better—Liberace joined Letterman and Killebrew on the set for no apparent reason other than the inevitable awkwardness. The Killebrew short film was shown, a pseudo-documentary "day in the life" for him, except with gags sprinkled throughout. For example, he was shown closing a deal at his car dealership, trying to squeeze a few more bucks from a cranky couple. "I guess we'll make it up on the undercoating," Harmon said, playing along. "Congratulations!"

And at the end of the show, naturally, Letterman raised Killebrew's navy blue blazer into the studio rafters while musical director Paul Shaffer, his whole band wearing Twins caps, serenaded him with a just-for-the-occasion ballad.

Surreal? Sure. But it was a lot more pleasant than some of the all-too-real things with which Killebrew was coping in his everyday life. Through much of the 1980s, his attempts to crack into business and find a reliable source of income failed. By August 27, 1989, the whole world learned of it when the *Minneapolis Star Tribune* carried a lengthy story by staff writer Jay Weiner who looked at Killebrew's unnervingly troubled financial and marital life.

"Somewhere between fame and 50, Harmon Killebrew lost his way, his marriage, and his financial security."

That was only the beginning. The story detailed Killebrew's tailspin into debt, the result of misplaced trust, poor judgment, and a lack of business savvy. He had gotten overextended with Killebrew Motors and a leasing company back in the Twin Cities. Construction costs on the family's home ran high. In the early 1980s, a hustler named Jack Dean Franks got Killebrew and Harding tangled in a bogus golf-course development scheme, a project promising luxury homes on a posh course in Rancho Mirage, California, that never happened. Franks used their names to snare investors and even plowed their $100,000 "commissions" back into the phony project—or rather, his pocket. Franks ultimately confessed to scamming more than $1 million. He pleaded guilty to wire and mail fraud and served a 60-day prison sentence.

"Jack Franks is one name I want to forget," Killebrew told *Forbes* magazine years later, when Franks surfaced in other financial transgressions. "It was horrible." Oh, and before that, there was a cattle ranch that Killebrew bought late in his playing days that went belly-up.

The story laid it all out there for a curious and disappointed fan base.

At the time he owed at least $700,000 to four banks, Calvin Griffith, and Reggie Jackson. He owed $270,000 on his dream house on 19 acres on top of an Oregon hill when he stopped making the $2,500-a-month payments and the mortgage company foreclosed.

His auto dealership in Ontario, Oregon, and a failed car leasing company in Blooming [Minnesota] pushed him close to bankruptcy. He lived in a rented condominium in Boise, Idaho. He traveled frequently to sign autographs, earning up to $5,000 an appearance. His name, signature, and wholesome image were his most valued capital.

His wife, Elaine, lived in Edina [Minnesota], separated from her husband of nearly 34 years of marriage.

"It's been a living hell. You have a lot of those days when you feel you're at the bottom," Killebrew said in 1989. "You get to feeling that sometimes you're out on an island by yourself. I don't feel anger, more sometimes frustration, sadness is another, loneliness is another one.... Stressful? That's an understatement."

There were family tensions, too. His first born, Cameron, was involved with the leasing company. Son Kenny, 23 at the time, hit a rough patch, ran afoul of the law, and pled guilty in 1982 to a charge of bank robbery. Then there was the separation from Elaine—she cited infidelity, Harmon declined to publicly address any issues—which soon enough led to divorce. It was not the sort of warm, rosy, post-playing life that anyone in the Killebrew household envisioned.

"He had that feeling, 'I was successful in baseball. I can do it again,'" Elaine Killebrew told the Minneapolis newspaper. "He's always been the type of person whose niceness gets him used. He didn't want anybody to be displeased with him."

Killebrew, as you might expect, didn't exactly treat his friends or family like Dr. Phil, opening a vein to reveal his innermost feelings and anxieties. But those who knew him best saw what he was enduring and understood.

"Harm was such an easy guy to take advantage of because he was so trusting," Kaat said. "Growing up—and I came from the same background in the Midwest—you tend to trust people. You think everybody's going to be like your neighbor was growing up, and then you find out you get taken advantage of, and that's what happened to him in a couple of cases."

Ron Manser, the boyhood friend who had gone into auto sales in Payette soon after high school, met Killebrew for a cup of coffee one day. "I was talking to him about the car business—I'd been in it all my life, and he was kind of new to it—and he said, 'Why in the world didn't you tell me how much money it took to operate a car store?' And I said, 'Well, you didn't ask.' Everybody thinks car dealers were making a helluva lot of money, which they weren't," Manser said. "He couldn't make it work, so he had to get out of it."

Kramer had written a sequel book in 1987 called *Distant Replay*, which caught up with many of the Packers players and coaches from his initial effort two decades earlier. What he learned about Killebrew's bad experiences as a former pro athlete out in the real world Kramer had already seen with a few old Packers teammates.

"In sports, you take the measure of a man and say, 'Let's line up and see what you've got,'" Kramer said. "You get to a point where the people you can't trust, they just don't last. So you're dealing only with people who do what they say they're going to do and can do what they say. Then you get out and you're trusting people and depending on people and trusting people to be like the guys you played with. And they aren't."

That seemed to be the widespread reaction to Killebrew's predicament—he was snookered, but he wasn't the one with the dishonest intentions. "All of us have had our setbacks and difficulties, we've all had reversals," Kramer said. "We all understand that that's life. I never held it against someone. Coach [Vince] Lombardi used to say, 'It's not that you never get knocked down in life. It's that you get up every time you get knocked down.' Us country boys, maybe because we didn't have better sense, kept getting up."

Griffith loaned Killebrew $100,000 in 1986 or 1987 to relieve some tax issues with the IRS. Jackson filed a lawsuit, seeking to recover the money Killebrew had borrowed from him. (The two sluggers had struck up a friendship even as they battled for AL home run supremacy in the late 1960s and early '70s—Harmon hit 49 in 1969 to Jackson's 47 and they both went deep at the 1971 All-Star Game.)

"Harmon's been at the bottom of the pit, and he's climbing out of the hole," said Jackson, who coincidentally closed a Chevrolet dealership he owned in the '80s when it spiraled into debt, too. "All he has left is his word, and he wants to keep it."

Killebrew was driven to make things right. He found new sources of income, new projects that didn't rely as much on some outsider's expertise. He launched a premium collection of autographed bats, featuring replicas of the ones he used to hit the milestone home runs of his career, with a price tag in 1989 of $1,495 for the bunch. He appeared on home-shopping channels to sell other mementoes and souvenirs, and he traveled to collectibles shows where a lot of ex-players make their livings nowadays. And as much as he dreaded the stigma of it, Killebrew did file for bankruptcy in 1993.

"Maybe I've made some wrong decisions, but I'm still an honorable person," the former Twins great told reporter Weiner, "and I intend to take care of all of my obligations."

Said Jackson, who reportedly did get the money owed to him, "He's moving in the right direction. His only chance is if people give him a chance."

Baseball had helped to get Killebrew into the position he was in, good and bad. The fame he achieved through it made him a target. The short career it presented him put him back out in the marketplace with time to fill and years to cover. But the game also prepared him, when Killebrew thought of it the right way, for coping with the failures. Pitchers, after all, got him out six or seven times for every 10 he stepped to the plate (career .376 on-base percentage). Killebrew struck out almost three times as often as he hit home runs, a ratio that surely would sting in real life, yet he's remembered much more for the latter than the former.

"I struck out an awful lot—1,699 times," he told the Minneapolis newspaper. "I always bounced back."

One of Killebrew's few home runs in the 1980s traveled farther than most and bounced around the bleachers at Doubleday Field in Cooperstown, N.Y.

Chapter 15

"We're Raising Boys, Not Grass"

As you enter baseball's great cathedral, there are walls of plaques to your left and to your right. Straight ahead, at the far end in the rotunda, are more plaques, featuring the original five—Babe Ruth, Ty Cobb, Honus Wagner, Walter Johnson, Christy Mathewson—from the Class of 1936. More recent classes, starting with this millennium's first inductees, are down there, too.

The alcoves on the left and right are ordered chronologically, starting with the right side, down to the atrium and then along the left. The Class of 1984 is about halfway into the gallery on the left, and that's where Harmon Killebrew's plaque is located, among the best baseball players the game has ever known. There he is, in bronze, looking out from under a familiar cap with a "TC" logo, with a shy smile, a couple of bats, and some garland. Beneath that, there's a concise and permanent resume:

HARMON CLAYTON KILLEBREW
Washington A.L. 1954–60
Minnesota A.L. 1961–74
Kansas City A.L. 1975

Muscular slugger with monumental home run and RBI success. His 573 homers over 22 years rank fifth all-time and second only to Ruth among A.L. hitters. Tied or led A.L. in home runs 6 times, belted over 40 on 8 occasions and is third in home run frequency. Drove in over 100 runs 9 times. A.L. MVP in 1969.

Don Drysdale, the former Dodgers pitching star, is to Killebrew's left. To his right, St. Louis outfielder Lou Brock, inducted in 1985. Catcher Rick Ferrell's plaque is mounted right above Killebrew.

It's a peaceful place of awe and implied exploits in this gallery of honorees at the National Baseball Hall of Fame and Museum in Cooperstown, N.Y. Like ditching the office for a ballpark on a sunny Thursday afternoon in the spring, there isn't a bad spot in the joint. This is baseball's ultimate velvet rope—either you get in or you don't.

But the fact is, had there been a little more smarts applied by Hall voters of the early 1980s, Killebrew might be a whole alcove over, his plaque grouped among an entirely different bunch of immortal neighbors.

It seems hard to fathom now—actually, it was pretty hard to fathom at the time, too—that there was much debate or disagreement over Killebrew's candidacy to the Hall of Fame once his career was over and he had waited the required five years for eligibility. But there were enough skeptics, doubters, and maybe even fools involved in the process that Killebrew whiffed three times before he was finally invited into baseball's shrine. Fortunately for him, "three strikes and yer out" isn't a Cooperstown rule. These were more like at-bats, really, so sticking with the analogy, Harmon's big fly came in his fourth trip to the plate.

Ultimately, like a lot of elections, Killebrew's four-year wait for the Hall says more about voters and the process than about the candidate. It wasn't anything heartbreaking like the 2012 election of former Cubs third baseman Ron Santo, who died on December 3, 2010. It was 36 years after he played his last game, after his long wait on the writers' ballot and deep into his consideration by the Veterans Committee when he was finally accepted in by that committee 367 days after his death at age 70. Others who merited induction have had to wait—Drysdale needed 10 ballots and Luis Aparicio, also part of the 1984 class with Killebrew and Ferrell, waited six. It's just unfortunate that for a while in middle age when the cheering had largely stopped, Killebrew saw several peers head to Cooperstown while he was made to feel as if he'd have to buy a ticket to ever get inside.

Testimonials in favor of his election weren't hard to come by. Rod Carew, his old Twins teammate, said around that time, "Minnesota gave me perspective, peace of mind, really. Tony Oliva taught me. Harmon Killebrew showed me. Here was this big mammoth guy. They called him Killer. So gentle, though. Whether he hit two homers or struck out three times, he handled himself the same way afterward. The only time I think about the Hall of Fame is to think that Harmon Killebrew isn't in it."

Or this from Ron Luciano, an umpire moved by the dignity with which Killebrew did his job, "The Killer was one of the most feared sluggers in baseball history, but he was also one of the nicest people ever to play the game. He was one of the few players who would go out of his way to compliment umpires on a good job, even if their calls went against him. I'd call a tough strike on him, and he would turn around and say approvingly, 'Good call.' And he was the same way in the field. And he never did this to get help on close plays as some players do. The man hit 573 major league home runs, and no umpire ever swung a bat for him."

Testimonials or pedigree weren't going to cut it with the baseball writers who did the voting. A homogenous group demographically with wildly divergent opinions, members of the Baseball Writers Association of America (BWAA) who had served 10 years or longer made this a cantankerous, arguing bunch mindful of regional rivalries and sometimes with limited exposure to those whose famous fates they were determining. This was back in the days before interleague play when the World Series was baseball's only cross-pollination. Television options often were limited to the local club, and a Game of the Week offering in those pre-cable, pre-satellite days. It wasn't easy even for the diehard fans and the diligent writers in an American League city to see a National League star, or vice versa. With the exception of the large markets—New York, Chicago, Los Angeles—cities were limited to one or the other.

Then again, even the eyeball test might not have swayed some voters once they got it into their heads this way or that on a fellow. When Killebrew came on the Hall ballot in 1981, there was as much chatter about his batting average, his strikeouts, his defense, and his foot speed as there was about his home runs, RBIs, walks, or good-guy personality. It continued for three years until it became unnecessary.

Consider this position statement in 1982 from Allen Lewis, a writer and voter from the *Philadelphia Inquirer*, "After each of the last two Hall of Fame elections, there has been an outcry from some quarters over the failure of Harmon Killebrew to garner enough votes for election. On the other hand, I find it hard to understand how he was given 239 votes in 1981 and 246 this year, the latter total only 65 shy of the necessary 75 percent of the ballots cast.

"It would seem that too many voters are overly impressed by only one or two statistics when preparing to vote. In Killebrew's case, it is his 1,584 RBIs and his 573 home runs, a total that puts him fifth on the all-time list. Other than those figures, Killebrew did little to merit being in the Hall, although he was a friendly, cooperative person who was liked by all.... Killebrew, a husky 6', 200-pounder in his prime, couldn't run, couldn't field, and never hit for average. He spent his career moving back and forth from third base, first base, and left field as his eight managers with the Senators, Twins, and Royals tried in vain to hide him in a spot where he would do the least damage defensively while still supplying homers and driving in runs."

Lewis went on for a while, criticizing Killebrew's lifetime .256 batting average, his yearly hit totals, and his inability to crack .290, never mind .300, in a season. "Had Killebrew come along 20 years later, he probably would have spent his entire career as a designated hitter. I hope the Hall of Fame is never tarnished by a player who was nothing more than a DH."

It was true about Killebrew's batting average and hits, and he wasn't a fast runner. He did get moved around defensively more than just about any Hall of Famer, but capability and cooperation had something to do with that. But that dismissal of his power numbers made Lewis look silly, certainly in hindsight.

Other veteran baseball writers, such as feisty Dick Young in New York and Joe Falls in Detroit, backed Killebrew from the start, figuring he did one thing—one mighty thing—better than all but four people who had ever played the game by the time he retired. Wrote Falls in June 1982, "He hit more home runs than Mickey Mantle, Jimmie Foxx, Ted Williams, Ernie Banks, Mel Ott, Lou Gehrig, and Stan Musial. Yet he can come into my town, as he did recently as a telecaster with the Oakland A's, and go into the press room and order dinner and sit down there by himself and eat in silence, with nobody even aware he was there. He is a very quiet, polite, and shy man, and I just hope this doesn't work against him.... If 3,000 hits is the magic number for the hitters and 300 victories the magic number for the pitchers, why shouldn't 500 home runs be the same for the sluggers?"

Killebrew, though, was no one-issue candidate. The years during which he played were the second coming of baseball's dead-ball era. Pitchers, until his final seasons, were dominant. Runs were hard to come by. In 1966, the year Harmon turned 30, AL teams averaged 3.89 runs per game. By 1982, the second year he was kept out of the Hall, that was up to 4.48. That was an extra half-run available every night per team. Context always shifted like that in baseball, one reason the BBWAA kept players on the Hall ballot for 15 years, allowing for fresh looks and new perspectives.

Killebrew, for instance, looks better to modern voters who give him more credit for his batting eye. That .256 batting average jumps to a .376 on-base percentage when his 1,559 walks are folded in. He ranked seventh all-time in drawing walks when he retired after the 1975 season and is still 15th, compared to his before/after move on the all-time strikeout list (from second behind Mickey Mantle to a mere 24th now).

Let's not forget, either, the glut of all-time great players who walked the earth during Killebrew's career, not just Hall of Fame–worthy but those among the game's truly elite. "There are any number of players now who are as good as anyone has ever been," Roger Angell of *The New Yorker* wrote in the early 1970s. Those were the guys he had to compete against. Those were the guys vying for votes around the same time on the Hall ballots.

In 1981, only Cardinals pitching great Bob Gibson got voted in, receiving 84.0 percent of the vote (337 of 401). Killebrew was fourth, his 239 votes leaving him 62 shy of the 301 he needed (a candidate needs to be named on 75 percent of ballots cast, with writers allowed to vote for up to 10 players). Drysdale was second, Gil Hodges was third (Hodges would never get in via the writers' ballot).

In 1982, Hank Aaron and Frank Robinson breezed in on their first ballots. Aaron was named on 406 of 415 ballots—it makes you wonder what those other nine guys were thinking, doesn't it?—for 97.8 percent, and Robinson pulled 89.2 percent with 370 votes. Juan Marichal was third, seven votes short of the 312 he needed. Killebrew was fourth with 246.

In 1983, it was Brooks Robinson's turn for instant induction, getting 344 votes on 374 ballots for 92 percent. Marichal made it this time, too, with 313 votes (83.7 percent) in his third try. Killebrew placed third, a dozen votes shy of the 281 he needed.

By that point, the wait and the frustration were getting to him a little. "Naturally I'm disappointed. Not bitter, just disappointed," he told a reporter who contacted him in Boise. "I certainly was hopeful this might be the year. I think I'm more disappointed this year than in the past."

Like others who had fallen short, Killebrew started to focus on the flaws in the BBWAA's system. "One of the things that concerns me is that maybe some of the writers have not seen some of the players play, maybe some don't use all the votes they can, and maybe some vote for somebody who was a friend," he said. "I think they should vote exactly on what the players' stats show. Another thing I'm thinking is that radio and TV people see the players day in and day out; maybe they should be included in the voting. I think I agree with what Don Drysdale said last year, that it's not the Baseball Hall Fame, it's the Baseball Writers' Hall of Fame."

Drysdale finished sixth with 242 votes, one vote behind relief ace Hoyt Wilhelm. Like frustrated Hall of Famers who were made to wait in future years, such as Bert Blyleven and Jim Rice, Killebrew wondered what he could do to convince any voter who wasn't already convinced. "Well, I'm not going to hit another home run in my life," he said. "What I've done is either enough or it isn't enough."

In congratulating Brooks Robinson, Harmon inadvertently might have touched on something that linked the two men and their candidacies. "He took a lot of hits away from me," Killebrew said of the slick-fielding Baltimore third baseman.

In the winter of 1984, Killebrew was said to be unusually quiet as the Hall's announcement day approached. He was at home in Ontario that afternoon when the phone rang, with BBWAA secretary-treasurer Jack Lang on the other end from New York. This time the news was good. Very good.

"[Harmon] began to talk about all the things he had to do before taking the plane to New York," Lang said afterward. "I told him, 'Harmon, the first thing you have to do is kiss your wife.' He was off the phone for about five minutes. I thought we had been disconnected. When he got back on, his voice was hoarse.

"'I'm okay now,' he said. 'I couldn't talk for a while.'"

Drysdale, Sandy Koufax's sidekick with the Dodgers and the pitcher Killebrew hit his World Series homer against in 1965, was going in, too. So was Aparicio, a shortstop for Chicago, Baltimore, and Boston who seemed to single-handedly keep the stolen base alive for many of his 18 years in the AL. Wilhelm was the one with his nose and his knuckleball pressed against the Cooperstown glass, though he was at the head of the Class of 1985.

Several of Killebrew's friends from the Twins shared their thoughts after hearing the news:

Calvin Griffith: "If our fans knew Harmon was coming up in the ninth inning, they never left the ball game, no matter what the score was. He hit home runs like few people can in the category of height and distance. Harmon didn't hit many line-drive home runs. He would hit the ball so blooming high in the sky, they were just like a rocket ship going up in the air.... Today, a Harmon Killebrew would command well upward of $2 million plus per year. He'd put Dave Winfield's contract to shame." (Winfield had landed a deal with the Yankees before the 1981 season worth a reported $21 million over 10 years.)

Zoilo Versalles: After noting that he tried to copy Killebrew's home run stroke, "Then I said forget it, there's no way.... Killebrew was an unusual player because when he hit the ball, it looked like it was inside the ballpark. The only way you knew it was a home run was when you'd see the outfielder go back and back and back."

Tony Oliva: "If I was a pitcher, I would have been scared because whenever he was up, there was a chance the ball would disappear."

Years later, Killebrew reflected on the impact of Lang's phone call. "He said, 'From this moment on, your life will never be the same.' It really didn't sink in as to exactly what Jack meant when he said that, but I've grown to understand that a lot more over the years. When they put 'HOF' behind your name, it's something magical.... I'm very proud of that and still don't believe it and can't believe that I deserve it... but it's something that has been wonderful."

Killebrew didn't need the Hall of Fame's validation or seal of approval to elevate his career and accomplishments. But it was a special honor all the same and would open up a new world to him. From a practical standpoint, it boosted his value in the marketplace as a speaker and as an autograph signer at collectibles shows. The demand for and asking prices of Hall of Famers can be several times what it is for members left in the Hall of the Very Good. For a fellow looking to move from red ink to black and dig out of crippling debt, it would prove to be helpful.

More than that, though, Killebrew blossomed as a Hall of Famer, truly enjoying the camaraderie, the ability to reunite every year with his peers for induction ceremonies and old stories at the stately Otesaga Resort Hotel. Nothing can make a ballplayer—regardless of how super his stardom might have been in his prime—feel like he's just passing through something much greater than himself than a stroll through the exhibits and gallery at Cooperstown.

Jeff Idelson, the president of the Hall, said in 2011 that Killebrew and Brooks Robinson acted as if they felt a special responsibility to the shrine and the game. In return, they often seemed to generate the most enthusiastic responses from the crowds that descended on each induction.

Jane Forbes Clark, chairman of the Hall of Fame, talked upon his death about Killebrew as an ambassador for the Cooperstown set. "Since joining the Hall of Fame family in 1984," Clark said, "Harmon was a beacon of light among his fellow Hall of Famers, always smiling, always enjoying every moment that life delivered at his doorstep. We have so many fond memories of this wonderful baseball hero, and we will miss him enormously."

So it took Killebrew three extra years to get in. Looking back across three decades, that means...not much. Sometimes the players who don't get in right away get more attention while they're waiting anyway. The bottom line was that Killebrew was 47 when he got elected—still a young man—and 48 when he stepped to the microphone on the front steps of the Hall library on that Sunday in August. He got to enjoy that status for the final 27 years of his life, five years longer than the baseball career that got him there. Not a bad bargain.

Here is Killebrew's Hall induction speech in its entirety, as he gave it on August 12, 1984:

Thank you, Commissioner. I don't know, I was used as a clean-up hitter a few times, but this is the toughest clean-up hitting I've ever done. To follow guys like Rick Ferrell and Don Drysdale and Pee Wee Reese, Luis Aparicio. This is a tough job. Commissioner, inductees, honored guests, families, ladies and gentlemen and friends—and I do mean friends, because if you weren't a friend of baseball you wouldn't be out there today and we're very thankful that you could join us: Thank you very much.

I was born and raised in a little town in Idaho called Payette, and when I was eight years old, my father gave me my first baseball glove. He was a great athlete. He played football for James Milliken University in Illinois, and then he played at West Virginia Wesleyan under the great Greasy

Neale, who not only was the great football coach for the Philadelphia Eagles but he also played baseball for the Cincinnati Reds. And it was through my father's insistence and persuasion, I guess, to insist that I participate in sports, not only in baseball but in football and basketball and a little track, that I became acquainted with this great American pastime.

I grew up in this small town in Idaho, and my father used to like to go to the movies, and I'll never forget that a lot of times on warm summer evenings like this my father would take my brother, Bob, and I to the movies and then after the movie was over he would race us home. He'd always win. He was a man that took a great deal of pride in his children. I'll never forget, we used to play a lot of ball out in the front yard and my mother would say, "You're tearing up the grass and digging holes in the front yard," and my father would say, "We're not raising grass here, we're raising boys." Harmon Clayton Killebrew Sr. would be very proud today, and I wish he were here. And somehow I know he is. Believe me, I know he is.

Excuse me. I don't know how these fellows ahead of me kept from being too emotional because to me this is an emotional experience. There's another person that I wish to thank today that's still living in that small town in Idaho. She's 89 years old, and that's my mother, Katherine. She encouraged me with the unique great attitude about life and she couldn't be here today, but my awe at her in a very special way and thank her for, I really thank her for, my very being. And I would also like to thank my brothers, Gene and Bob, and my sister, Eula, who encouraged me in my early formative years when I was growing up. But there's a certain blonde girl from Idaho that's here today that encouraged me about as much as anyone else and she's still doing that. She's here today, and I'd like to introduce her, my wife Elaine.

I'm also very proud of my family, and many of them traveled from great distances to be here with their spouses and I'd also like to introduce them. My son, Cam, his wife, Monica, and their son, Todd. Todd's a little sleepy right now, but he's there. They came from Austria to be with us. My son, Ken, came from Seattle. Ken, I'm glad you're here. My daughter, Shawn, and her husband, Rick, came from England. Kathy and her husband, Scott, came from Scottsdale to be with us. And the baby of the family, Erin, will be a sophomore at Brigham Young University this fall. I'm glad they're here to enjoy this great experience.

I've also got so many friends here that came for many, many miles to be with us here on this great occasion. My two business partners, Ralph Harding and Doug Harper. I'm glad that they could make it. They've been great supporters since my retirement from the game of baseball. I started playing baseball at eight years old. Not organized, of course, because in those days we didn't have the great Little League programs that produce such great baseball players as we have today, but we had what they call Knothole Baseball, and then I played five years of American Legion baseball and, of course, in high school. I played some semipro ball before I started to play professionally. And I want to thank those teammates in those years that I played with, at least one of them is here today, because they gave me a great deal of help, too, in those early years.

If you'll permit me, I'd like to tell a story that I've told on many occasions but I think you'll realize why I'm telling this story. I talk to a lot of major league scouts like all these gentlemen up here have talked to over their formative years, and I had decided to play baseball and football at the University of Oregon. And we had a United States Senator from my home town by the name of Herman Welker, and Herman Welker was a great friend of Clark Griffith of baseball, and he used to go out to old Griffith Stadium a lot. And he told Mr. Griffith about a young boy out in Idaho he thought could hit the ball pretty well, and I think more than anything else, just to keep Senator Welker quiet, Mr. Griffith sent Ossie Bluege out to see me who was the farm director of the Washington club at that particular time. A former great third baseman with Washington. And Mr. Bluege came out to that little town in Idaho. He rented a car in Boise, Idaho, and drove through the rain 60 miles to that little town, and it didn't look like we were going to play the ballgame that day, it had rained very hard.

And I'll never forget that I sat in Mr. Bluege's car and we talked about going to Washington, that the club wanted me to work out with them, and I said, "Well, I really appreciated that, but I was going to play football and baseball at the University of Oregon," and we talked and the skies cleared. And the townspeople there, knowing that a major league scout was there, hurriedly got the field in order, and we played that ballgame that night. And that night I happened to hit a ball over the left-field fence, and I'd been going to that ballpark since I was a small boy and never had seen anyone hit a ball over that left-field fence. It was over 408 feet down the left-field line, and no one that I can recall had ever hit one over there in previous years. And when I hit one that night, Mr. Bluege went out the next morning and stepped it off and he immediately called Mr. Griffith, and he said it was 435 feet or so in a beet field—not a potato patch—and he thought that was a pretty good hit for a 17-year-old boy from Idaho.

He left a contract in Senator Welker's law office and went back to Washington, and I talked that over with my older brother. My father had passed away by then, and my mother decided that baseball was what I wanted to do with my life and so I signed the contract. And it was so… it was through the recommendation of Ossie Bluege that I am standing here this day. Mr. Bluege is here, and I would like to recognize him. Thank you, Ossie.

I'll never forget joining the ballclub in Chicago and I'd never seen a major league ballgame before, and the second day I was there they put me in as a pinch runner if you can believe it. I got to first base and Walter Dropo was playing first and he was about, looked like he was—at least to me—he looked like he was 9 feet tall. Nellie Fox was at second. I happened to get to second base, though I can't remember how I got there, and before Luis Aparicio they had another Latin American shortstop with the White Sox, Chico Carrasquel, he was a shortstop. And I was beginning to wonder what in the world I was doing there with those fellows.

Well, I stayed with that ballclub for a couple of years, and then I went to the minor leagues and then finally one spring, I happened to be playing a little third base. And of course in those days Washington had a great third baseman by the name of Eddie Yost, and it took a trade of Eddie Yost to the Tigers to give me an opportunity to play at least, or a chance to play, but that in itself really didn't do it. In the spring of '59 at the insistence of one man, who at that time took over the running of the Washington ballclub, Calvin Griffith, I was inserted in the lineup at third base. Opening day I hit a home run and as the commissioner told you I hit one the last day of the season to tie Colavito for my first home run championship. And Calvin Griffith is here today, and I certainly want to recognize the fact that I appreciate Mr. Griffith insisting that I be put in that lineup. Calvin, thank you very much. Calvin's been a credit to baseball in the American League and I, for one, and I know many, many people, are going to miss you when you are no longer in baseball. Thank you.

One of my great heroes in baseball was Ted Williams, and I'll never forget, I wish Ted was here today, I'll never forget Ted saying to me, "You know it's a shame that you didn't grow up in California where the weather was great. Maybe you could have been a better hitter." Well, maybe I could have been a better hitter, Ted, if I'd have grown up in California, but I'll tell you one thing, I'm thankful that I grew up in the great state of Idaho and for the great people in the state of Idaho that have supported me over the years. What a wonderful place to be born and raised. Many people from Idaho are here today, and I'm happy to see them here.

I was extremely appreciative when the Minnesota organization moved to, or the Griffith organization moved to Minnesota from Washington, although I was apprehensive about it because I loved to play in Washington. Those were great years playing for the Washington Senators. But I quickly learned that Minnesota was my kind of place, and the fans there were my kind of people and are my kind of people.

We enjoyed some great years in Minnesota. We had some great ballclubs, at least four former Minnesota Twins that I played with are here today. A couple of them were on the 1965 pennant-winning ballclub that we played against. A couple of these guys that are up here, Koufax and Drysdale. Jim Kaat and Bob Allison are here today, and I want to thank them for being here with me. I think I'd be remiss if I didn't thank all the teammates that I played with over the years because you certainly can't get here by yourself and I thank you.

I thank all the managers that I played for over my career. From Bucky Harris, who was my first manager, right on down the line to Dressen, Lavagetto, Mele, Ermer, Bill Rigney, Quilici, McKeon, Herzog, they were all great. They helped me tremendously. Although I didn't finish my career at Minnesota, I played my last year at Kansas City; I thank the Kansas City Royals organization, too. They're great. Mr. Kauffman, I thank you for the opportunity of playing with the Royals. I'm especially proud today to be here to take part in the last official act of our great commissioner, Bowie Kuhn. In my book, an excellent job well done, and I for one will certainly miss him running this ship. A great man and he's been great for baseball. Thank you, Bowie.

I'm thankful for the ability that my father in heaven gave me to play baseball, or I wouldn't be here today. I'm thankful to be honored in such a special way by a group of individuals that do an outstanding job, the Baseball Writers of America. Thank you for honoring me. I'm thankful to the Baseball Hall of Fame for this opportunity of being here and it's a special treat to me to go in with this special group that's going into the Hall of Fame this year. Rick Ferrell, Don Drysdale, Pee Wee Reese, Luis Aparicio.

I'm delighted. I love baseball, and I consider this baseball's greatest honor. Thank you very much.

Chapter 16

Back in the Game

Estranged would be too strong a word. That word is better reserved for personal matters, family, relationships, kids, divorce—the emotional stuff Harmon Killebrew went through the same as anyone else, real life playing out away from his talent and career in the major leagues. No, what crept in between him and the team for which he starred was more of a distance, a chill, the result of inattention and different directions and probably an awkwardness that just made it a little harder each day for anyone to pick up the phone or take the first step.

Finally, Dave St. Peter picked up the phone. The Minnesota Twins reached out to Killebrew, and Killebrew quickly reached back.

"From an organization's perspective, we felt there was, on some level, a responsibility to work to at least patch up that relationship, even though this predated me," said St. Peter, the Twins president who worked as the team's communications manager back in the 1990s, when this healing began. "I felt very, very strongly that our organization, frankly, needed a relationship with Harmon. And I like to think Harmon needed a relationship with the Twins.

"I think he symbolized everything about our franchise, and specifically the introduction of major league baseball to the Upper Midwest starting in 1961. He was really in many ways the first star on the Minnesota scene, and I think in that respect, his legacy, his brand so to speak, was very, very important in terms of our fan base."

Playing their games in a football stadium, stuck indoors on plastic grass under a Teflon sky, the Twins had missed out on the nostalgia kick MLB teams went through, building and moving into beautiful throwback ballparks that stirred memories of all those father-son or mother-daughter baseball moments. Minnesota had gone to two World Series and won them both during the first half of Killebrew's retirement. It even had distinguished itself with a hustling, defense-first, fundamentally sound brand of "Twins baseball" famous for its follow-through from Class A right to the big leagues.

But embracing its legends, restoring and strengthening the links across generations of Twins clubs, reaching back to the Calvin Griffith/Met Stadium era never seemed to be a top priority. St. Peter got things moving, with the blessing of the Pohlad family that owned the franchise, and it wasn't long before the team's staff directory had a listing for "special assistants," the title given to Rod Carew, Kent Hrbek, Paul Molitor, Tony Oliva, and Killebrew.

"People wanted to have a chance to interact with Harmon," St. Peter said when asked specifically about the slugger, "and ultimately to know that he was part of the organization. Over time, I learned how important it was to Harmon. He was very appreciative and often articulated that directly to me, about how great it felt for him to be back as part of the Twins. He took a lot of personal pride and pleasure in seeing the organization return to prominence throughout the... really, 2001 on, in terms of many postseason appearances, MVPs, Cy Youngs, and batting championships. He was very involved with our club and really was an ambassador in every sense of the word."

Mind you, the Twins had always had bits and pieces of Killebrew around, remnants of their many years together. They had photos, clippings, and documents ranging from the telegram that announced his signing by the Washington Senators as a 17-year-old unknown out in Idaho to the notes he typed and scribbled on his Hall of Fame speech 30 years later. Thanks to Clyde Doepner, the team's official curator—"Clyde the Collector," he calls himself—they had the bat with which he clubbed the final home run of his career (No. 573 off Eddie Bane) and the traveling bag he used for years, its bottom perforated from countless days and nights dropping his spikes in first and packing heavy items on top of them.

"I've got his Hartland statue and the original box it came in," Doepner said one afternoon in 2011, on an informal tour of Target Field and its troves of Killebrew treasures that had made the move to their third ballpark. Hartland action figures are highly sought collectibles, a series of baseball stars produced in the late 1950s to early '60s. "The irony is Harmon and Nellie Fox were the two lower-end stars back then, so they're the ones that didn't sell as much. Well, because of rarity, they're the two most expensive ones, more than Babe Ruth, more than Hank Aaron, more than Ted Williams.

"I have a lot of different bats—he hit the longest home run in the history of Met Stadium, and I have the bat he hit it with. It lasted for 27 days, and when he finally broke it, they used it to stir the pine tar—it was just thick with pine tar—because they said maybe some 'Harmon' would come off it. And little stories like that are just what makes it all worthwhile.

They had Killebrew stuff but, for that stretch of a decade or so after he stopped broadcasting, the Twins did not have Killebrew. Until St. Peter invited him back to be part of the team's forever family. It started small—an early-season series against Detroit in 1997, the Kirby Puckett jersey-retirement party a month after that, then as a guest at the 20-year reunion of the '87 Twins team. "It's nice to be back on occasion," he said that spring. "It's been a few years now." Then it grew. Soon, Killebrew was making promotional appearances for the club, joining the players and coaches in Ft. Myers, Florida, for spring training and, sure enough, moving from talking about "Twins baseball" and slipping back to speaking of the organization from "they" to "we."

"I thought that was really cool that day to see him in my office, shaking my hand and telling me he was so excited to be on the field," said Ron Gardenhire, who took over as Twins field manager in 2002. Gardenhire stepped in after Tom Kelly, the winningest (1,140–1,244, two World Series championships) and longest-serving manager in team history (1986–2001), stepped down. Gardenhire would top the seniority chart of MLB managers, too, posting an 866–755 record with six AL playoff appearances in his first 10 seasons.

"That was as great a moment as you can have as a manager, knowing you rubbed elbows with Harmon Killebrew," Gardenhire said. "We want our players to emulate him. There aren't too many people who met Harmon and walked away disappointed. He means everything to the organization."

Pitcher Scott Baker met Killebrew in 2004 while working his way up through the farm system. "More than anything, guys are just happy to see him and happy to know him," Baker said a few years later. "He means a lot to this organization, and he's fun to be around. He always has a smile on his face. It didn't matter if you just got called up or if you were 15 years in the big leagues. He treated everybody the same."

Killebrew's presence was felt across several generations of Twins. Randy Bush, an outfielder with the club from 1982 to 1993, remembered his trip back to the Metrodome for a Series-team reunion in 1997, soon after Minnesota had drafted a young power hitter named Michael Restovich in the second round of the amateur draft. Bush's best friend was Paul Mainieri, the baseball coach at Notre Dame (later LSU) who was trying to recruit Restovich to college, and he asked Bush to give a little sales pitch as a favor. "I said, 'I'm going to do it. When I see Restovich, I'll tell him it worked out well for me to go to college,' and I'll give him the scoop," Bush recalled.

At the Metrodome that weekend, Bush was talking with a group of people—including Killebrew—when a Twins staffer walked in with Restovich in tow. Said Bush, "I'm thinking, 'Perfect, I'll get to talk to Michael Restovich, this will be great.' He comes walking over and—before I say a word—Harmon grabs him and says, 'Michael, my name is Harmon Killebrew. Nice to meet you! You're a good, strong-looking young man—when am I going to see you out on that field out there in a Twins uniform? We need you out there!' He lays it on like nothing you have ever heard. Restovich signs with the Twins, like, two days later."

There was the time Tim Laudner, catcher on the 1987 champs and for nine Twins seasons, hopped aboard a small twin-engine plane with Killebrew to speak and play in a golf fund-raiser at a tiny parochial school in Watertown, South Dakota, as a courtesy to a priest who was friends with the Pohlads. After the golf and a meal, there was a Q&A session with some students. "One little kid raised his hand and asked me, 'What was it like to be a major league player?'" Laudner remembered. "I said, 'Matter of fact, it's been so long since I played that sometimes I've forgotten.' But I tried to answer the question best as I could. Well, it wasn't two or three minutes after we left the kids that Harmon came up to me. He grabbed me with those paws of his, right around my upper arms, he pulls me close and he says, 'Hey, what you told those kids about not being able to remember much about being a player?'—he goes in all seriousness—'I feel like that, too.'

"And I'm thinking, 'Wait a minute, here's a guy who's a Hall of Famer, 573 good flies, whose career went into the 20-year mark...' There were certain instances whether you were a two-year journeyman or a 20-year player, there's still a commonality that, for whatever reason, Harmon was able to bridge the gap just like *that*."

This was a two-way reconnection. The Twins got the benefit of Killebrew's wisdom, popularity, and personality, but he got a lot in the bargain, too. Like so many who spend their time around younger people, Killebrew—he had turned 60 in 1996—felt younger for the experience. A win-win was awfully nice at that point in his left.

"I think in some ways over the last 15 years of Harmon's life, you know that was a pretty special gift that he gave to our organization," Laudner said. "For a new generation of Twins that had the chance to interact with him—not even so much on the field but in the clubhouse, in the dugout—just how to deal with failure, how to deal with success, how to deal with a manager, a beat reporter, with people in general... how to be a man, and how to wear that Twins uniform with pride. I think we were very fortunate to have him and, frankly, other alumni in spring training."

No mere back-in-my-day old-timer, Killebrew anchored his tales and advice in the "now" so modern Twins could apply it. When he befriended veteran slugger Jim Thome after he joined the Twins for the 2010 season, Killebrew promptly put the new guy at ease. Thome, after all, arrived with 564 career home runs and figured to surpass Harmon's 573 total and bump him from Major League Baseball's top 10 while wearing a Twins uniform, with Minnesota fans cheering him on. It could have been awkward. It wasn't.

"I told him, 'Don't feel bad if you pass me up because I passed up a lot of guys in my career,' Killebrew said, and he cheered right with the others on July 3 when Thome took sole possession of 10th place with his second HR of the game off Tampa Bay's Wade Davis.

Another piece of Killebrew's baseball legacy was taken from him—good-naturedly, even amusingly—in a quirky episode stretching back 40 years, thanks to some anniversary attention focused on the MLB logo. You've seen the image a thousand times—a simple silhouette in red, white, and blue, a batter at the ready, bat held high, locked and loaded as a pitch arrives. Killebrew had been rumored to be the model for the design, making him baseball's equivalent to Jerry West, the NBA legend whose tiny dribbling self was turned into that league's logo. In fact, "Logo" became one of West's nicknames in his later years, an instant reminder of the lofty perch he occupied in NBA annals.

The timing of the MLB logo's commission—1968, in anticipation of the game's centennial celebration—seemed right, with Killebrew headed toward his MVP season. Also, he had recalled being in the commissioner's office when they were marking up a draft of the logo and noticing a photograph of himself among the artists' materials. Innocently enough, Killebrew told and retold the story. "It did look like me," he told ESPN.com in a 2008 interview. "The only change was the angle of the bat. They changed that to kind of make it fit more into the design."

Four decades passed before Killebrew and everyone else learned the truth—he wasn't the inspiration, at least not alone. He was introduced over the phone to Jerry Dior, the graphic artist who drew the original sketch. Dior said he used photographs of several different batters and couldn't even remember if Killebrew's image was among them. "He asked me if I was sure and I said yes," Dior said of their conversation in an ESPN.com story. "It was a great phone call."

The design *is* as simple as it is iconic, and the silhouette can be seen as representing either a right- or left-handed batter. The MLB's official stance: "No one player has ever been identified as the model of the 1969 Major League Baseball logo."

And that's about as controversial as Killebrew ever got when it came to his baseball career.

That's not the case for more modern players, though, and being back in the game—more so than at any previous point in Killebrew's retirement—meant facing some of baseball's thornier issues. Steroids was one that hit especially close to home as the all-natural power hitters of Killebrew's vintage, as well as those who played before and for a decade or two after, got crowded by a rush of brawnier types.

Sluggers of yore might not have always looked like the greatest athletes—suddenly, they were built like superheroes and changing the numbers in baseball's record books like prices at the gas pump. In 1950, the start of the decade in which Killebrew made his big league debut, the 500 Home Run Club had just three members (Ruth, Foxx, Ott); Chuck Klein's 300 was good for No. 10 on the all-time list, and the player who ranked No. 25, Bill Dickey, had hit 202. By 2000, confessed steroids abuser Jose Canseco was at No. 25 with 431. Mark McGwire, who had broken in as Canseco's Oakland teammate, had already cracked the 500 Club with 522 and counting.

At that point, 15 players in major league history, spanning a century or more, had hit 500 home runs in their careers. During the next 10 years—from 2000 to 2010—another 10 sluggers crossed that threshold. Most of them—Sammy Sosa, Rafael Palmeiro, Manny Ramirez, Alex Rodriguez, and of course Barry Bonds—got there while testing positive for performance-enhancing drugs, acknowledged using them, or at minimum were swamped by circumstantial evidence that they had used PEDs. Only Thome, Ken Griffey Jr., and Eddie Murray gained entry without generating allegations or speculation that they had broken rules, possibly laws, and stomped on the sense of history and sportsmanship that had linked baseball's previous generations.

Power stats inflated like banana republic currency, and Killebrew—rarely a cynic about much of anything—cast a critical eye toward those whom he felt cheated the game, past sluggers, and himself. "It's a dark cloud over baseball. Anything that hurts baseball, I'm saddened by," he said in the thick of it. "I just hope that Manny Ramirez being suspended for 50 games [in 2009] sends a message to the other players that if you are using that stuff you better stop because more than likely you are going to get caught."

A threat even more near and dear to Killebrew's heart came in 2001 and 2002 when the Twins started to be talked of as a contraction target for MLB. The franchise's financial woes were severe, the result of a vicious circle of poor performance, meager attendance, low revenue, and a lousy ballpark that for an uncomfortable time nearly turned into a death spiral. Maybe, commissioner Bud Selig and the game's powers-that-be mused, the simplest solution would be to smite Minnesota and Montreal from the scene entirely.

Killebrew was agitated. It would be bad enough losing the franchise with which he had so recently, so happily, become re-acquainted. It would be worse to have his achievements, as he saw it, wiped from baseball's living record—would people have to drop by Clyde Doepner's house to know that he had ever played, that the Twins had ever existed?

"It gave me a sick feeling," Killebrew said. "I was very disappointed that a ballclub that had such a tremendous history and won, not so long ago, the world's championship could be eliminated. I would feel like a guy without a country if there was no baseball in Minnesota. There's no more Washington Senators where I played, and if they eliminate the Minnesota Twins, I don't know what happens to my history.... [The franchise] history is about a hundred years old. So for that to happen would be, I think, just a terrible, terrible thing."

The arc of Killebrew's career had taken him through other rough times and milestones. Racial inequity was one. He had seen teammates turned away from restaurants or refused admittance to hotels where white players stayed. Labor relations were another—Marvin Miller arrived during Harmon's career to lead the baseball players' union, transforming it into arguably the most powerful union in America,

Teamsters included. Free agency became a reality as Killebrew was exiting; the pay structure that exploded after that might not have prevented his money woes in the 1980s, but it surely would have eased them.

Killebrew was no fan of what Pete Rose brought upon the game, either, with his lifetime ban for gambling and endless arrogant denials. Nor was he persuaded in 2004 when Charlie Hustle finally admitted to the allegations—as a way to boost book sales after 14 years of claiming he was clean. "The timing wasn't very good," said Killebrew, active in the Hall of Fame Veterans Committee (Rose was deemed ineligible for Cooperstown consideration at the time). "I think it was probably more detrimental to him than if he hadn't said anything. If he'd [admitted] it immediately 14 years ago when everything started, said, 'Gee, I don't know what I was thinking,' he'd probably be in the Hall of Fame."

Killebrew had one more baseball crusade that really was his alone. But it was one, too, that delighted fans who hoped someday, years into the future, to gaze upon the baseball they'd gotten signed in a special moment with a favorite star—and to be able to actually read the name written on the ball. Taking care with an autograph, that simple, even silly request that players and fans alike have turned into big business, became a pet cause of his.

Twins outfielder Michael Cuddyer wrote about his Killebrew-triggered moment of clarity in 2011 for the website of the team's regional sports network and told his tale again at the slugger's memorial service at Target Field. In the winter of 2005, the outfielder participated on the team's Winter Caravan promotional tour, with a particular stop in Mankato, Minnesota, about 75 southwest of Minneapolis. After a dinner and some questions from the audience, the current and former Twins on board faced a line of maybe 1,000 fans seeking autographs.

"We were about a third of the way through the line," Cuddyer wrote, "when I heard, from one of the tables, Harmon ask someone about an autograph he didn't recognize. Now at that time, I didn't have the prettiest of signatures. As a matter of fact, it was downright awful. It was pretty reminiscent of an EKG that you would get from one of your physicals. You could make out the 'M' and the 'C' but after that it could have been Miley Cyrus who signed your ball, for all you knew.

"Harmon [walked over and] told me that if he saw this ink spot go through the line again, he was going to walk away and stop signing. The only person the people would have been mad at if Harmon had stopped signing was me. From that moment on, I have made it a point to sign my autograph so fans can actually read it. Every single autograph I have signed since then, I have heard Harmon in my head saying, 'If you are going to take the time to sign your name, you better make sure people can read it.'"

The tale became another amusing part of Killebrew's legacy—the stickler for legible signatures. One glimpse at his and people immediately understood why: Elegant, forceful, with an upstroke flourish at the end and always readable. No guesswork required, no scribbling involved. The Twins reminded their fans at Target Field after Harmon's death by displaying his classic autograph, XXXL-sized, on the wall in right-center for the balance of the 2011 season.

Other Twins—Torii Hunter, Justin Morneau, Joe Mauer—could relate similar lessons by the end. There was the day Killebrew stood behind the batting cage at the Metrodome, for instance, watching as Mauer—three-time AL batting champ, 2009 MVP—smacked line drives, one after another, to all fields. "Your swing is perfect, Joe," Killebrew said. "Now work on that autograph."

Sometimes Killebrew's advice went deeper. After Morneau's 2008 season ended in disappointment both for the Twins (failed shot at the playoffs) and himself (late-season slump), he reluctantly answered the phone one day to hear, "Hi Justin, it's Harmon Killebrew." Said the 2006 AL MVP (who had batted .300 with 23 HR and 129 RBIs in 2008). "He knew I was down after we lost. He knew I blamed myself for everything, and he just told me, 'It was a great year. You did a great job. Don't worry about what didn't happen.' That was pretty cool. He's probably the nicest Hall of Famer you'll ever meet."

Killebrew talked again with Morneau the following spring, suggesting a few adjustments at the plate. Morneau didn't hesitate to test them out, moving closer to the plate before later stepping back to his old stance. "If he told me to stand with my back facing the pitcher, I'd try it because he's got 573 homers," Morneau said. "He obviously knew what he was doing. So I definitely tried it. I just feel comfortable with what I'm doing."

Killebrew had other lessons for young Twins, if they cared to listen. He never was one to force anything, but if they chatted him up or stayed within earshot, they invariably would pick up observations and tidbits similar to what Harmon dropped one day on a St. Paul reporter:

- "I wasn't grumpy after a loss.… You should try to keep the peaks and valleys not too high and not too low. I've tried to pass that along to a lot of players. Some listen. Some don't."
- "Not a whole lot makes me angry. I don't get easily angered. Early on, I got some good instruction from my father and probably got some good genes from him, too.… He said, 'Don't let people try to get you to lose your composure. Keep a cool head. If they get the best of you, they can beat you at anything.'"
- "There's something inside a player that makes them either try to excel, or they don't. Why do some players get to a certain point and don't improve? Desire is the thing. I had the desire to excel."
- "What's the best day of my life? I try to make every day the best day."

Killebrew had a bunch of best days at this senior point in his life—some through the reconnection with the Twins, some simply from his status as one of baseball's all-time greats and the satisfaction of enduring so much while motoring along. In 2001, he was one in a group of legends invited to the White House to celebrate the start of that baseball season. Fellow Twins Kirby Puckett and Dave Winfield were along, too, to visit with President George W. Bush, a former owner of the Texas Rangers and a pal who knew his ball.

"Baseball isn't just in the stats—though of course, that's part of it," Bush said. "It isn't just the money. It really isn't who makes the Hall of Fame. As much as anything else, baseball is the style of a Willie Mays or the determination of a Hank Aaron . . . the kindness of a Harmon Killebrew and the class of Stan Musial, the courage of a Jackie Robinson or the heroism of Lou Gehrig. My hope for the game is that these qualities will never be lost."

In 2003, unrelated to the game he mastered, Killebrew focused on the game he never did, traveling to Scotland with some boyhood friends to play at St. Andrews, Troon, and other famous courses. He was playing on two store-bought knees by this point but had an 11 handicap and didn't mind a bit when his Scottish caddy gave the six-time AL home run champ putting tips.

In 2004, Killebrew even reconnected with his old pal Dave Letterman. On the brink of induction weekend in Cooperstown that summer, Letterman's *Late Show* producers brought 10 Hall of Famers to the CBS studio. One by one, a baseball Murderer's Row featuring Bob Feller, Ralph Kiner, Rollie Fingers, Ozzie Smith, Phil Niekro, and Lou Brock read down the "Top 10 Perks of being a National Baseball Hall of Famer."

Brooks Robinson had No. 8 ("I once saw Earl Weaver naked"). Bob Gibson was No. 5 ("'I gotta do Hall of Fame stuff!'—perfect excuse to get out of plans the wife made"). Former Montreal and New

York Mets catcher Gary Carter, the 2003 inductee who would battle brain cancer before passing away in February 2012, got the big finish at No. 1 ("One free swing at a costumed mascot of my choice").

The line fed to Harmon by the writers at No. 9, meanwhile, was as hilarious as any of them. "If I don't have the money for the Domino's kid, I just hand him any old bat and say, 'I used this one for my 500th home run.'" When Letterman worked his way down the line, shaking the players' hands, there was a little extra nod of recognition for Killebrew, dating back to their oddball and enjoyable 1986 visit on the other network.

Those were diversions or larks compared to the work into which Killebrew and his second wife Nita threw themselves for two decades. He had become an avid spokesperson for hospice care after his own serious health scare and remarkable return to health in 1990. In 1998, they started the Harmon Killebrew Foundation as a way to assist a variety of charities, including VistaCare hospices, the Payette High athletic program, children's hospitals, and relief efforts to assist the victims of Hurricane Ike in 2008 and the 2010 earthquake in Haiti.

He had the Danny Thompson Memorial golf event each year in Sun Valley, which was set to tweak its name in 2012 (to the Harmon Killebrew–Danny Thompson tournament). Killebrew added two more in Arizona and Minnesota, including one in 2010 for a granddaughter facing her own health issues, to meet the foundation's needs. And he became a driving force in the Miracle Fields project, which was dedicated to providing safe opportunities for special-needs children to participate in baseball. The specialized fields require rubberized synthetic turf, accommodations for wheelchairs and other walking assistance, and additional safety precautions, each with budgets from $150,000 to $250,000 or more. Killebrew's foundation brought many of them to life.

One field begun in Lakeville, Minnesota, late in May 2011, soon after Killebrew's death, was named for him. It was the seventh such venue built in Minnesota. He was told of the naming decision deep into his battle with esophageal cancer. "He was moved to tears because it was so important to him," Kelly McDyre, executive director of the foundation, told a Twin Cities newsman. "It was really neat because Harmon got to hear it before he died."

Killebrew had also worked through the Twins when the organization helped to renovate inner-city baseball fields. He couldn't help but reflect on his own days in the park, planting the seeds for his love of the game. "We feel everyone has the right to be able to play baseball," Killebrew said. "It's so great to see the smiles on these kids' faces."

In 2006, the World Sports Humanitarian Hall of Fame, established in Boise, Idaho, called for Killebrew—he was to be inducted in a class featuring Pro Football Hall of Famer Steve Largent and former NBA star and Olympic gold medalist Steve Smith. They joined previous inductees such as Steve Young, Mary Lou Retton, Tony Gwynn, and Drew Bledsoe. Killebrew cracked some jokes during his speech, at one point reminding the audience that—if his walks and strikeouts were combined—"That's well over 3,000 times at the plate. That means I went to the plate in my career a total of six years and did absolutely nothing."

But the gist of his talk was more sincere. "Steve Largent said it best—we're really not here because it's another award," Killebrew said. "What it does is to draw more attention to what we should be doing as former players and giving back to the communities in which we played or lived. That's the real significance to the whole thing."

Another time, Killebrew said, "I'd want my friends to say that I was helpful. I'd hate to have them say, 'He didn't want to help me when I needed help.' A lot of people helped me along the way, and I was very thankful for that. My mother told me when I was a young kid that the No. 1 reason we're here on Earth is to help people. She was right. What else is there?"

One gift Harmon continues to give to baseball lovers throughout the Upper Midwest is Old-Fashioned Killebrew Root Beer and Cream Soda. Brewed in Minnesota and sold at Target Field and in stores from the Dakotas to Wisconsin and Iowa, it was a project driven by Ken Killebrew, Harmon's younger son. It was a fitting product choice given Harmon's conversion in the 1960s to the Mormon faith and a lifestyle free of drinking and smoking (though not ice cream). Killebrew's older son Cam came the closest to following his father in sports, playing in the Rangers and A's minor-league systems from 1978 to 1981 before settling in Atlanta. But Ken was the only member of the family who stayed in the Twin Cities.

Early in Killebrew's career, when pressed for an answer by a writer from *Sports Illustrated* who asked him about his hobbies, the young slugger had said, "Washing the dishes, I guess." But he always enjoyed hunting and fishing, eventually switching to golf. Later in his life, Killebrew would cook family recipes handed down from his mother; his best work was a dish of rice, tomatoes, peppers, onions, and ground beef. He liked Clint Eastwood movies, watched the various *CSI* crime shows on television, and still considered Ted Williams' *The Science of Hitting* the best book he had ever read. He had wide tastes in music and admitted that he enjoyed singing. "It's one thing I wish I could do: be a piano player and a singer," he said. "If Simon Cowell heard me sing, he's say, 'That's enough. See you later.'"

Talking with baseball fans qualified as a pastime, too, presenting Killebrew an endless supply of strangers to whom he apparently meant a great deal. "I go around to different places, especially in the Upper Midwest, and someone will still say, 'I was on the tractor the day you hit that home run in Cleveland,' or, 'I was in the milking barn when you hit that home run against the Yankees.' It's great to hear things like that," he said.

More often than not, fans and friends would get around to asking what, to him, was a tricky question—did Killebrew wish he played baseball today? "If you're talking about the money, that would be nice," he'd say. "But I can honestly say I'm very glad I played baseball when I did. I think the '50s, the '60s, and the '70s were the golden years of baseball. More great players played during that period than any other. You had Willie Mays, Mickey Mantle, Hank Aaron, Ted Williams, Sandy Koufax, and Whitey Ford."

So rather than switching eras, Killebrew sounded like a man who wouldn't mind hitting a "reset" button and doing it all over again. "If I could trade places for a day with anyone? I don't think I'd trade with anybody except a younger me. I'd like to shave 50 years off."

Someone ultimately did that for him. As part of Target Field's inaugural season in 2010, the Minnesota team commissioned sculptor Bill Mack to fashion a bronze statue of Killebrew, one of several former Twins honored as part of a new-millennial craze at ballparks and arenas across the land. Mack's stunning final version of Killebrew in his prime shows the slugger taking a ferocious rip at a ball, fully extended, based on his swing that sent Jim Maloney's offering over the fence in the 1965 MLB All-Star Game at Met Stadium. Mack worked from photos and even got a much-older Killebrew to pose, replicating the explosive, upper-cut stroke.

"It doesn't look like Harmon was trying to use the whole field," someone said at the statue's unveiling, prompting Twins broadcaster and former Killebrew teammate Bert Blyleven to say, "That probably would get him in trouble with today's coaches. It was a beautiful thing to see him swing."

In this case, Killebrew is finally Paul Bunyan-esque; the statue weighs more than 750 pounds and truly is larger than life. Same, come to think of it, as him.

Chapter 17

Farewell

Harmon Killebrew described the pain as a piercing sensation in his back and neck, and it was severe enough that he was taken to the hospital—and treated for a collapsed right lung and damaged esophagus. Months later, he still wasn't feeling healthy, so doctors kept looking. Tests revealed an abscess near his lung, and the surgery required to address that left the baseball Hall of Famer, then 53, with a gaping hole in his back. A staph infection developed and swiftly spread, with Killebrew hospitalized again but getting worse instead of better. Doctors were stymied and when they sent him home, they doubted they would see him again.

That ordeal of six months in 1990 was the first thing a lot of Killebrew's friends and fans thought of when they got bad news about the slugger's health 21 years later. That scare had been the worst of times—also in 1990, Harmon and Elaine divorced after 34 years of marriage—but he survived it and soon experienced some times as good as any that had come before. In 1991, he married Nita, his fiancée who had helped him through the near-death episode. He eventually would return to the Minnesota Twins' embrace, and vice versa. He would see his children, and his four new stepchildren, tackle life and raise families of their own.

So when the announcement was made on December 29, 2010, that Killebrew had been diagnosed with esophageal cancer and would begin treatment immediately at the Mayo Clinic near his home in Scottsdale, Arizona, those who knew him and loved him were nervous. And hopeful.

"With my wife, Nita, by my side, I have begun preparing for what is perhaps the most difficult battle of my life," Harmon said in the statement. "I am being treated by a team of medical professionals at the Mayo Clinic. While my condition is very serious, I have confidence in my doctors and the medical staff, and I anticipate a full recovery." He and Nita requested privacy as they dealt with his condition.

Esophageal cancer attacks the muscular tube that moves food from the mouth to the stomach. It most often occurs in men over 50 years old. Often it isn't discovered until it is in an advanced state, reducing the chances of long-term survival. When surgery alone isn't possible, chemotherapy, radiation, or both are used to relieve symptoms and fight the cancer. Some familiar with Killebrew's earlier health crisis heard that word again—esophagus—and wondered how this one might be related. Others just knew he was in for a formidable fight.

Earlier in December, Killebrew had been in the Twin Cities and had breakfast one morning with Twins president Dave St. Peter. Upon learning of his condition, St. Peter said, "That's one of the great things about Harmon. He's a glass-half-full guy. He understands that he's in a battle, but he believes he is going to beat this."

In January, with the MLB meetings in Phoenix, St. Peter, Twins CEO Jim Pohlad and general manager Bill Smith drove over to visit Killebrew. "As you would expect, Harmon lifted our spirits more than the other way around," St. Peter said. "One of the first things he did say was, 'What are you waiting for? Get [Jim] Thome signed.' So we were happy to get that done, for Harmon and for our ballclub." St. Peter said that as they left, Killebrew shook hands with that same, familiar "Killer" grip.

Killebrew was able to attend spring training in March—in fact, his doctors at the Mayo Clinic encouraged it, knowing how much he enjoyed baseball's rebirth each year in Florida and pulling on a Twins uniform again. He stayed in camp for five days, and though he had lost a little weight, he smiled readily and seemed chipper. The ballplayers he worked and talked with knew what was going on, adding to the reward of having Killebrew as a mentor again.

"It meant a lot because we knew what he was battling and what was going on with him," outfielder Denard Span said. "For me, I didn't ask him how he was doing, but I wanted to so bad. I didn't want him to think about what was going on. I just wanted him to get his mind off what was going on. So for him to be around us, it lifted us up."

Jim Rantz, Minnesota's longtime farm director and a Killebrew friend dating back 50 years to his days as a minor league pitcher, asked the Twins legend to talk with approximately 150 young prospects for the brush-with-greatness zapping that it always gave the minor leaguers.

The brush with baseball at its best in Florida in March was meant to zap Killebrew a little, too. "This is my job, trying to get well," he said while in camp. "That's what my whole day is focused around. I couldn't have done it without my wife [Nita]. She's been my rock and my caretaker. She has done a tremendous job of trying to get me well."

On one of his five days in Ft. Myers, with most of the squad out of town, Killebrew stayed behind with his friend and former teammate, Tony Oliva, to watch Justin Morneau get some extra work in the batting cage. Morneau, the slugging first baseman, had suffered a concussion in 2010 and was still suffering some ill effects. Afterward, Killebrew talked again with one of his prize pupils. "The conversation was about how I was doing," Morneau said. "That is what Harmon was like as a person. Even though he was going through his battle, he wanted to make sure I was feeling all right and ask how *I* was doing in *my* recovery."

Before leaving the clubhouse at Hammond Stadium that day to fly back to Scottsdale, Killebrew gave Oliva a hug. Oliva said he would see him up in Minnesota for Opening Day.

Killebrew wasn't there on Opening Day. He had been scheduled to throw out the first pitch before the home game against Oakland on April 8, and he also wanted to be there for the unveiling of a new Oliva statue, a bronze tribute similar to Killebrew's own outside Target Field. But it was left to Killebrew's sons, Cam and Ken, to officially open Gate 3—designated for their father's uniform number—and when Oliva threw the ceremonial pitch in his pal's place, the "catcher" was Harmon's grandson, Casey.

Cam Killebrew said the outpouring of letters and cards pulling for their father had been overwhelming as he continued chemotherapy. Oliva sounded like he still planned to see Killebrew at a Twins game soon, reflecting back on days that sometimes didn't feel so long ago. "He would hit them so high," Oliva said of Killebrew's home runs. "I would be yelling, 'Run, Killer, run!' and he would just watch the ball, and slowly drop the bat, and slowly start to jog, and the ball would just keep flying. He hit them so far."

Oliva added, "I tell everybody he's too nice to be a baseball player. He's a gentleman.... His family is my family. His wife and my wife are very close. [When] he first got to spring training, he called and told my wife, 'Don't forget about my black bean soup.' So we brought him some to the hotel and talked about a lot of things."

A Twin Cities TV station, covering Opening Day, wrapped up its report from that afternoon this way, "Harmon Killebrew's sons told us he most certainly will be back in the Twin Cities in June for his annual golf tournament. And if he's here for the golf tournament, there's no way that he's not making a stop here at Target Field."

It wasn't to be. On May 13, 2011, Killebrew announced through a Twins press release that he was ceasing treatment and entering hospice care. "It is with profound sadness that I share with you that my continued battle with esophageal cancer is coming to an end," his statement read. "With the continued love and support of my wife, Nita, I have exhausted all options with respect to controlling this awful disease. My illness has progressed beyond my doctors' expectation of cure.

"I have spent the past decade of my life promoting hospice care and educating people on its benefits. I am very comfortable taking this next step and experiencing the compassionate care that hospice provides. I am comforted by the fact that I am surrounded by my family and friends. I thank you for the outpouring of concern, prayers, and encouragement that you have shown me. I look forward to spending my final days in comfort and peace with Nita by my side."

The news was devastating. Yet the dignity and courage of Killebrew's determination and decision were staggering. Friends wept, and admired him anew. Many wondered if they could possibly handle life's toughest challenge so nimbly and with such nobility. Some, as badly as they wanted to reach out again to him, were left speechless.

"It's one of those things, you want to call him but you don't know what to say," said George Brett, the Kansas City Royals third baseman and Hall of Famer who got to know his hero when they played together in 1975. "I had heard for a while things weren't well. There were numerous times I picked up the phone just to say 'Hi' but then just didn't know what to say. As a result of that, I never said my goodbye I never told him he was a great friend, I never told him probably a lot of things I should have told him. I'm just not good at that.... I'm not good at that."

Others did speak to Killebrew. A few traveled to see him in his final days. Oliva and former Twins teammate Julio Becquer visited in Scottsdale over the weekend. Molitor made the trip. So did St. Peter. "Harmon made a point of asking me how [manager Ron Gardenhire] was doing because he knows we're scuffling on the field," St. Peter said. "It was kind of classic Harmon. He was worried about everybody but himself."

Said Oliva, "I was thinking I would go see him in very bad shape, and when I saw him laughing and talking, it was a big surprise for me. That was Saturday, and I was happy for me to have that opportunity to get there and see him in person. Sunday was a different story. I came back and was visiting and he was very down. You could see he was hurting. He said, 'You know I love you.'"

The family closed ranks at the end. "We were all there, all his kids, and we had a really good time," son Ken told the *St. Paul Pioneer Press*. "We put on the David Letterman show [DVD] that he hadn't seen since Dad was on it, when they had Harmon Killebrew night.... We laughed. All five of us kids sat around and watched it. Dad got a good kick out of it."

On Tuesday, just four days after entering hospice care and barely a month shy of his 75th birthday, Killebrew died. He became the fifth baseball Hall of Famer to pass in slightly more than a year, following Robin Roberts, Sparky Anderson, Bob Feller, and Duke Snider. That, along with the stats (573 home runs, 1,584 RBIs, and so on) and the diamond achievements, was all about Killebrew the baseball player. Those who had been touched by him, or even felt as if they had, mourned Killebrew the man.

"The one thing I'd admired about him since the day I met him is how he treats everybody the same. You wouldn't know he's a Hall of Famer when he walks into the room," said Twins catcher Joe Mauer, who first met Killebrew when Mauer was 18. "When I learned the news about Harmon today, I felt like I lost a family member. He has treated me like one of his own."

"At first it was disbelief, shock," said Mark Heleker, the principal at Payette High in Killebrew's hometown. "I tried to call him last week, but I was not able to talk with him because he was resting, and it never occurred to me how sick he was. And to get this news…I thought, 'This cannot be true.'"

Jack Morris, the nasty right-hander who had helped the Twins win the 1991 World Series with his masterful 10-inning performance in Game 7, heard his voice crack and eyes tear up as he told reporters, "I lost a hero." Growing up in St. Paul, Morris said, he looked up to Killebrew because of the All-Star he was. "But as a grown man," Morris said, "I look back at him now not as that guy but as the guy who tried to show me that you don't have to be angry, you don't have to be mad. You can love and share love."

Pitcher Jim Kaat, Killebrew's teammate in Washington and Minnesota, said the Twins' reputation as a "gentlemanly organization" was due to Killebrew. And Kaat marveled at the timing of everything—"almost like there was divine intervention"—with the Twins in Seattle on a West Coast trip and headed to Arizona, where they could attend his funeral service.

The flag at Seattle's Safeco Field was flown at half-staff the night of Killebrew's passing. A moment of silence was observed, and the Twins players took the field with a No. 3 patch on their uniforms. After the first inning, the Mariners showed a video of Killebrew highlights on their giant flatscreen. Michael Cuddyer, the Twins outfielder whose autograph was forever changed by his friendship with Killebrew, smacked a two-run single in the first inning for the only runs Minnesota needed that night; beating the Mariners 2–1, snapping a nine-game losing streak, and winning the first of three victories in a row.

Playing that night, Cuddyer said, actually gave the Twins "three hours to get our minds off the tragedy, even though you can't." Reporters pressed him for more, knowing Cuddyer was the Minnesota player closest to Killebrew. "In talking about Harmon, I've always said you want to be a better person when he's around, you want to be a better player when he's around," the outfielder said. "So maybe tonight, you don't want to say you tried harder, because you try hard every day, but I don't know. Coincidence or higher power? Maybe he was looking down on us tonight."

Cuddyer said that night he wished all the Twins could wear Killebrew's familiar No. 3, "But obviously that can't happen." He did, however, address that over the winter when he signed a three-year, $31.5 million contract as a free agent with Colorado—Cuddyer said he would wear Killebrew's number rather than the No. 5 he had worn through 11 seasons with the Twins.

At Target Field, with the team out of town, officials and members of the grounds crew buried a black-and-white photo of Killebrew beneath home plate. They made preliminary plans for a public memorial on May 26 and soon announced other tributes to the popular slugger.

- A Killebrew jersey would hang in their dugout for the rest of the season, a practice the players had begun as soon as they heard Killebrew had entered hospice care.
- At home, the Twins would wear the cream-colored 1961 throwback jerseys at Target Field for the rest of the season with a memorial patch on the shirt.
- Killebrew's familiar, elegant signature would be displayed on the wall in right-center field.
- His number, among the five retired by the Twins through 2011, would be draped in black.
- A large No. 3 was displayed from a water tower atop a nearby Minneapolis building, visible from the stands at the Twins ballpark.

Thome added a little individual tribute in August after getting to 598 in career home runs but failing to get to No. 600 on a six-game homestand. Eleven days elapsed before he got the milestone by hitting two in the same game on August 15 at Detroit. Forty years earlier—on August 10, 1971—Killebrew had gotten No. 500 by hitting two in the same game (Nos. 500 and 501, to be precise). "He was such a special guy," Thome said. "He was a wonderful man, a wonderful human being who touched so many people's lives in a positive way. He was truly one of the best baseball men I've met in the game."

Another slugger of some clout, Henry Aaron, sifted through his own memories of Killebrew. Aaron, while playing with the Milwaukee Braves, used to listen to night-time broadcasts of Twins games on the radio. "That's basically the way you got to know other players, through the radio. Wasn't TV at that time," Aaron said. "And I would sit there listening to 'Harmon Killebrew,' and even his name sounded like someone very special."

Aaron was on the old *Home Run Derby* TV show the same as Killebrew, but they never went head-to-head in an episode. For a long time, Killebrew was an All-Star from the other league that Aaron saw in the spring and then once or twice in the summer (MLB staged two All-Star Games each season from 1959 through 1962). But later the two home run heroes traveled to Japan and got more acquainted, a friendship taking root.

"I think Harmon and I got along about as well as any two ballplayers could get along," said Aaron, who, like Brett, did not talk with Killebrew near the end ("too chicken-hearted"). "We understood each other. In some ways, we were almost alike.... He was a wonderful human being. I got to know him as a man first, baseball [player] second."

Charlie Manuel, the 25-year-old rookie outfielder in 1969 who was awed to find his locker in between Killebrew's and Bob Allison's, had his Philadelphia Phillies in first place from the start in May 2011 and would manage them to 102 victories by season's end. But the bad news hit hard. "Honestly, when he passed away, I was really kind of down," Manuel said. "But the more that I think about the fact I got to know him, got to know who he was and everything...he lived a pleasant life. He was a guy who was very proud and happy. He was a very honest person. He was everything they said he was, maybe more. He was that good."

People in Minnesota—those who rooted for Killebrew at the ball games in Bloomington soon after the Twins arrived in 1961 as well as those born long after his career there was over in 1974—laid flowers at the base of his statue outside Target Field. They brought messages and memories, not just of the player but of who they were in his time. "It kind of makes you feel like your childhood years are gone—like a part of your life is taken away," Kevin Lindquist, a fellow from Fridley, Minnesota, told the Minneapolis newspaper the day Killebrew died. "I know it sounds stupid...but I've never been so sad about someone I didn't know." Another fan, John Grabow, was 14 when Killebrew played his last season with the Twins "I always had the feeling here that the Twins were never out of a game if Killebrew had an at-bat left," he said.

On Friday, three days after Killebrew's death, the entire Twins team attended his funeral service in Peoria, Arizona. Players Cuddyer, Morneau, and pitcher Joe Nathan were pallbearers, along with manager Ron Gardenhire, Molitor, Oliva and Frank Quilici. Baseball Hall of Famers Robin Yount and Frank Robinson were among the estimated 750 or so mourners who attended the service. Son Cam talked of the deluge of get-well cards, prayers, and good wishes sent his father's way in his final days. "I don't think he really realized how much he was loved," the oldest Killebrew child said. "That's the kind of man he was. He was so humble. He got a lot of things, but I'm not sure he really got that, and it was beautiful."

Former teammate and Twins broadcaster Bert Blyleven asked those in attendance to cheer one more time for Killebrew like the fans did when he strode to the plate at Met Stadium. He remembered his early encounters with Killebrew that day. "Being a rookie pitcher, Harmon treated me like one of the guys," Blyleven said. "More like a son than a teammate because I was so young. But when I think of Harmon Killebrew, I think of class. Not just a Hall of Fame player but a guy who just loved life and gave so much back."

Jim Pohlad, the Twins' chief executive who took over the franchise when his father Carl died in 2009, said that day, "It was universal, the feeling about Harmon. You could've had 50 people up there, and they would've said the same thing."

That same day, 1,000 miles north, a moment of silence was observed, too, before the Idaho 3A baseball tournament game—Payette vs. South Fremont at the Elks Memorial Field in Ontario, Oregon. There it was—Killebrew's old high school team playing a big game in the town across the river, the place where the big leaguer and his growing family lived in the off-seasons of his Hall of Fame career. The Pirates jumped out front on Colton Bullington's solo home run, then kept on going to win 11–0. Starting pitcher Spencer Pollock pushed the emotional needle hard to the right by striking out five, walking three, and allowing no hits at all. Payette lost to Fruitland the next day but got an ovation from its fans.

"Yeah, I thought about it a little bit," Pollock said of Killebrew's passing. "I wanted to come out here and do something for him for all the things he's done for our program. I wanted to pay my respects to him a little bit."

Three days later in Payette, on May 23, there was a private burial for family only. A memorial service was held at the high school gym, with Idaho Governor Butch Otter, football's Jerry Kramer, and another 400 friends and neighbors. Harmon Clayton Killebrew Jr. was laid to rest that afternoon in the family plot at Riverside Cemetery, alongside his father, Clay, and his mother, Katie. His brother, Eugene, sister, Eula, infant sister, Patricia, and sister-in-law, Ann, were there, too. Baseball had taken Killebrew around the world—to the nation's capital, to Minnesota, to all those cities in the major leagues and to stops big and small across the United States. He had traveled to Alaska, Vietnam, Europe, Japan, and beyond, thanks to the sport he loved... until the day he came back home to stay, one mile from the house in which he grew up.

There was no headstone right away, of course, but the man whose place it would mark already had done the hardest part of the engraver's job. Deep into an interview one time, when asked about a day that presumably would come far into the future, Killebrew said, "I want my epitaph to say, 'Here lies Harmon Killebrew, who was a good friend and tried to help others.'"

He was and he did, and those long fly balls were just a marvelous bonus.

Chapter 18

Memorial

The size and scope of Target Field made the crowd that night—May 26, 2011—seem rather uncrowded. The folks in the stands were gathered mostly between the bases, down low, close to the field. Great seats for a ball game? Great seats to honor a ballplayer and a man, too. As estimated by those in the business of doing so that evening, the crowd numbered somewhere north or south of 4,000, which might not have seemed like many in a ballpark that seats nearly 10 times that.

Then again, throw open the gates to your own memorial service and see how long it takes for 4,000 of *your* dearest family, friends, and admirers to show up.

Harmon Killebrew hadn't played for the Minnesota Twins in 37 years. He hadn't swung a bat in anger or clubbed a ball over a fence in 36. And while the Twins organization had done a terrific job of putting Killebrew before the public as an ambassador and icon—at TwinsFest, on the Winter Caravan tours, at reunions and other functions—he spent most of his time in Scottsdale, Arizona, and in Meridian, Idaho, living life as your average, ordinary baseball Hall of Famer.

But the love, respect, sense of loss, and ultimately appreciation from those who attended—not to mention the thousands more watching on live television in the Twin Cities—filled that gorgeous ballpark in downtown Minneapolis, regardless of the number of fannies in the seats.

One seat, with one particular fanny in it, drew extra attention about an hour into the event. A highlight reel on the videoboard (and in home viewers' living rooms) told the tale of Killebrew's mammoth, 520' home run off Lew Burdette, forever remembered as the longest ball hit at old Met Stadium after the Twins slugger crushed it on June 3, 1967. That one settled finally in the second deck of the left-field pavilion at the Bloomington ballpark, a location matched in its distance from home plate by just one lonely seat at Target Field.

The video ended, replaced by a live shot of that spot, a mystery man planted in that faraway chair to illustrate the mighty blast. There, sitting high, higher, as high as one possibly can sit, way out yonder in the left-center field stands, was Bob Uecker—wait, no, it was Jim Thome. The camera zoomed in to reveal Thome, the modern-era slugger considered most reminiscent of Killebrew's style, power, and personality. He had a big smile on his face and was waving a 1962 game-worn No. 3 Twins jersey.

"I'll be honest, when I went up there—let's just say, I don't go up and sit in the upper deck. We're old baseball players, we don't go sit in the crowd—so when I walked up there, it started getting a little bit eerie," Thome said afterward. "I have a new respect for fans that get to sit up there because it's *really* high. I can only imagine if Harmon hit a ball close to that area—that is unbelievable to think about."

For many of those closest to Killebrew, the day had begun in the south suburbs at the Mall of America in Bloomington where old Met Stadium used to be and where all of the ballplayer's top Minnesota feats (in home games, anyway) occurred. That's where Killebrew Drive, still there, delivers shoppers to a megamall rather than fans to a ballgame, but at least the developers took care to preserve the location of home plate, aligned just so. And then there's the red seat bolted high above the amusement park in the center of the mall, approximately in the same place—520 feet away—where Killebrew's home run landed. It is there without fanfare, a surprise really, something that began as a novelty but turned into a tribute with Killebrew's passing from esophageal cancer at age 74 on May 17, 2011.

"That's where we started the memorial service," former Twins pitcher Jim Kaat said. "They took us out to the Mall of America that day, and everybody got the chance to see the seat and home plate. Then we jumped on the light rail and made our way into Target Field."

In the nine days that had passed since Killebrew's death, there had been a funeral service in Arizona, where he and his wife Nita had lived for much of the past two decades. There had been a public service and a private burial in his hometown of Payette, Idaho, with his grave at Riverside Cemetery maybe a long Killebrew poke from the Snake River at the Idaho-Oregon border.

So by the time the gates of Target Field opened free to the public—the Twins honoring Killebrew, the identities of player and team inseparable—the idea was to celebrate him for who he was both on and off the field. Oh, there would be tears, but less from the mourning and the pain than from remembering the good times and from gratitude at having been around for even a little bit of Harmon.

The ceremony went off without a hitch. Twins broadcasters Dick Bremer and John Gordon did a masterful job as emcees and narrators of the various video packages. The choice of speakers—from MLB commissioner Bud Selig and home run great Henry Aaron to past Twins Kaat, Rod Carew, Paul Molitor, to active players Michael Cuddyer and Justin Morneau—was spot-on. Harmon's many family members sat to the side, most of them happy to leave this one to Killebrew's team and fans.

The music was right, from the Minnesota Chorale to Minneapolis folk singer Jeff Arundel (who performed his original composition "Harmon Killebrew"). Same with the staging, out near the pitchers' mound with flowers and a large No. 3 on each side of the lectern and Killebrew's jersey number on display all over the park. The National Baseball Hall of Fame had permitted Killebrew's plaque to make the trip from Cooperstown to Target Plaza so fans could see it prior to the ceremony. Then it was displayed, front and center, below the microphone. It was the first time a plaque had been allowed to leave the shrine since Ted Williams was similarly honored by the Boston Red Sox at Fenway Park in 2002.

The Twins, unfortunately, had some practice at these sorts of things. The organization had been shaken in 1995 when Bob Allison, so strong, so robust, died at age 60 after falling victim to a rare neurological disease (Olivopontocerebellar atrophy) seven years earlier. Then it endured the sudden loss in 2006 of the only player who could challenge Killebrew in popularity and certainly in association with the Twins as known by a younger generation of fans.

Kirby Puckett had been the face and personality of the franchise almost from the moment he arrived in 1984, catching his famous $83 cab ride from the airport to meet up with the club in Anaheim. He was the sparkplug center fielder for the teams that went to and won the World Series in 1987 and 1991, an All-Star and eventual Hall of Famer whose production—a lifetime .318 average, five seasons of 200-plus hits, six Gold Gloves, and six Silver Slugger awards—was all the more remarkable given his physique. A short, stocky chunk of a player, Puckett won fans with his enthusiasm, his hustle, and the joy with which he played. Certainly he had more impact defensively than Killebrew, frequently swiping home runs by leaping high against the Metrodome's outfield walls.

Puckett's career ended prematurely in 1995 when he woke up with blurred vision in his right eye, a victim of glaucoma. His reputation suffered several years later with a very public divorce, published accounts of infidelities, and from an incident at a Twin Cities night spot, a sexual misconduct charge that stuck to him even after he was acquitted in 2003. His days as a Twins VP were over, and Puckett relocated to Arizona. Sadly, on March 6, 2006, eight days before his 46th birthday, Puckett died after suffering a stroke.

During the Twins memorial for Puckett at the Metrodome that spring, Harmon Killebrew watched quietly from a press box. The voice on the P.A. system called Puckett the "greatest player in Twins history," and in that moment Killebrew smiled. Charley Walters—the longtime St. Paul sports columnist who had played with Killebrew briefly in 1969, a hard-throwing pitcher nicknamed "Shooter" who got a shot with the hometown team—noticed.

"For sure, Puckett was a great player, as great as any Twin," Walters wrote years later. "But he wasn't greater than Killebrew. So I walked over to Harmon and whispered that not everyone in the stadium considered Kirby the greatest player in Twins history. Maybe it was a generational thing. Killebrew, a proud but humble man, smiled again. I think he appreciated that."

Five years removed from Puckett's death, with Killebrew's achievements renewed and fresh in Minnesota fans' minds, there seemed to be a shift in that "greatest Twin of all-time" claim, with sentiment turning Harmon's way. Certainly it sounded and felt that way as friends, teammates, and family honored him at the Target Field service. The biggest challenge for those involved was to come up with fresh material; the risk of sounding redundant was high. As former Twins shortstop Roy Smalley said in his role as commentator for Fox Sports North, "We could have 100 people give a tribute to Killebrew and they all could wind up saying similar things about the man's grace and class."

Not to worry. There was variety, there were laughs, and there was emotion. Among the highlights:

- Kaat, Killebrew's longtime teammate, spoke in detail of his friend's unassuming technique for wreaking so much havoc. "When you look at some of the clips that you've seen there, his off-field demeanor, his calmness carried over into the way he swung the bat. If you notice when Harm took his stance... there wasn't a lot of excess movement. He got in the box, the bat was on his shoulder, the hands moved back, cheeks puffed out a little bit, and then he would do what our old teammate, the late Jim Lemon would say, 'Swing the bat like a hammer, not like a broom.' And he swung it so much on balance—I never saw him lose his balance on a swing. That [was why] he was able to hit the center of the ball with the barrel of the bat so often, that he had that effortless power."
- Mudcat Grant, a pitcher and a Killebrew favorite during their time together in the mid-1960s, remembered Harmon's inquisitiveness about the civil rights movement, engaging the African-American Grant in long discussions about race relations. Then Grant played and sang one of Killebrew's favorite songs, "What a Wonderful World."
- Hank Aaron, whom many—Killebrew included—considered to still be MLB's homer king, cheated by the "steroids era," handed off that title to his departed friend. "Really, in all fairness to him, he was No. 1 really," Aaron said. "He hit 1,000 home runs because he did so many great things off the field."
- Bud Selig praised Killebrew during the service but was most eloquent talking with reporters beforehand. "He is a great lesson for future generations of baseball players. That's the way you're supposed to carry yourself. That's the way you're supposed to act."
- Michael Cuddyer read the column he had written for *Fox Sports North* about Killebrew's scoldings over scribbled autographs, and

- Justin Morneau shared a similar tale. "To this day when I sign an autograph," the first baseman said, "I try to do better because Harmon was inspiring me and my teammates to be better people."
- Carew's memories of Killebrew—whom he called "Charlie" to Harmon's "Junior" nickname for him—turned especially heartbreaking when he recalled sitting at his friend's bedside the day before Killebrew died. "He said, 'I love you, Junior.' I said, 'Charlie, I will always love you, too.' No matter how many players pass through the Twins organization, there will only be one face of this organization, and that's Harmon Killebrew."

At the end, it was Killebrew's widow, Nita, who stepped into the spotlight, rare for her, to share her feelings while expressing her thanks to those who so honored her husband. At one point, she asked those in the ballpark to literally "Stand Up To Cancer" in support of the charitable organization dedicated to fighting the disease that took Harmon.

"He was a gentleman to the end," she said. "Always composed, never complaining. If only you could have seen what I was blessed to have seen.... I was truly honored to be his caregiver. He left me inspired, awed, amazed, and humbled."

Finally, Nita Killebrew provided a sense of place for the man loved by so many at so many levels. "Harmon's body is at rest in his hometown of Payette," she said. "His soul is at peace in that big ballpark in the sky. But his heart will always be right here in Minnesota with you."

Sources

Anderson, Dr. Wayne J. *Harmon Killebrew, Baseball's Superstar*. Deseret Book Co., 1971.

Bouton, Jim. *Ball Four*. Wiley Publishing, Inc., 1970.

Brackin, Dennis and Patrick Reusse. *Minnesota Twins: The Complete Illustrated History*. MVP Books, 2010.

Butler, Hal. *The Harmon Killebrew Story*. Pocket Books, Inc., 1966.

Freedman, Lew. *Going Yard: The Everything Home Run Book*. Triumph Books, 2011.

Grow, Doug. *We're Gonna Win, Twins!* University of Minnesota Press, 2010.

Moffi, Larry. *This Side of Cooperstown*. Dover Publications, Inc., 1996.

Thielman, Jim. *Cool of the Evening*. Kirk House Publishing, 2005.

Vincent, Fay. *We Would Have Played for Nothing*. Simon & Schuster, Inc., 2008.

Wright, Dave. *162–0: The Greatest Wins in Twins History*. Triumph Books, 2010.

Index